HAWK

I Did It My Way

Ken Harrelson with Jeff Snook

TRIUMPH
B O O K S

Library of Congress Cataloging-in-Publication Data

Names: Harrelson, Ken, 1941- author. | Snook, Jeff, 1960- author.
Title: Hawk / Ken Harrelson, with Jeff Snook.
Description: Chicago, Illinois : Triumph Books LLC, [2018]
Identifiers: LCCN 2017058357 | ISBN 9781629375847
Subjects: LCSH: Harrelson, Ken, 1941- | Baseball players—United
    States—Biography. | Sportscasters--United States—Biography.
Classification: LCC GV865.H28 A3 2018 | DDC 796.357092 [B]—dc23
LC record available at https://lccn.loc.gov/2017058357

This book is available in quantity at special discounts for your group or organization. For further information, contact:
Triumph Books LLC
814 North Franklin Street
Chicago, Illinois 60610
(312) 337-0747
www.triumphbooks.com

Printed in U.S.A.
ISBN: 978-1-62937-584-7
Design by Amy Carter
Page production by Nord Compo
Photos courtesy of the author unless otherwise indicated

To Aris, the love of my life. I told you it would never be boring…thanks for the journey together. I love you!

CONTENTS

1 SOMEHOW, I DODGED ALL THE BULLETS

I WAS ONLY 12 YEARS OLD THE FIRST TIME A GUN WAS FIRED in my presence.

It happened one afternoon in 1953 in the tiny kitchen of the two-bedroom, one-bath house in which I grew up on Causton Bluff Road in Savannah, Georgia.

It also was a culmination of the final confrontation my parents would ever have. At least in person, that is.

I am not ashamed to say that my mother, Jessie Harrelson, was the love of my life. She was a beautiful woman and I was a mama's boy, which I say proudly. She doted on me, her only son. In turn, I did anything I could to put a smile on her face or to make her life easier.

On this particular day, that required coming to her defense by punching the man she had married several years before I was born. Later, as I grew up and when I became an adult, I never referred to him as "my father" or "Dad," even though that's who he was biologically. I never respected him enough to honor him with those designations, ones that should mean so much to any kid.

Smith Franklin Harrelson was a cheater and a mean drunk.

When he drank, he and my mother argued. When he drank a lot, or was caught cheating, they fought.

On this particular day, he had done both.

1

Earlier that day, he said he had to visit the hospital for whatever reason and that is when Mama had caught him cheating on her again, this time with a nurse.

I knew that Mama always carried a pistol in her purse for protection. As their verbal squabble was about to escalate into a physical fight, I was reading a book in my bedroom. I was used to hearing them fight, but I knew this one was different. Mama screamed even louder than usual. I walked into the kitchen to see if I could break it up.

I immediately noticed her holding that gun—and I could tell by the look on her face that she meant to use it.

I guess she'd had just about enough of his bullcrap. Every woman has a tipping point with a bad husband and she had reached hers. I was afraid she would kill him right then and there. Or worse, I thought he might take that gun away from her and shoot her. He wasn't a big man, but he was very strong and he had big hands and arms.

He grabbed her by the wrist as I charged at him. Suddenly, the gun went off. Fortunately for all three of us, the only casualty was the living room ceiling, since he had stretched Mama's arms up over her head.

I reared back with my small right hand and caught him square in the jaw. I must admit it was a pretty good punch for a kid in the seventh grade. But no punch from a 12-year-old would do much damage to a grown man. He looked down at me, somewhat in disbelief, and let go of Mama's arm.

He then turned and walked out the door—and that was the last time I saw the man who was married to my mother for many, many years.

"Kenny, you and I are on our own now," she told me soon after that. "But I will always take care of you."

That episode was just a prelude of what was to come for Kenneth Smith Harrelson.

Over my lifetime, I would get into more scrapes than I can remember and more bar-room brawls than most career bouncers. I had a temper, developed some fighting skills, and never backed down from anybody.

Unless they had me outgunned…

Four years after that bullet pierced a hole through our ceiling, in the summer of 1957, I was walking down the street in a low-income area of Savannah with my friend Hennon Warren. Hennon was one heck of a shortstop on my American Legion team. I don't remember where we were headed that night when we came upon a bicycle lying straight across the sidewalk.

"Some kid must have left it here," I told Hennon. "I'll take care of it for him."

I picked up the bike and carried it to a narrow spot between two houses where I figured it would be secure. I gently set it down, thinking the kid who owned it would easily find it the following day. Suddenly, just as that bike left my fingertips, the front door of the house swung open and a man walked out. He saw me immediately.

"You trying to steal my kid's bike? I am going to shoot you!"

I didn't even get a chance to explain my good deed before that man bolted back inside.

In that part of town, I knew exactly what he was headed for. But I was pretty fast and I also knew it was time to put my speed to use. I looked at Hennon and neither of us needed to say a word.

We took off running across the street as if our lives depended on it.

As it turned out, they did. The man was not bluffing.

Pop! Pop! Pop!

Where I grew up, I recognized the sounds of gunshots.

I dashed for a used-car lot across the street, spotting a chain across the entrance in the darkness just in time. I hurdled it as the bullets whizzed by me onto the pavement. I didn't have time to warn Hennon about that obstacle, turning just in time to see him trip over it, landing head-first on the pavement.

Of course, a little asphalt-rash heals much better than a bullet hole. It was a good thing the man was shooting at me and not at Hennon.

He was lying prone on the pavement and would have been an easy target.

It also was a good thing this guy was not a very good shot.

Or maybe the darkness of the night saved me.

I will never know.

I would have loved to go back there at some point to inform the trigger-happy father I was only securing his kid's bike, but I didn't want to risk it.

That was not the last time I'd be shot at. One time when I was in my twenties, I planned on doing a little duck-hunting in Savannah. I walked about a half mile down to this river and noticed a car, sitting on a beaten path, rocking up and down like a boat on the Atlantic. Curiosity got the better of me, so I walked up to the car. I got about five feet away before I could see, well, let's just say some carnal relations were occurring in the back seat.

Suddenly, the man looked up and saw me peering inside.

Rather than stay and try to talk myself out of this jam, again I took off running.

I ran about 30 yards by the time I heard the familiar *Pop! Pop! Pop!* of a pistol again. I zigzagged through the open field and cut behind a tree just as a bullet carved a big hole into the bark inches from my head. I took a deep breath, turned, and continued running out of range, figuring the guy could not chase me with his pants around his ankles.

I never even considered leveling my shotgun and shooting back at him. In times like those, I figured the safest thing to do was to run for my life. So that's what I did—again.

Years later, after I had already made it to the big leagues, I was on a road trip in Oakland. By then I was well known as "Hawk" Harrelson, which didn't stop a 6-foot-5 guy from beating my butt pretty good in a bar. That one I probably deserved, since I had started it.

He threatened revenge moments before the police hauled him away, declaring, "I know who *you* are."

He was half right, anyway. He had met the Hawk, but he didn't know Kenny Harrelson.

You see, not only had I received a nickname that stuck like glue, but I admit that the Hawk became my alter ego.

There was a huge difference between me and the Hawk. I didn't want to fight, but the Hawk did. Sometimes pressure ate Kenny up, but it wasn't a problem for the Hawk, whether it was on the baseball field or the golf course in front of a big gallery.

A prominent psychologist once told me the Hawk developed his own personality to help Kenny deal with his issues.

Anyway, the day after that scrum in an Oakland nightclub, I showed up at the ballpark sporting a huge black eye. I had to plead with my manager to put me into the lineup. I then hit a long double off the wall with only one eye open.

That episode illustrated a theme in my life.

When I was growing up, some of my friends made bets with each other about whether I would live to see the age of 20. And if a few guys had been more accurate with a gun, I wouldn't have. Not only did I fight a lot, but I was a daredevil. I often did stupid, dangerous things, like drag racing on the streets of Savannah.

I could have died a dozen times in about a dozen different ways over the years. Not only have I been shot at, but I have had a gun stuck to my ribs in a foreign country, taken part in more bar-room brawls than I can remember, and survived white-knuckle, out-of-control rides in cabs over mountainous terrain in faraway places.

I feel fortunate to have lived long enough to put my life story into words.

I like to think I learned something from those near-death experiences. They not only leave you alive, they make you *feel* alive, if that makes any sense. Let me tell you, there's nothing that rattles your nerves like the sound of lead flying by your head.

I have been beaten up—physically and mentally, figuratively and literally—a lot during my lifetime. I have taken my share of butt-whippings and delivered quite a few myself.

You see, the Hawk was a fighter.

The Hawk never cared how many he faced or how big they were, he knew somebody was gonna get knocked out.

I never quit fighting in the middle of one, even when I was taking a beating. I didn't care if I got my butt kicked once in a while. I always figured a good butt-beating gives a guy some humility. Sometimes, it taught me a lesson or kept me grounded. It's not the worst thing in the world to get the crap beat out of you, and I never let it interfere with my work.

Many a day and night throughout my life, I worked my way out of a tough situation with my 10 knuckles. That's just the way it was where I was raised, when I was raised, and I certainly won't apologize for it all these years later.

In some ways, disputes were better solved that way than they are in today's world. You wiped off the blood, said your peace, and sometimes you even shook hands when it was over. Then you went back to what you were doing to begin with.

Nobody ever died.

Today, they carry the loser of a confrontation to the morgue. The winner, if caught, often goes off to prison.

Fortunately, I avoided both destinations.

Not that my body didn't get damaged along the way. My nose has been broken five times and is somewhat of a mangled, yet prominent, mess. I have had five operations on my eyes and I don't have much peripheral vision. I have screws and pins in my right ankle.

A doctor, while examining my broken right hand once after a fight, told me, "Hawk, you just hit *too* hard."

These days, my wrists are very painful. Doctors have told me I basically wore them out. It's no wonder, because I spent my life swinging away at something—with a baseball bat, a golf club, or my fists.

Now, just because I have been in a ton of scrapes, and owned a bad temper, don't get the idea that I couldn't get along with people.

I made more lifelong friends along the way than a guy deserves to have, from the biggest sports legends on the planet such as Michael Jordan and Arnold Palmer to my teammates from baseball, golf partners, not to mention hundreds of everyday Joes, clubhouse attendants, bartenders, bellhops, and restaurant owners the public wouldn't recognize, as well as some of the biggest business titans America has ever known.

I love people.

I love meeting them, talking to them, getting to know what makes them tick. I just never put up with the rudeness or insults, or what I thought were insults back when I could do something about it. But when I became a professional athlete and a public figure, it seemed I was often a target for the drunkest or brashest guy in the joint. Also, I often defended friends or acquaintances who were unwilling or unable to defend themselves.

I may have grown up without a father in my life and I may have been a mischievous kid, but I still knew right from wrong. Mama taught me well, and I never crossed the line or broke the law.

Along the way, my teachers, schools principals, the media, a manager or two, and some of my critics have called me anything from unruly, wild, outspoken, and flashy, to a showboat and a rebel.

The truth is I probably was all of the above at one time or another.

I went from being a great high school athlete in three sports to the bright lights of Major League Baseball. I played professional golf for a few years and then quit because my terrible temper made it impossible for me to make a living and keep my clubs intact at the same time.

I finally answered my calling: I found a home as a baseball broadcaster.

I was recently hitting a bucket of balls at my favorite course outside Chicago when an older gentleman walked up to me.

"Mister Harrelson, I don't mean to interrupt you," he said, "but I've been reading about you lately and you really have led some sort of amazing life."

I thanked him, finished my bucket, and as I started my 34-mile drive back to my house in Indiana, I thought about what he had said.

"That guy is right," I said to myself. "It has been an amazing life."

Looking back on it, I really believe my timing couldn't have been more perfect.

It is a special thing to be the first person to do something significant. Neil Armstrong was the first man to walk on the moon. Amelia Earhart was the first woman to complete a transatlantic flight. Jackie Robinson was the first black player in the major leagues.

Me?

I was the first big-leaguer to wear a batting glove, albeit by accident. (Actually, it was a golf glove, but the idea caught on and later morphed into the common-day batting glove.) Watch today's hitters at the plate. Is there anyone, outside of a pitcher hitting in the National League perhaps, who doesn't wear one or even two?

I also became baseball's first free agent, even though Curt Flood was credited with that distinction a few years after I did it. But I will explain that later.

No records are kept on this, obviously, but I believe I was the first player to ever have a full-time bodyguard—and I sure needed it.

I was the first major leaguer to quit baseball to play professional golf for a living. Or at least try to.

Then I became the first professional golfer to quit the sport to become a baseball broadcaster.

I know there is nobody else who can claim to have played in the MLB All-Star Game, a World Series, and the British Open.

How many guys have been given golf clubs by Ben Hogan, Jack Nicklaus, and Palmer, or a putter by Payne Stewart only weeks before he died, beaten Sam Snead in match play, or sang on stage with Roy Clark, Jerry Reed, and Chet Atkins, or hung out with the likes of Rocky Marciano and Mickey Mantle, or movie stars like Richard Burton and Liz Taylor, or kneeled in the on-deck circle as the great Carl Yastrzemski ripped a homer at Fenway Park, or sat next to Frank "Hondo" Howard as he ripped into a steak, had a drink with Robert Mitchum, been called a buddy by Frank Sinatra, or even got the chance to meet John Wayne?

I witnessed quite a bit of history, too. I was with Joe Namath the night before he fulfilled his famous guarantee, leading the New York Jets to one of the biggest upsets in sports history, in Super Bowl III. I joked around with Bobby Kennedy at my locker just weeks before he was assassinated. (I never told him that I almost punched his brother Teddy in the face one night.)

I have enjoyed America's greatest venues, from the White House to Air Force One to Fenway Park and Yankee Stadium to the greens of Augusta National.

I played with or against some of the greatest legends of America's pastime. I shared a broadcast booth with several more and played golf with hundreds of people who wound up in Cooperstown.

I know it may seem as if I am bragging about my life, but I sure don't want it to come off that way. Like I said, I just happened to frequently be in the right place at the right time.

There were times I felt invincible, that I could succeed at just about any event or game I tried athletically. I was never afraid to take risks or try something new and I learned the nuances of most sports very quickly.

I was a high school All-American in basketball and a quarterback whom all the big schools wanted to sign. I was a scratch golfer as a high school junior. I could shoot pool with anybody. I averaged around 200 as a bowler. I won my first eight boxing matches as an amateur—until I got knocked on my butt and gave up that sport.

And baseball?

It may have been my worst sport.

Then I made a living at it. Well, if you describe a $6,000 salary when I came up to the big leagues in 1963 as a "living." When I wasn't playing baseball, I supplemented my income betting on myself in arm-wrestling, shooting pool, and, of course, playing golf. I was a pretty good gin player as well.

I admit that I once loved living in the fast lane, at least until I found the woman who settled me down. I traveled by helicopters and limousines. I had long hair and could have passed for a member of the Mod Squad in the 1960s. I used to wear the flashiest, most outrageous clothes of anyone in professional sports, including Broadway Joe. Then there was a period during the 1970s and '80s when I usually sported a cowboy hat on my head and cowboy boots on my feet, with big sunglasses propped on my prominent nose.

All the while, I considered myself "old school," although a few of my former teammates surely would laugh about that label now.

I always believed in standing proudly and singing loudly during the national anthem, holding doors and pulling out chairs for women, running hard to first base, and signing as many autographs for the fans as possible. My mama's favorite player, Rocky Colavito, taught me that. And if the other pitcher knocked down one of our hitters, I believed in knocking down two of theirs. Two eyes for one eye, right? Then I was more than happy to have a drink or two with those same combatants after a game.

I played nine seasons in the big leagues, but my greatest contribution to baseball has been the millions of people who have invited me into their homes over the past six decades. Not literally of course, but via the airwaves from Boston or New York or Chicago or whatever city my team played in that particular day or night.

I sincerely hope I gave more than I received, not only to the game of baseball but to help make people's lives more enjoyable.

Since 1959, I have spent every year but one in the game of baseball, outside of my three years in professional golf in the 1970s.

I realize it's coming to an end soon. My goal is to work in baseball until the year 2020, joining a very small group of men who have worked in baseball for parts of eight decades.

You can say that I owe the game everything for the blessings in my life, such as my family, my friends, and all of my fond memories. I tried to make the most of every moment in my career. It is no secret I wanted to win every game I either played or called on the airwaves, which is why my critics have labeled me "the biggest homer in broadcasting."

They may mean it as an insult, but I sure don't take it as one. It's a compliment in my book. I love to win. I love to see the people I am close to win. I have been insulted once, twice, or a hundred times over the course of my life, but that description doesn't hurt me in the least.

I have no complaints, few regrets, and probably wouldn't change a thing even if I could.

I am just thankful I dodged the bullets and survived the punches to make it this far.

2 PROUD TO BE A MAMA'S BOY

I HAVE HAD MY PICTURE TAKEN THOUSANDS OF TIMES OVER my lifetime. I smiled in most photos, though sometimes I was serious. I was often either swinging a bat or a golf club, and wearing a cowboy hat or even a fake mustache.

My picture has been placed on baseball cards, in newspapers, on huge billboards endorsing a product, and even in national magazines such as *Sports Illustrated* or *Golf World*.

But my favorite picture hands-down is the one of me and Mama walking down the street in Savannah.

I was only eight or nine years old and she was holding my hand. It was just a simple black-and-white snapshot that was framed, sitting on a shelf in our living room for years.

I don't know who snapped it and I have no idea what happened to it, but I would give anything to still have it.

That one moment in time captured a theme of my life while growing up, and perhaps even as an adult: I was an unapologetic mama's boy. Unlike most kids who were tagged with that usually unflattering term, I was proud of it. It was anything but derogatory to me.

My mother, Jessie Harrelson, was *everything* to me. I won't reveal her full name because she absolutely hated her middle name.

She was large but not overweight, and a very beautiful woman.

I was not an only child, however.

My sister, Iris, was seven years older. She had to quit high school to get married at the age of 14, which wasn't uncommon in our town during that era. She wasn't around much while I was growing up. Her first marriage didn't last and she later married six more times. Despite her Elizabeth Taylor–like approach to matrimony, she was a genius, having an IQ of more than 160.

I was born, September 4, 1941, just three months and three days before Pearl Harbor was bombed by Japan.

In my eyes, the man Mama married wasn't a great man by any means, as I have detailed in his shameful exit from our lives.

They called him "Smitty."

I got my size from Mama, but I must have gotten my strong hands from him. I was told later by some of his friends that he wasn't a bad athlete, either. He played baseball for one of the mill teams in town and he batted cross-handed. Apparently, he could hit the ball a long way, too.

He owned two bakeries, one in Spartanburg and one in Woodruff, where he taught me how to knead dough. One day his bakery in Woodruff burned to the ground. After that, he began to spend more time out of town and we didn't see him as often.

Eventually, we moved from Woodruff to Charlotte to Savannah, Georgia, where we settled.

Mama's husband did teach me a few things besides kneading dough. When we visited my grandparents in the country, he would wrap electrical tape around cow chips to make baseballs. I knew I had some talent at a young age because I could hit those cow chips pretty far, just like he could. So that must have been where I got my power.

He taught me to hit cross-handed like he did, which I didn't realize was the wrong way to grip a baseball bat until I started playing Little League.

He also taught me how to drive when I was only six or seven. There were a lot of bridges where we lived—those narrow, wooden one-lane bridges that cover the many rivers and creeks across South Carolina and Georgia—requiring my steering to be perfect. One time I sat on his lap, steering the car as he controlled the pedals. When we came to one of those bridges, which must have been 100 yards long, I wanted to climb over into the passenger seat.

"No, no, no, no," he said. "You're doing it!"

He actually forced me to steer that car across that narrow wooden bridge. That was the first time in my life I remember being absolutely petrified.

After his Woodruff bakery burned down, he got a job at an atomic-energy plant in Barnwell, South Carolina.

As I grew old enough to understand their relationship, I resented the man because of what he put Mama through. I could see the pain in her eyes almost every day. She was forced to put up with a lot because of him. He drank a lot, cheated on her, and made life tough for her.

They argued and fought constantly, although he never hit her to my knowledge. And after he left us, he never gave Mama a nickel to help raise me.

That punch I landed on him might have been my first but it surely wouldn't be my last. But it was the only one I had thrown against the man who once claimed to be my father.

I can remember my first real fight vividly and I will regret it until the day I die.

A very nice boy by the name of Douglas Allen was one of my best friends in my first-grade class. One day we were playing baseball and something happened on the field between us. I don't remember the particulars, but I know I got angry. I was big for a six-year-old kid and I hit Douglas a couple of times. He stopped fighting back and complained of a headache.

"Stop it!" he yelled. "My head hurts!"

Then I hit him again. He was crying by the time the coach came over to break it up.

I felt bad almost immediately for fighting him. I didn't see him over the next few days for me to apologize, so I walked the mile and a half to his house.

His mother answered the door.

"Can Douglas come out?" I asked her.

"He's really not feeling well right now," she told me.

She went inside and he walked out a few minutes later, sitting down next to me on the front stoop.

"I am sorry, Douglas," I told him. "I didn't mean to hit you like that."

We talked for a few minutes and I tried my best to patch things up before I left. I didn't see him at all in the ensuing weeks and months. Then I heard from a few other kids that Douglas had to undergo an operation to remove a tumor in his head.

It turned out that he had brain cancer and died shortly after that.

I thought back to that fight and how he had complained of a headache and I will never forgive myself for hitting him one more time. His headache must have been a symptom of the tumor and I believe our fight resulted in his diagnosis.

Still, I can't say I am over what was nothing but a childhood squabble, because I never will be.

I will regret punching him until my final day on earth.

I also wish I could say it was my final fight, but it wasn't even close.

A kid by the name of Eugene Jeffers was a really good fighter who was about my age. One time during a field-day competition for all the junior high schools in Savannah, in which they held events such as the football throw, softball throw, 100-yard dash, etc., I stood talking to a group of kids when a high school bully by the name of Bubba walked up to me.

He pointed to Eugene.

"Eugene over there says he can kick your butt," Bubba told me.

I walked over to Eugene.

"You got a problem with me, Eugene?" I asked.

"Yeah," he said, just before he took a swing at me.

I ducked his punch and hit him with a few good shots. There must have been 30 people watching us go at it and somebody called a nearby cop, who came and pulled me off Eugene. Later, I think we both realized Bubba had instigated the whole thing, and from that day on, Eugene and I became pretty good buddies.

The great thing about Woodruff for me was that it wasn't segregated. Black people lived all around us and most of my friends were black kids from the neighborhood. Those were my buddies. We played basketball and football together, fought together, and ate lunch together. I very seldom played with a white kid when I was little.

I like to think I never had a prejudiced bone in my body, even though I grew up in the Deep South, because of that time in my life.

When we were playing and fighting together, I don't even think we noticed the color of our skin wasn't the same.

I thumbed for a ride a lot while growing up, but sometimes I hopped on a bus. That is when I discovered that black people could not ride in the front of the bus. If the bus was full, and I had a seat, I always made it a point to give it up to a black lady who was standing in the aisle. I remember the two separate water fountains when I went to get a drink. I remember separate public toilets.

I was a kid growing up in the Deep South, where those things were normal and accepted, but I remember thinking how wrong it all was.

I was baptized a Baptist and Mama and I went to church often.

Our house was a tiny two-bedroom place. When the screen on my bedroom window ripped, I stuffed a sock in the hole to keep the mosquitoes out. We didn't have air conditioning, either, so Mama bought me a fan for my room.

The only major league team I could get on my small transistor radio was the Cardinals on KMOX out of St. Louis. Their games brought me the voices of two legends—Jack Buck and Harry Caray. Jack was my absolute all-time favorite to listen to when I was a kid. I would fall asleep almost every night to his voice.

Protected from the mosquitoes by my socks and cooled by that fan, I would lie in bed tossing a baseball toward the ceiling and catching it while listening to Jack and Harry broadcast some game thousands of miles away from my tiny bedroom. I could imagine the plays, the hits, the pitcher going into his stretch—everything they described.

Those memories made me believe the baseball gods created the game specifically for radio. While listening to a game, I used my imagination, envisioning each hit, each home run, and each double play.

My grammar school, Eli Whitney Grammar, was directly across the street from my house.

When it came to girls, some things you never forget—like your first kiss.

Her name was Anne. I was in the fourth grade and she was in the sixth. We had been playing in the cemetery one day when she sat down on top of a tombstone.

"I am going to kiss you," she said bluntly.

Who was I to object? She wasn't bluffing, either, and I'll never forget that moment.

When I visited my grandparents' farm in the country, my grandpa often encouraged me to shoot his .22 rifle. He and I would sit on the front porch and practice shooting at flowers about 60 yards away. One day, I shot what I thought were eight or nine wild turkeys and brought them up to the house, proudly displaying them for my grandma.

"Look, Grandma! I got some wild turkeys," I stated.

"Those are my guineas!" she screamed.

I didn't know one big bird from another and I had killed her pet guineas.

All in all, it was a fun childhood and I never really thought much about growing up without a real father in my life. Mama was both my mother and father, and everything in between, in my eyes.

She sacrificed so much for me, because the man she had married left us and stopped providing for us.

The day he left wasn't the final time I ever saw him, but I wish it had been.

When I was playing in the big leagues almost 15 years later, he found my telephone number somehow and called me, wanting to meet one day. I was curious as to what he had made of himself, so I agreed.

Within a few minutes, I knew the reason he wanted to see me and it was colored green. It wasn't to reconnect or to catch up on lost time. He needed money and he figured I had plenty to lend. He asked to borrow a few thousand dollars, but I turned him down.

I saw him one more time, years later near Savannah. He had remarried and had another son with him, but this time, for whatever reason, I loaned him $500 when he asked.

I never saw that $500 again, or him for that matter.

I guess I have a younger half-brother, whom I have never met, living somewhere in this world. I don't know his name or where he lives, and I don't really care to meet him because of who his father was.

A few years after I loaned him that money, Mama's sister, Aunt Errol, called me. She said that he was in the hospital and that he soon would die. She wanted to know if I wanted to see him one final time.

I didn't.

When he died a few days later, she called again and asked me to come to the funeral.

"I am not coming," I told her.

"But he was your father!" she told me.

My father?

He didn't fit that definition in my eyes and he hadn't been around for me for most of my life. I wasn't about to take the time and effort to be there for him when he died.

I really never forgave the man for the way he treated the most important person in my life.

I had Mama and that's all that mattered to me.

She was a very wise woman and taught me so many things. She imparted her wisdom in so many ways. She didn't have much formal education, but she was a genius when it came to common sense. I like to say she was street smart.

We had only one tiny bathroom, but every morning I looked into that bathroom mirror and read a small newspaper clipping she had stuck in the lower-right corner:

There are two days of the week of which and upon which I never worry…two carefree days kept secretly free of fear and apprehension. One of those days is yesterday. The other day I should not worry about is tomorrow, which is beyond my immediate control. Let me, therefore, live one day at a time.

I really don't know if Mama placed it there for her to read every day, or for me to read, or for both of us, but I read it whenever I brushed my teeth or combed my hair. And I tried to live by it every day of my life.

I am sure raising me had to be a big burden on her, but she never showed it.

Mama would do anything she could for me. She couldn't afford much, but she busted her butt working every day for me. Sometimes, I needed to be reminded of that.

One time during my junior year, I needed a new shirt for a dance that was coming up. She didn't have the money, simply because she was making only $56 every week from the meat-packing company. Still, she found the money somehow and then went out and bought me a new shirt. She brought it home and pulled it out of the box.

I got very upset once I saw it. I didn't like the shirt at all and we argued about it. Finally, I told her that I wasn't going to wear it and I ripped it in half.

My mother, the woman I loved more than anything, started to cry.

I will never forget that moment as long as I live. What an ungrateful jerk I was, taking advantage of that poor woman who had spent her hard-earned money to buy something for her only son. The thought of that moment makes me want to cry right now. I will wish forever that I could go back in time and change that moment.

Nobody on this earth ever loved me like that woman.

But I know she had to realize how much I loved her back.

I was born a mama's boy and someday I will die a mama's boy.

3   IT JUST CAME EASY

WHEN I WAS NINE YEARS OLD, MAMA ALLOWED ME TO SKIP
school one day during the spring.

The New York Yankees were passing through Savannah at the
end of spring training, on their way from Fort Lauderdale to New
York, and they were scheduled to play the Cincinnati Reds at Grayson
Stadium.

Mama knew I loved baseball and she took me to the game.

I had been reading about this hotshot rookie coming up and I wanted
his autograph.

The Yankees arrived by train, played the game, and then were hurry-
ing to their bus to head back to the train station. As the players walked
from the dugout to the bus, I spotted him.

He wore No. 6 on his back.

"Mister Mantle," I stammered. "Can I have your autograph?"

"Beat it, kid!" the Mick told me, spitting on the ground while not
breaking stride.

That rejection just about crushed me that day. *If I ever become a big-
league baseball player*, I thought, *I will never do that to a kid.*

(And in case you are wondering about Mickey's number, he didn't
start wearing No. 7 until the second half of his rookie season.)

I tried emulating the big-league players when I played baseball,
despite that autograph snub.

Mama's street smarts helped me when it came to athletics.

She once told me, "Kenny, at times you will be playing against boys who are bigger and better than you, but don't let them ever outcompete you. You play as hard as you can and you always play to win."

I took her advice to heart.

I had played plenty of pickup games back in Woodruff. During one of them, I was kneeling in the on-deck circle, trying to do it just the way the big-leaguers did. The kid at the plate took a mighty cut and took off running as my eyes followed the ball. Unbeknownst to me, he had let go of the bat upon contact. It hit me squarely in my nose.

I was lying there in the dirt, my nose gushing blood as tears ran down my cheeks. There is no pain like getting your nose broken. I was a bloody mess, as the older guys tried to clean me up a little and help me to my feet. I walked home covered in blood that day.

Mama started crying the moment she saw my face.

It was the first time I broke my nose, but there would be many more to come.

It didn't take long to do it a second time—on the same playground but in a different sport.

This time, playing football, the running back's shoulder pad caught me right in the schnoz. I knew the feeling. It was broken again. The director of the playground drove me to the hospital, where a doctor grabbed it with both hands and tried to set it straight. He then wrapped it in adhesive tape and sent me home.

The third time came on the team bus before a football game during my sophomore year in high school in a dispute over a pair of socks, of all things.

Our Benedictine High School team would travel to Parris Island for a week for spring football practice each year. On the bus ride there, I got into an argument with Billy Robinson, a buddy, over who owned a pair of socks lying on the seat. Just as we stepped off the bus, he turned around and caught me with a punch right in the nose. I returned with one to his jaw.

Those two punches left me with a broken nose, again, and this time, a broken right hand.

I was the quarterback and every time I took a snap from center over the next week, I winced in pain. It took months for my hand to feel normal again.

I got into another senseless fight in an oyster bar when I came home after my first year in the minor leagues. Some guy came over to me and asked, "You're Ken Harrelson, aren't you?"

"You know who I am," I replied.

Without warning, he just sucker-punched me. I didn't know his name or why he hit me. Maybe I sounded cocky or condescending to him, I don't know. I then whaled on him and won the fight, knocking him out cold. Anyway, his one and only punch had broken my nose yet again.

My fifth and final broken nose came after another bar fight, this time in Sarasota, Florida, during spring training one year when I was with the Kansas City Athletics.

It's almost as if my nose had what doctors today call "concussion syndrome." Once you have had one, it's much, much easier to get another. Or maybe it was because of its size and shape. I don't really know.

I do know how Jerry West feels. They say he has broken his nine times. So I got a few more to go to beat him.

Savannah was a huge sports town and I was considered a sports prodigy of sorts.

It was big news in town when Savannah instituted its Little League program when I was 12. In the city's very first game, which was played at Coke Field, I hit three home runs and a double. From that day on, it seemed most people in town knew my name.

I scored 49 points as a third-grader in a basketball game in which my entire team scored only 60. Basketball was my first love. I could dribble well, handle the ball, pass, and, of course, shoot it. I also played football like all of the other kids.

I played golf for the first time during my junior year in high school at a nine-hole course that the Union Camp Corporation, one of the largest paper mills in the world, had built for its employees.

I fell in love with the game of golf from the moment I hit my first tee shot. Back then it was considered a rich man's game and we were anything but rich. So I took up caddying and usually earned 50 cents or maybe a dollar for a round. That is when I met a man named Hobart Manley, one of America's most legendary amateur golfers. When I caddied for Hobart, he usually paid me five dollars and sometimes gave me a new sleeve of Titleist balls. Hobart was such a good player that he never lost a ball, so he had plenty to give me.

He played in three U.S. Opens as an amateur, six U.S. Amateurs, and he won the North-South Amateur at Pinehurst in 1951 when he finished the final round with five consecutive threes. He never turned professional, because his father convinced him to stay in business, and because in the 1950s there wasn't huge prize money available on the PGA Tour.

Hobart could hit the ball a mile, had a great short game, and was a clutch putter. And he did it all with great style.

He was my first sports idol, and, as I write this, he is in his nineties, still lives in Savannah, and plays golf almost every day when the weather is good.

I got my driver's license when I was only 13 years old because the coach of my baseball team was a local deputy sheriff. He fixed some paperwork and did me a favor so I could drive earlier than most kids. Mama had bought me a beautiful 1941 Plymouth for $50, but my sister Iris had bought a new Studebaker Silver Hawk, ironically, which I loved to borrow whenever she was around.

That car could really move. I frequently pestered her to let me drive it—and I frequently drag-raced in it, rarely losing.

One night while I was in high school, I was returning home from Savannah Beach after I had a fight with my date, when I noticed a classmate sitting next to me in his new Chevy at a red light.

"Hey, Kenny, you want to race?" he asked.

"Heck, yes," I answered.

It didn't take long to get Iris' Studebaker up to 100 miles per hour, as I blew by that Chevy. Then I spotted a flashing red light in my rearview mirror. My buddy had turned off the road to the right, so I took the first left I could find, thinking I could hide out for a while to avoid what surely would be a speeding ticket.

I waited 10 minutes and then re-entered the highway, where the cop was waiting for me. He pulled me out of that car in a very rough manner, and I already had been in a foul mood after the fight with my date, so I did something really stupid—I took a swing at him.

Fortunately, I missed.

He hauled me off to jail, where I was told I would get one telephone call. It was 2:30 in the morning, so I wasn't calling Mama. I found the number of a lawyer in town who I knew was a big sports fan.

"If you are stupid enough to get yourself put in jail at this hour, you can stay there," he told me.

Then he hung up.

I was stuck. I looked around my cell, noticing the feces-filled toilet and the thin soiled mattress on top of a cot. I sat down on it and cried. The stench of urine, feces, and vomit was overwhelming. Now I added a few tears to the room.

I sat there, crying my eyes out, wondering when and if I would get out of the place.

Within a few minutes, the cop came back and opened my cell door.

"You're the luckiest kid in town," he told me.

It turned out the kid who I drag-raced had a father who happened to be the mayor of Savannah Beach. The kid obviously had witnessed the cop hauling me off to jail from down the road and then went home and told his dad.

Unfortunately, it wouldn't be the last time I spent a night in jail.

I didn't get into any drag-racing duels with my own car, but I did have a near-death experience once, only because my windshield wipers didn't work very well.

It was raining one day when I pulled out of the street where we lived. I couldn't really see anything but raindrops. All of a sudden I heard a loud horn—a car traveling way too fast for the conditions was headed directly at me. Suddenly, the car veered to the left, narrowly missing me. That car went up on two wheels and almost flipped over before it landed on all four.

I knew my mistake had almost killed me or whoever was in that car. The other driver hit the brakes and turned around, so I figured it was a man wanting to come back and beat me up. I hit the gas pedal and got out of there quickly before they could return.

There were three high schools in Savannah—Commercial High, Savannah High, the largest school enrollment-wise in the state, and Benedictine, a military academy.

By the time I finished middle school, sports fans in town wondered which high school I would attend. I wasn't sure myself.

While I was in the ninth grade, the coach at Commercial, M.A. Spellman, invited me to play in their annual Blue-Gold spring game, which always attracted a huge crowd. He was recruiting me, trying to get me to come to the school before my sophomore year.

I was told to meet the other football players at the school at 6:00 that night and ride the bus to the stadium with the team. I had hitched a ride and arrived at Commercial at about 4:15 PM and had plenty of time to kill, so I walked five blocks to a pool hall.

I had learned how to shoot pool when I was only 11 or 12 years old. By the time I was a freshman, I could handle a pool cue probably much better than any golf club or baseball bat that ever touched my hands.

I had about two bucks in my pocket that day when a guy in his forties walked in, looking for a game. I asked him if he wanted to play nine-ball at 50 cents per game.

He sized me up and down and jumped at the chance, figuring he could easily take whatever money a ninth-grader had in his pockets.

"Okay, but I have to quit at five minutes to 6:00," I told him.

I ran the table during the first game. I won the next. I continued winning. I was up about $25 when I noticed it was 6:00.

"I have to leave," I said.

"You can't leave now," the guy told me. "You have $25 of my money."

I came up with a brilliant idea.

"Double-or-nothing on one final game?" I asked.

I ran the table and took the guy's $50 just as Commercial High's trainer John Pappas walked in.

"I knew you would be here," he said. "We have to get you to the stadium!"

John drove me back to the school, but the team bus had just pulled out of the parking lot. I threw my street clothes into a pile on the locker room floor and put on my pads and uniform. John drove me to the stadium but by the time we arrived, I could tell Coach Spellman wasn't happy.

"Where in the world were you?" he asked.

I lied. I knew I couldn't possibly tell him I had been shooting pool for money only a few blocks away.

"I couldn't get a ride," I told him.

He inserted me into the Blue team's lineup as the quarterback. Even though I was younger than all the other starters, I threw four touchdown passes that night.

"You are my starting quarterback next year," Coach Spellman told me after the game.

But I hadn't committed to attending Commercial. All three high schools started to court Mama about the decision. A man by the name of R.C. Haupt, who owned the Coastal Butane Gas Company, came to the house. His son Reginald went to Benedictine High.

He told Mama, "I will pay all of Kenneth's tuition, books, and expenses."

The Savannah High head coach told her, "You know he'd be best off at Savannah High, because it's the biggest and best school in town."

And I liked Coach Spellman, too.

In the end, Mama figured Benedictine would provide the discipline I needed. I had known a few kids who attended Benedictine and I was worried, knowing the type of hazing they endured at a military school. I also feared having to "walk the jug," as they called it—marching up and down a courtyard with an M-1 rifle on my shoulder. I could picture myself doing that day after day, since I would probably accumulate a few demerits along the way.

At least I would get a uniform.

Mr. Haupt also gave me a job at his company, paying me $40 a week to paint butane gas tanks by brush for two hours each Saturday.

While working for him, I also went out on service calls and sometimes had to crawl under narrow crawl spaces to fix whatever the problem was. I ran into a rattlesnake three or four times under there.

Another of Benedictine's athletic boosters was the guy who owned the only Chevy dealership in town. He was wheelchair-bound, loved all sports, and had plenty of money. If I drove in a run in baseball, he would give me a dollar. If I hit a home run, he gave me five. The same went for scoring touchdowns.

On days when we didn't have a game, I mowed lawns for 50 cents.

The toughest part of attending Benedictine was the annual St. Patrick's Day parade, in which we had to march in formation wearing our dress whites. It usually was very hot and several freshmen would faint along the three-to-five-mile route. Most of the guys had to carry an M-1, which weighed about nine pounds, over their shoulder.

My job was to carry the Browning Automatic Rifle, which weighed about 19.5 pounds.

I was in great shape, but carrying that big thing was brutal.

We got hazed some, too, as I had feared, but mostly the school administrators and coaches took care of me because of my athletic ability. On game days, they allowed me to take a nap on the couch in the library. Sometimes, they allowed me to go home early to rest up before a big game.

When I once was given a few demerits and was ordered to walk the jug, my football coach, Vic Mell, told me, "I will take care of that."

Coach Mell wanted his sophomore quarterback at practice, using his shoulder to throw passes, not carry rifles.

I had strange taste in music then, at least according to my friends.

My sister bought me a recording of Ravel's "Bolero" and I listened to it before every big game. I would lay on the couch, close my eyes, and picture myself riding across the desert on a big white horse as that familiar "bump...bump...bump" roared throughout the house. That record was 10 minutes long and I played it over and over as a relaxation tool before big games.

While everybody else about my age was into Elvis, I was a high school kid who loved Ravel. Go figure. I did see the King perform once, however. When I was 14, Elvis came to town and some buddies and I went to his concert that day. At the end of that performance, I finally agreed with them: I too thought he was the greatest. If there were three performers I always wanted to meet but never got the chance, they were Elvis, Dean Martin, and Neil Diamond.

With my earnings playing pool, mowing lawns, painting butane tanks, caddying, and what I was getting paid for my high school sports exploits, most weeks I made more than Mama's $56 paycheck.

Ironically, baseball was my worst sport among the big three. I didn't even play baseball during my junior year, because I had convinced the principal to start a golf team. In our school's first year competing in golf, I won the city's high school championship.

I went back to playing baseball during my senior year. I was a good player, but I was much better as a basketball guard and a quarterback.

We had a heck of a basketball team during my three years and we made it to the state semifinals during my sophomore season, in which I started at guard and led the team in scoring. By the time I was a senior, we had a new coach who didn't like to run up the score on other teams. So I would score about 25 points in the first half and then not play in the second half.

Richmond Academy in Augusta was our big rival in basketball. One year I had a great game and we beat them at their house before a large crowd. That night, our team stayed at a hotel in Augusta that was located up on a hill. The guys were celebrating in one of our rooms when somebody popped out a small bottle of Four Roses bourbon.

I had never sipped booze before that night. In fact, I had been the one teammate to yell at the other guys who did drink. Even the smell of alcohol turned me off.

But that night, I took a few sips. Then I took a couple more. The small bottle was soon empty. Then I reached into my travel bag for some reason and took a few sips of my Old Spice cologne, which was all I wore in high school. Don't ask me what I was thinking by swallowing cologne, but before long, I was puking my guts out. I eventually passed out in the bathtub of that hotel room.

As I tried to sleep it off, one of my teammates came into the bathroom and shook me.

"We need you! We need you!" he screamed.

I got up and ran downstairs to see two of my teammates sprawled out on the putting green in front of the hotel. They had been beaten up by two older boys who had gone to Richmond Academy. I later learned their names: Pat and Nat Dye. (Pat later became a star football player at Georgia and a well-known coach at Auburn University.)

They had brought some friends over to start trouble, since they didn't appreciate us beating their school.

But by the time I arrived on the scene, Pat and his brother were long gone. I stood there covered in vomit, smelling of Four Roses and Old Spice. To this day, I have never met Pat Dye, but I owe him one. And to this day, I have never had another sip of bourbon—and I never wore Old Spice again.

Only 211 kids attended Benedictine and 29 of them were on our football team. That was all we needed, because we were very good. I think 11 were offered football scholarships after their senior seasons.

By my senior season, I grew to love the discipline that Benedictine required. I knew I was treated better than most of the other kids because of my athletic ability, but I still liked military school. That doesn't mean I always behaved as I should have.

During one game late in my senior season, I missed a tackle and Coach Mell jumped all over me about it. He started cussing me out and I didn't respond as I should have. I walked off the field that night. With Ronnie Braddock replacing me at quarterback, we beat our rival Savannah High, the largest school in the state enrollment-wise, 40–6.

But I loved playing quarterback and attracted recruiters from some big-name schools such as Georgia, Auburn, USC, and Notre Dame. Wally Butts, the head coach at Georgia, came to town and met with me and Mama. At the time, Charlie Britt was the Bulldogs' starting quarterback and his backup was a guy by the name of Fran Tarkenton. (Freshmen were ineligible to play at that time.)

"If your son signs with us, he will start at quarterback as a sophomore," Butts told Mama.

Joe Espy, who owned a paving and construction company in town, also loved the Bulldogs. He offered me $50 every week and a one-year-old car if I signed with Georgia.

Notre Dame's football coach, Joe Kuharich, pleaded with me to visit South Bend. The school's basketball coach, Johnny Dee, told me I could play both sports if I signed with the Fighting Irish, but I don't think Kuharich had agreed to that.

In the end, I liked Butts and also realized that Espy's generosity would help both me and Mama, so I signed a scholarship to play at Georgia. Along with Ronnie, I visited Athens for the only time the spring after my senior year to watch them scrimmage. They just beat the crap out of each other physically that day and I stood there thinking I had made a big mistake.

I really didn't want to play football anyway, and seeing that scrimmage reinforced my doubts. Mama did not want me to play football in college, anyway. She loved baseball and was pushing me in that direction. There was no player draft in baseball then, so I could sign with whatever professional baseball club I chose.

Clyde Kluttz, a Kansas City scout who had followed me through high school and during American Legion ball, talked to me often during my senior year. The Los Angeles Dodgers and Chicago Cubs scouted me consistently, too, and let me know they would be offering contracts, which they were not allowed to do until I had graduated.

Clyde, a former catcher, had a great demeanor and I liked him the moment I met him. He was a good-looking guy with a great head of hair. He didn't sign many guys, but the ones he did usually made it to the big leagues. He later signed Jim "Catfish" Hunter and Dick Howser, among others who made it to the bigs.

Clyde told me and Mama he believed I would get to the big leagues much quicker with Kansas City than with any other club. The Athletics had only five minor league teams, while most teams had many more. By contrast, the Dodgers had about 20.

Once I graduated and could listen to offers, Leon Hamilton of the Dodgers said the organization would offer me $50,000.

"Look, I have to go down to Key West to see another prospect. Let me know what you want to do," Leon told me. "If another scout comes in here and asks what you have been offered, tell them the Dodgers are up to $50,000. Don't accept anything without giving us a final chance. I will come back after I go to Key West."

The prospect Leon went to see was none other than Boog Powell, who was graduating high school at the same time I was. Boog ended up signing with the Baltimore Orioles and became a great player for them.

Clyde told me the Athletics' best offer would be $30,000.

I knew I had a big decision to make. Would I follow through with that scholarship to play quarterback at Georgia or sign with a professional baseball club and head to the minor leagues? And if I chose baseball, which organization was the right one for me?

Clyde's opinion about my reaching the big leagues easier with the Athletics had been very convincing, even though I would be sacrificing $20,000 if I did not take the Dodgers' offer.

"I know that's a lot of money to give up, but if Ken signs with us, he will be in the big leagues by the time he is 20," Clyde told Mama.

What did I know about money? I let Mama handle the details, so I signed with the A's and suddenly had some real money in my pocket. I also believed in Clyde and what he had told us. I promised Mama I would buy her a car with my bonus money. My football coach Vic Mell sold Pontiacs on the side and got me a great deal.

The Athletics didn't want me to start playing until the following spring, so once I signed the summer after I graduated I started goofing off at the beach. I was putting peroxide and lemon juice in my hair to turn it blond, getting sunburned every day and just waiting for the following spring to begin my pro career.

After a few weeks of that nonsense, I grew bored, so I called Clyde.

"Listen, I want to play baseball now and not wait until next season," I told him. "Is there anything you can do?"

He said he would make a call.

Clyde called Hank Peters, the farm director in Kansas City, and talked him into letting me report to Olean, New York, a Class D team for the rest of the season.

I packed my bags and baseball equipment and headed out the door. Mama drove me to the airport, where I boarded a plane for the first time in my life.

I was anxious to start my climb to the big leagues.

4 NO MORE "HENRIETTA"

CLYDE KLUTTZ, THE KANSAS CITY SCOUT WHO SIGNED ME, once told me that my American Legion team was the smartest amateur team he ever saw play.

We were well coached and we knew the game. We knew which base to throw to, how to hit the cutoff man from the outfield, and how to move runners along the bases. Not that we weren't talented, but we beat other teams strictly with our fundamentals.

So what I discovered after a few games of professional baseball shocked me.

Most of my new teammates in Olean didn't really know how to play the game.

Bill "Robbie" Robertson, my first professional manager, was a peanut farmer in the off-season. He was a great guy and he knew the game well. His players, however, didn't have a clue. They usually made a habit of throwing the ball to the wrong base or doing something stupid on the basepaths.

Not that I got my pro career off to a blazing start.

I struck out against Geneva three or four times in my very first game as a professional. By the end of the night I thought to myself, *Maybe you should have taken that football scholarship and gone to Georgia.*

It wasn't like I was living in grand style, either. The lower the class in the minor leagues, the less the quality of the amenities. And Class D was the lowest of the low.

We traveled in a real small bus with only about 15 seats. Problem was, there were about 18 players on the team. There were no trainers, bus drivers, or equipment guys at that level. The manager did everything. We would pile all of our equipment in the back of the bus, and since I was the new guy on the team and there were more butts than seats, guess who had to sit on the equipment during those long bus rides?

There were so many mountains on our trips that we learned to use them to our advantage when we had to relieve ourselves. We hopped out of the bus at the bottom of a hill or mountain, knowing that the bus was so overloaded with players and equipment that it would creep along at about five miles per hour. We would jump out of the bus, take a whiz, and then start running alongside the bus to catch up to the door as it slowly chugged up the mountain.

I was making about $400 per month and an extra $1.75 each day for meal money. When we went on the road, the home teams would provide names of boarding houses where we could stay and eat all we wanted for one dollar.

We were overcrowded, not making much money to play in tiny ballparks in front of few fans, running to catch our bus after taking a pee, all while sleeping and eating in boarding houses—and we loved every minute of it.

There was no complaining about the conditions, because we didn't know any better. We were among the select few who had the opportunity to play baseball for a living. We weren't being forced to do it. We were living our lives the way we wanted and everybody seemed happy, unless they were slumping at the plate.

I hit only .192 with three home runs in just 43 games at Olean that summer, not quite good enough to receive a promotion. But I was not even 18 years old yet, either, just a few months removed from high school.

When I signed with Kansas City, I had never smoked a cigarette or even drank a beer in my life. My only indulgence had been that drunken night in Augusta when I sipped Four Roses and Old Spice and then got sick as a dog. I hadn't yet been introduced to the bad habits that seemed to come with being in pro ball.

But Lew Krausse Jr. changed all that for me.

One night before a game in Elmira, they held a long-throw contest. The club had entered my name, but I didn't take any time to warm up my arm, since I was too busy hiding under the bleachers with Lew, who was teaching me how to smoke.

Suddenly, I heard my name over the PA system: "Ken Harrelson, please report to center field!"

I took a final puff of a cigarette and ran out there, coughing along the way. The distance from home plate to the center-field fence was 410 feet. The contest was being held from about 10 feet in front of the fence and we were told to throw toward home plate. On my first attempt, I threw the ball half-way up the screen behind home plate to win the contest.

The next morning, as I lifted my toothbrush to my mouth, a sharp pain shot through my right shoulder. I couldn't even finish brushing my teeth or comb my hair. If only I had warmed up my arm, instead of puffing on a cigarette, I knew the injury wouldn't have happened.

Even worse, I continued smoking after that day, anywhere from one to two packs each day.

Thanks, Lew.

Lew, whose father was the pitching coordinator for the A's, had his first start in the big leagues at the age of 17, only one week after signing a $125,000 contract out of high school in 1961. All he did that night was shut out the expansion Los Angeles Angels, throwing a three-hitter. But he later hurt his elbow and had been sent down to the minors, where he became one of my all-time favorite teammates. He didn't make it back to the big leagues for three years.

We had just finished a game in Charleston, West Virginia, one night early in the 1962 season and Lew was complaining of a sore arm. We started playing cards after the game and he couldn't get to sleep that night because of the pain. The club wanted him to catch an early morning flight back to Kansas City to have his arm evaluated.

"Screw that flight," I told Lew. "You need to go to bed and get some sleep. You can catch a later flight."

Lew didn't think he should wait, but I talked him into it. So he slept in that morning, May 22. The second leg of his scheduled flight, Continental Airlines Flight 11 from Chicago to Kansas City, exploded in midair over Missouri. A passenger had detonated a bomb aboard the plane as part of a life-insurance scheme to make his family rich.

All 45 passengers and crew members died, but thank God Lew wasn't one of them.

So Lew corrupted me into a sore arm and a bad habit that stuck with me for decades, and in turn, I saved his life.

It was common then for the organizations to send their best minor league prospects to Florida during the off-season to gain more experience in winter ball. I had just turned 18 when the A's sent me to Clearwater.

I struggled at the plate to start winter ball. I just couldn't hit a thing and I was growing frustrated with each strikeout, pop-up, or ground-out. One day, after striking out three times, I walked into the showers with my head down, wondering what the heck I was doing wrong.

One of my teammates was Dick Howser, a top prospect who Kluttz also signed. (Dick later would become a successful manager for the Kansas City Royals.) I called Howser "Slick."

Nicknames and sports go together like peanut butter and jelly. They are as much a part of the games we play in America as winning and losing. You can't name a sport that isn't filled with nicknames, but none more than baseball. Joltin' Joe, Stan the Man, The Lip, Mudcat, Catfish, Pudge, The Say Hey Kid, Yogi, Popeye, Spaceman, and the most-famous of them all, The Babe—I could go on and on and list about a million of them.

I had a nickname, too, while growing up. Because of my widow's peak, most of the guys around Savannah called me "Spider."

Little did I know, Howser was about to give me a new one.

"Hey, 'Henrietta Hawk,'" Howser said, looking at me. "You know, you are swinging the bat just like Henrietta Hawk."

Henrietta was a cartoon character at the time. Dick was not a very big guy, but I soon learned he had the quickest wit of anybody in baseball. I didn't say anything to him that day, because Dick was older than me. He was a pretty good shortstop, too, so I decided just to keep my mouth shut and figured his ribbing of me would pass.

The next day, I struck out three more times and walked into the showers to wash away my frustration.

"Here comes Henrietta Hawk again," Howser blurted.

This went on for a few days, until finally I had had enough of his name-calling.

"Listen, Slick," I declared. "I am sick of your crap. If you call me that one more time, I will knock you out!"

"Well, maybe if you swing the bat a little better," he told me, "I will drop the 'Henrietta' part."

I was frustrated like I had never been frustrated before. It was the biggest struggle in my life athletically up to that point and I started to doubt my ability. Any athlete who claims they never, ever doubted their ability is full of crap in my book. Everybody does it at one time or another.

And this was my time.

Wouldn't you know it? The very next day I hit a long home run. I couldn't wait to get to the showers now to see what Howser would say.

"Hawk!" Howser shouted.

There was no Henrietta.

Just "Hawk."

From that point on, it was Hawk. It stuck like glue. Everybody started calling me Hawk.

And I loved it.

The truth is, baseball had a Hawk before me; Bob "Hawk" Taylor was a catcher who played for the Milwaukee Braves among a few other teams. When I first heard of him, I had admired his nickname long before Dick Howser made it mine.

A lot of people in baseball over the years figured I received the name because of my prominent profile, which changed each time I busted my nose, and perhaps that was the reason Dick started calling me that in the first place. I really don't know for sure. I just know that once he dropped the first part of it, I was fine with it.

Dick was a great guy and I liked him, but I am sure he had no idea how it would become a large part of my identity.

I had little idea what marketing meant while I was in the minors, but I liked my new nickname enough to tell our team's PR guy, "Don't call me 'Ken' Harrelson anymore. Just use 'Hawk.'"

Before road games, I sought out the stadium announcers, too. I wanted to make sure they used my new nickname over the PA system. Within a season or two, nobody in baseball called me by my given name.

Following winter ball, I started my first full season in the minors with the Sanford Greyhounds, a Class D club in the Florida State League.

Just as I fought a few times growing up, not much changed in the minor leagues.

One night we were playing the Philadelphia Phillies' farm club, which had a big-bonus boy who stood about 6-foot-2 and weighed 235 pounds. Well, a big fight broke out during the game and I came flying in from the outfield. I squared off with the big-bonus boy. We started swinging away at each other, but I got my fists in there first, knocking him down. I jumped on top of him and planned to finish the job when I felt somebody pulling me off from behind. It was Andy Seminick, their manager.

"Okay, Harrelson, he's had enough!" he screamed.

I wasn't finished, however, and I decided to meet this guy after the game. Their locker room was located right next to ours, so I stood there waiting, but the big-bonus boy wouldn't come out. All of my teammates stood around watching me, anticipating what was about to happen. But the guy just wouldn't come out.

I guess that alone made an impression on my teammates.

Another time, my outside-the-clubhouse confrontation strategy was more effective. The opposing pitcher, a big guy, had been throwing at me during the entire game. I never charged the mound, but I noticed their clubhouse door was only about 25 feet from ours, so I waited for him after the game. As soon as he came out, I called him a few names just to provoke him.

He fell into my trap, swinging at me as I ducked. Then I just whaled on him.

The Sporting News was the players' bible in those days. All the guys read it. The paper got wind of both of these incidents and mentioned it in one of their minor league notes. That story and word-of-mouth resulted in me gaining a reputation as the guy who waited outside of the clubhouse to settle a score.

America still had a long way to go in the 1950s in terms of race relations, and I witnessed it firsthand during my time in the minor leagues. There was a lot of racism in all forms in those days, and it didn't come from just the competition, either. My teammates used racist terms at times too, and I threatened them every time.

"Shut up or we will go at it," I had to say way too often.

I became good buddies with a teammate named Bolivar Hinojosa, one of only two minorities on our Sanford club. "Hinny" was a great guy, an outfielder and first baseman who had decent power. I took it upon myself to be Hinny's personal food-delivery man, since black teammates could not eat with us in restaurants. Whenever the team bus stopped outside a restaurant, I looked at him and asked, "What's it this time, Hinny? Burger and fries again?"

A man named Lloyd Brown came to Sanford to replace Robbie as our manager midway through the 1960 season. Lloyd had been a left-handed pitcher for several major league teams in the 1930s and I loved listening to his stories of the old days. Somewhere along the line, he actually roomed with Babe Ruth. And like many of the players in those days, he hated Ruth.

"I really didn't room with Babe himself," he told me once. "I roomed with his *bags*."

This gives you an idea of Babe's lifestyle away from the ballpark. Lloyd's memories of him mirrored all the movies and books about the Babe that came along much later. He described him as crude to the core. He told me that Babe's only redeeming quality was that he loved children and always stopped to sign autographs or talk to them. On the other hand, he treated most adults like garbage.

At team parties, it wasn't uncommon for Babe to walk by a teammate's wife and grab her butt, Lloyd claimed. It was also true, Lloyd told me, that the Babe often ate eight to 10 hot dogs before games.

Now that's scary.

On the field, one of the few times I was ever scared occurred in a game against the Palatka Redlegs, Cincinnati's farm team.

They had a big 6-foot-5 left-hander on the mound and he threw really hard. One night, I hit a line drive up the middle and it caught him square in the forehead. He went down like he'd been shot and we all ran out there, fearing the worst. After a few minutes, he stood up and told his manager he wanted to stay in the game. So he finished the inning.

He came out for the next inning, picked up the ball, and stared into the stands with a dazed look on his face. He just stood there looking around the stadium as if he had no idea where he was. Then he walked toward the exit near his team's dugout and headed right out of the ballpark. They went and got him and took him right to the hospital. It turned out he had a bad concussion. I was relieved I didn't kill the guy.

I have talked about this over the years with dozens of baseball people but it bears repeating: it is nothing less than amazing that in the entire history of big-league baseball, only one player has ever been killed by a pitch or a batted ball. And his name, Ray Chapman, hit by a pitch by Carl Mays in 1920, will never be forgotten among those who played the game.

I had another serious scare at Sanford that summer. I lost 22 pounds in a couple of weeks and the doctors admitted me to the hospital for tests. They called Mama and initially told her, "We don't know what's wrong with your son, but he may have some form of cancer."

She drove from Savannah to Sanford immediately, but within days of being in the hospital, I slowly started to regain the weight. All the cancer tests turned out negative and the doctors never were sure what I had. One doctor told me he thought it may have been a case of German measles.

That was the week I first saw Sam McDowell.

I had regained about 10 pounds by the time we had a team party one day at a nearby lake. We had a game that night, so we weren't drinking. We spent the day water skiing and I always loved to water ski. However, water skiing takes your legs away for the day. It is not exactly something you should do before heading to the plate four times a few hours later.

That night, Sam, Cleveland's big-bonus boy, was on the mound for Lakeland. A lot of great pitchers had two pitches but Sam had four—fastball, slider, curve, and changeup—and they all were devastating. He had the best stuff I had ever seen to that point in my career and since. He struck me out in my first at-bat that night on three pitches. The next time up, he threw me a high fastball and I tomahawked it about 420 feet over the fence.

I got a full season under my belt with 547 plate appearances and I started to feel comfortable, leading the team in homers with 10. I also drove in 72 runs and hit .227. That earned me a promotion to Visalia, the Athletics' Class C team of the California League, in 1961.

It didn't appear the promotion would last, however.

Bobby Hoffman, who managed the club, called me into his office one day.

"I want to send you down," he told me.

"But my numbers are good," I said.

"I don't care about your numbers. I care about how you go about things. Your work ethic is terrible," he explained.

I really had no idea what he was talking about. I worked as hard as anybody else, so I pleaded with him to give me two more weeks.

He did. I didn't change a thing, either. I just continued doing what I was doing and I put together a Triple Crown–like season there, with 25 home runs to go with 114 RBIs and a .301 average in 135 games.

One of those home runs came in the most unusual way.

Joe Moeller was a big-bonus boy with the Dodgers who really was a right-handed Sam McDowell. His fastball reached the high 90s and you could hear his curveball. The first time I ever faced him, in Reno, he struck me out four times in four at-bats. When Reno came back to play us at Visalia, he struck me out the first two times I faced him. So I was 6-for-6 in strikeouts against Joe.

As I waited in the on-deck circle before my next at-bat, I noticed our bat boy had one of his Little League bats leaning against the fence.

"Hey kid," I asked. "Can I use that?"

He looked at me kind of strange, but he handed me his bat. It must have been only 29 inches long, a good six inches shorter than my normal bat.

Joe threw me a fastball and I hit it over the left-field scoreboard, which must have stood 30 feet above the fence.

One guy I became buddies with on another team was Jimmy Ray Hart, who played for Springfield in the Eastern League. He had great power and was one of the nicest guys you would want to meet. One day, his manager, who knew Jimmy Ray and I were close, approached me.

"Hawk, will you talk to Jimmy Ray for me?" he asked.

"Why?" I asked.

"Well, he's coming to the ballpark with a pint of Four Roses in his back pocket," he explained. "He's got a real drinking problem."

Later that day, I told Jimmy Ray, "You have a chance to be a great player in the big leagues someday, but you are not going to get there by drinking your way there. You've got to stop."

He listened to me and didn't say much. I don't know if he stopped altogether or cut down on his drinking, but I know he had a pretty good career. He played more than 11 seasons in the big leagues, mostly with the San Francisco Giants, and had 170 home runs and more than 1,000 hits.

I soon learned that Jimmy Ray's problem was a common one.

Our second baseman at Visalia was Jerry Leone, a 5-foot-9 fireplug who was as tough as they came.

One night at a bar in Spokane, four or five college guys started to give Jerry and me some crap, just because they knew we were baseball players. I didn't say much to them, but Jerry reached a boiling point with this one big guy who wouldn't leave him alone.

"Okay, let's go out back and see how tough you really are," Jerry told him.

The big guy landed a punch right on Jerry's jaw to start the fight. Jerry just stood there, shook it off, and proceeded to beat the crap out of this guy. I thought Jerry was going to kill him, so I had to pull him off.

Jerry was a fighter, and I knew how to spot one.

During the off-season while I was in the minors, I started to box in Savannah at a place called the Jefferson Athletic Club. A guy by the name of Ray Stuckey trained me. I always kept in shape during the off-season anyway, so going a few rounds in the ring was not a problem.

I never told Mama or the Athletics about my new hobby. Then Ray lined up some actual fights for me, so I had to pick an alias. I went by the name of Tommy Shocker.

I had some boxing talent, but my best attribute was that I hit hard. My punches carried some force and I won my first eight amateur bouts, most by either TKO or by knockout. Then, as Ray and I were driving to

Charleston one night for my ninth fight, he told me my opponent that night weighed more than 235. I weighed about 185.

"He won't fight me," I told him. I knew this guy and I don't think he wanted any part of me.

We got there and sure enough, the guy withdrew with an injury. There were more than 100 fans there who already had paid $5 to get in the gate.

Ray said, "Well, you have to fight *somebody* tonight."

They asked another fighter there to be my opponent. Somebody pointed him out to me, and it appeared that he weighed about 160 pounds.

I thought, *Heck, this will be easy.*

The fight started and the first thing I remember was lying flat on my back in the middle of the ring. He had hit me with a solid left I never saw coming. That was my final fight—in the ring, that is.

The next stop for me in baseball was with the Binghamton Triplets of the Eastern League, which had a reputation for being a pitchers' league.

We all had read in *The Sporting News* about this left-hander who threw over 100 miles per hour. He was already a legend in the minor leagues. Well, one night in Daytona Beach I walked into the Martinique Lounge and I recognized the guy sitting at the bar from his picture.

It was none other than Steve Dalkowski himself.

I introduced myself and told him I had read about him.

"I've read about you, too," he said.

In those days, bartenders often left the beer bottles in front of you after you drank them, if only to keep track of your tab. I noticed Steve had a lot of bottles in front of him. He confided in me that he had been an alcoholic since he was 17 years old.

He also told me that he was petrified to throw to left-handed batters. One time, he had hit a left-hander in the ear and the pitch basically tore off half of the guy's ear.

"I am scared to death I am going to kill somebody someday," he told me.

Steve never had even average control and he realized it, but he threw harder than any pitcher in baseball, including Sam McDowell and Nolan Ryan. He played for Elmira and when they came to Binghamton, I finally got to face him. When he threw his first pitch, I had never seen anything like it. The baseball just made a whooshing sound. He easily struck me out in my first at-bat.

At Binghamton, there was a three-story apartment building beyond the left-field fence. In my next at-bat, Steve threw me another fastball and I somehow hit it over that three-story building.

Steve is the only guy I ever knew who forced a manager to change his entire lineup. When he made the spring training roster with the Baltimore Orioles one year, the Yankees were about to play them in Miami. Casey Stengel, the Yankees' manager, had just turned in his lineup card to the umpire before the game. Teams never knew what pitcher they would face in spring training back in those days.

Well, as soon as Steve came walking onto the field after warming up on a back field, Stengel saw him.

He walked back to the umpire and demanded, "Give me that lineup card."

He walked back to the dugout and then filled out a new lineup card filled with nothing but backup players.

The sad thing was, Steve never made it to the major leagues.

He later became a fruit-picker in California, simply because he couldn't consistently throw strikes. His alcoholism didn't help his cause, either. Somebody later told me the central character played by Tim Robbins in the movie *Bull Durham* was based on Steve.

Jimmy Ray's and Steve's drinking issues were very common back then. Drinking was part of the baseball culture as much as chewing tobacco and scratching yourself. I knew dozens of guys in baseball who had drinking problems, including managers.

The old motto was, "We don't want any milkshake-drinkers on this club."

Once I started drinking in the minor leagues, I picked my spots after games and during off days. I didn't let it affect my performance on the field.

That season in Binghamton was magical for me: I hit 38 home runs to set the Eastern League home run record, which has been broken a few times since. I drove in 138 runs, which still stands as the league's single-season RBI record all these years later.

That season was notable for a few more things. The club had signed a 17-year-old bonus baby out of Tampa for $125,000, one of the biggest bonuses given during that period. After a few days of watching him, we all noticed the guy couldn't throw well, run fast, hit, or catch the ball. But he was a good-looking guy.

One of my teammates asked, "Who signed this guy?"

The guy's name was Tony La Russa.

I'll give Tony credit for perseverance, however, because he stayed in pro ball for 15 seasons in the minors and even reached the big leagues a few times over those years. I think Tony had more than 5,000 minor league plate appearances. That amounts to a lot of bus rides.

Travel in the minor leagues often disrupted my digestive system, causing irregular bowel movements, as it did with many of the guys.

This is when I first learned about hemorrhoids, a common condition among ballplayers. As I said, minor league managers did more than manage the team. My hemorrhoids were so big that my manager, Granny Hamner, would put a rubber glove on his hand, grease it up with Vaseline, and shove them back where they belonged.

Granny, our player-manager, was one of the oldest guys in the minors. He was 34 years old but he looked 50 to me. He had a good knuckleball and even made the league's all-star team that season.

I loved Granny and had only one problem with him. When we took those grueling 18-hour bus rides from Binghamton to Charleston, West

Virginia, he wouldn't let us sleep. We would leave right after a night game ended, drive all night, and get to the next stadium right before our next game. Granny loved playing cards and he would keep us awake playing Hearts or Pinochle or Euchre.

My hemorrhoids usually stayed in place for a few innings, until I started running or sliding. I wasn't a great slider to begin with, but having hemorrhoids made it extra unpleasant. I had to sleep on my side because they were so painful. My battle with the dreaded condition continued when I made the big leagues, too.

(Remember when George Brett was chasing a .400 average in 1980 and there was a ton of publicity about his fight with hemorrhoids, which led to his endorsement of Preparation H? I once told him, "I know your pain. I had them for years, but I didn't get any commercials from them!")

With parts of four minor league seasons behind me, I knew that the spring of 1963 would give me my first real chance to make the Athletics' roster, but I spent much of that spring training in awe.

For example, I walked up to the plate during a game in West Palm Beach against the Milwaukee Braves. Warren Spahn was on the mound and Bob Uecker was behind the plate.

That was my introduction to "Mr. Baseball."

"Man, I have been reading about you in *The Sporting News*," Uecker said, smiling. "You had some year last year in the minors…but you know that guy on the mound out there is a legend, don't you? He will go into the Hall of Fame someday."

I don't think I even said a word. I just smiled back at him.

Before Spahn's first pitch, Ueck told me, "We are going to start you off with a fastball!"

I thought he was playing mind games with me, but Spahn threw me a fastball. Strike one.

"Here comes another one!" Ueck said.

He was right again. Strike two.

"Here comes a third one!"

This time, Spahn threw a slider on the inside part of the plate. Strike three. I walked back to the dugout without taking a swing.

At that time, the legendary names of the game overwhelmed me. Spahn probably had nothing more than an 86 mile-per-hour fastball by that stage of his career, in what would be his final season. Ueck was right about that Hall of Fame thing, too. Spahn, who finished with 363 career wins, the most by any left-hander in history, was inducted 10 years later in 1973.

At least I can say I once faced one of the greatest pitchers in baseball history.

I also got thrown out by one of the greatest outfielders in baseball history.

We were facing the Detroit Tigers in Bradenton. I got a hit and was leading off from first. The guy behind me singled to right field, and I made the turn at second and headed to third. I had pretty good wheels early in my career, so I was surprised when I got tagged out by about six feet at third base.

That was my introduction to the great Al Kaline. He was one of my idols and I quickly learned there was no bigger competitor in baseball.

After being tagged out, as I ran back across the infield to our bench on the first-base side, I heard him yell, "You rookie son of a [expletive], don't you *ever* run on me!"

During one trip to St. Petersburg, I got off the bus and walked onto the field where the St. Louis Cardinals were taking batting practice. I looked into the cage and there stood "Stan the Man." Number Six. Musial was hitting rockets and I stood there in awe. I couldn't believe it. I had to pinch myself that I was standing right there on the same field with him.

I found the courage to introduce myself. We chatted a little and he was as nice as he could be.

That's the way it went most days during that spring. I saw baseball's biggest names through the lens of a fan, not truly grasping I was about to play on the same field with them.

We were in Bradenton before a game against the Pittsburgh Pirates one day when the wind must have been blowing straight in from center field at about 30 miles per hour. I was taking batting practice in one of the last groups as some of the Pirates walked out and stood behind the cage.

I noticed Roberto Clemente standing there. He was shorter than I had expected, but he had broad shoulders. I knew his reputation of being somewhat aloof and never speaking to players on an opposing team.

Just before I re-entered the cage for my final round, I heard, "Hi, Hawk."

He followed it up with something else, but his English wasn't very good and I had no idea what he had said, so I just smiled. It was enough knowing that the great Robert Clemente knew my name.

Another time, before a game against the Orioles, a certain third baseman walked up to me.

"Hello, I am Brooks Robinson. Welcome to the American League," he said, extending his hand.

Brooks was one of the nicest men to ever play the game, but I have to admit, he must have taken 10 points off my average by the time I finished my career. I hit a few rockets his way over the years and he would suck them up like a vacuum cleaner and turn a double play.

There was another day that spring in Fort Lauderdale I will never, ever forget, but I wish I could.

It was my first time seeing the famed Yankees in person.

They had Mantle—the guy who snubbed me for an autograph—and Maris and Yogi, while Joe D. would sit right behind their dugout as he often did after he retired.

I started at first base that day, planning on making a big impression on all of them.

Bobby Richardson led off the game with an easy grounder to me, but I booted it. Maris then hit a hard grounder right through my legs. Mantle then hit a shot to me, which should have been an easy double-play ball, and I let it bounce off my chest. I had committed three quick errors in three batters—in the *first* inning.

I noticed fans were laughing at me.

Then I saw the Yankees laughing at me in their dugout.

I saw Joe D. chuckling.

I even saw some of our guys in the third-base dugout trying to hide their laughter.

Then the first-base umpire, Eddie Hurley, said, "Okay, Hawk, you've filled the bases. Now you got 'em where you want 'em."

Unfortunately, it got even worse.

Joe Pepitone hit one off my glove. The next batter hit one to third baseman Ed Charles, who made a great stop and threw to first. Problem was, I didn't get to the bag in time and his throw sailed down the right-field line. A few batters later, somebody hit a grand slam. The Yankees scored seven runs in the first inning—all because of my errors.

I finally made a play, knocking down a grounder, crawling on my knees to reach it. I grabbed the ball and then crawled to the bag to make the third out, ending my nightmare of an inning.

When I came to the plate, I received a standing ovation, albeit a sarcastic one, from mostly Yankee fans. I didn't know how to react, so I bowed and tipped my cap. Our manager, Eddie Lopat, never said anything to me because he was so laid back, but the next day I was relegated to the club's B team to play the Reds' B team.

One of Lopat's coaches, Mel McGaha, managed the team that day. On the bus ride to Tampa, he asked me to sit down next to him.

"Hawk, I suppose you thought you were funny yesterday," he said. "I didn't think you were funny. If I had been managing, I would have hauled your butt out of there the first time you cracked a smile. You had better not pull any of that crap today."

Before the game, he hit ground ball after ground ball to me at first. He drilled me over and over. I was worn out.

After that, he added, "If you want to act like a ballplayer, you might make this club. If you want to act like a clown, go get a job in the circus."

I realized he was completely right. I had acted like a fool in Fort Lauderdale after I had been embarrassed and I regretted it.

Nevertheless, I had a great spring other than that one terrible game and I was sure I had made the big-league club. Then one day near the end of spring, I jumped back into first base on a pickoff play. I heard a loud pop, which was the twisting sound of a ligament in my ankle.

Off to the hospital I went again. By the time they released me, the club sent me to the Portland Beavers, Kansas City's AAA team in the Pacific Coast League, to rehab my ankle. It eventually healed and I joined the Beavers in Salt Lake City, hitting a towering home run in my first game. After 37 games in Portland, I was hitting over .300 and leading the league with nine home runs and 31 RBIs.

One of the best things about playing in Portland were the road trips to Hawaii.

Bob Flynn, a pitcher, was one of the franchise's first big-bonus boys. I think he got something like $100,000 to sign, or about $70,000 more than I did. He was one of the strongest guys I have ever seen in my career. Everybody called him "Goon."

On one trip to Hawaii, we were staying on the sixth or seventh floor of a hotel and Goon had too much to drink one night. I heard screaming coming from his room. The screams were coming from my buddy Lew Krausse Jr. I ran into Goon's room and saw him dangling Lew upside down over the balcony, holding him by his ankles. If he had dropped him, there was no way Lew would have survived the fall.

Goon was laughing as Lew screamed bloody murder.

"Goon!" I screamed. "Get him back in here! If you drop him, he's dead!"

Goon pulled Lew up and Lew then bolted for his room. A minute later, Lew emerged in the hallway holding a gun. Goon could fly for a big man. He had no choice but to start running down the hall, just as Lew squeezed off a few shots. Fortunately, they all missed Goon and left holes in the wall.

Lew was just that crazy when he got ticked off. When that road trip ended, we were sitting in our cars in Portland, waiting for someone to arrive and unlock the gate to the players' parking lot.

To kill the time, Lew pulled out his pistol again and practiced his marksmanship by taking a few shots at the scoreboard beyond the outfield fence.

The highlight of that road trip wasn't Lew firing bullets at a teammate, however.

One night, I had gone down to the hotel bar to have a drink when I noticed this big, strapping guy sitting there by himself. He looked familiar. I pulled up a stool about three stools down from him, ordered a drink, and looked again.

It was John Wayne.

I introduced myself and he was as nice as he could be. We made small talk for a little while before he finished his drink and left. Here I was, an unknown minor league baseball player talking to the Duke himself.

After starting the season at Portland on a hot streak—I even broke the league record with home runs in six consecutive games—I started to struggle. I was in the midst of an 0-for-14 streak and had struck out four times one night in a game at Seattle, so I headed to pitcher Moe Drabowsky's room to play some poker.

I figured a game of cards and some adult beverages would get my mind off my slump.

Unfortunately, my slump carried over to the card table, where I was in the midst of losing a couple hundred dollars (I always was a terrible poker player, because I raised every hand no matter what I held).

At about 1:00 in the morning, the phone rang.

"Who is that at 1:00 in the morning?" Moe asked.

He answered the phone and handed it to me. It was Athletics owner Charlie O. Finley.

"You are coming up to Kansas City," he told me. "Go back to your room and gather your stuff and we will have a reservation for you tomorrow to get from Seattle to Kansas City."

I was shocked. If I was going to be called up, I thought it would be during my home-run streak. I had started—and finished—the game earlier that day in a terrible slump. I had struck out four times. I had just lost a few hundred playing poker.

And now I was being called up to the big leagues?

"They must be crazy in Kansas City," I told Moe, "because they just called me up."

Who was I to question the timing of it all?

5 MAKING THE SHOW

I GOT NO MORE THAN THREE HOURS' SLEEP THE NIGHT OF June 8, 1963, because I realized I would awaken as a big-league ball-player for the first time.

I climbed out of bed in Seattle, left my minor league uniform behind, gathered my suitcase, and caught a flight to Kansas City. I arrived at Municipal Stadium in the fourth inning of the game between the Athletics and the Chicago White Sox.

In the bottom of the ninth, with one out, we trailed 4–3 when I heard manager Eddie Lopat call my name.

"Harrelson, grab a bat," he said. "You are pinch-hitting."

Before my first big-league at-bat, I walked to the plate in a daze. Juan Pizarro, a reliever, was on the mound for the White Sox. He was a real hard thrower and I happened to be sleep-deprived. He had just blown away two of the three previous batters. The last thing I needed was to see a big-league fastball.

I saw three hard fastballs and that was that. Let me correct myself: he threw me three hard fastballs. I don't think I saw any of them.

I struck out swinging.

The next day we hosted the Angels. I didn't start, but I got to pinch-hit again, grounding out to third base in the bottom of the sixth. The following night I didn't even get off the bench. We had an off day on my fourth day in the big leagues and we flew to Minnesota to open a three-game series against the Twins.

That next night, in the first game of a doubleheader, the Twins started left-hander Jim Kaat. Lopat put me in the lineup for the first time. I was batting seventh and playing first base.

We jumped on Kaat early and I hit a bullet up the middle for my first major league hit in the bottom of the first. I then grounded out, flew out, and struck out before I came up with one out in the eighth. We had a 10–4 lead when I hit a bomb over the center-field wall off reliever Bill Pleis for my first home run.

In the second game of the doubleheader, the Twins started right-hander Camilo Pascual and I was back on the bench. I did get to pinch-hit, but I grounded out.

That's the way my rookie season went, platooning and starting mostly when the other team pitched a left-hander.

Life as a rookie in the big leagues for me was a continuous learning process.

Our fifth infielder was a guy named Sammy Esposito, who happened to be a world-class handball player, although I didn't know it at the time. He was one of about five players, myself included, who lived in a hotel close to downtown Kansas City. The place happened to have a brick wall in the back that some of the guys used for a handball court.

One day, Sammy approached me.

"You play handball?" he asked.

"Some," I replied.

"I'll tell you what I'll do," he said. "I will spot you 20 points...for $100?"

I made him repeat his proposition, just to make sure my ears had not deceived me. He said it again.

"You got a game!" I declared.

Of course, the game of handball is played to 21, but the winner must win by at least two points. Sammy beat me 22–20. I never scored a point. He was that good.

Sammy got me again later on a matter of semantics.

We didn't draw many fans, usually 3,000 to 9,000 fans per game, unless the Yankees were in town. After we came home from my first road trip in the big leagues, I was sitting on the bench this particular night early in the game when Sammy remarked, "Man, this is one of the best crowds we've had this season."

I looked around the stadium and I could have counted the heads. There were probably 2,000 fans in the stands at the most. Normally, they announced the game's attendance over the PA system during the last few innings.

"What are you talking about?" I asked him. "There aren't many people here."

"I will bet you there are between 10 to 12,000 fans here tonight," he said. "Twenty dollars?"

"You are full of it, Sammy," I told him. "And I will take that bet."

They later announced the attendance at a little more than 3,000.

"You lose!" Sammy said. "Pay up!"

"What are you talking about?" I asked.

"I said there would be between 10 fans and 12,000 fans—and I was right!"

I paid him his $20, but I remembered the prank, waiting to find an unsuspecting rookie so I could get my money back. When Rick Monday arrived in Kansas City, after being the first pick in the first baseball draft in 1965, it was common news that he had received a $100,000 bonus.

I got Rick the same way Sammy got me, but this time I made the bet $100.

Rick handed me the cash that night, but he was shipped back down to the minors a few days later. I felt bad about taking his money, so I folded a crisp $100 bill into an envelope and mailed it back to him. He still loves to tell that story.

Before he got sent down, his speed was obvious to anyone who saw him play. Rick could flat-out fly.

"How many bases did you steal at Arizona State?" I asked him one day.

"A lot," he answered.

"Well I will *run* you 30 yards for $100," I told him.

We had some teammates mark off the 30 yards and Rick left me in the dust.

"Pay up!" I said.

"But I beat you!" he told me.

"I didn't say I would *beat* you. I said I will *run* you for $100," I said, laughing.

Rick handed me a $100 bill, but I gave that back to him, too.

Players frequently made silly bets in those days, sometimes just to pass the time.

One night during a rain delay in a game at Minnesota, one of our pitchers, Johnny Lee Odom, whom Charlie O. Finley had nicknamed "Blue Moon," bet a teammate $10 that he could walk around the entire field on his hands. He had to start at home plate, go all the way around the warning track, and back home. I heard the guys talking about the bet and I told Blue Moon, "Bullcrap! You can't do that."

"Then I will bet you, too," he told me.

He had $10 bets from seven guys riding on it. Believe it or not, he did it. Do you know how far that is? He walked on his hands more than 110 yards down one line, clear around the warning track, and then more than 110 yards back to home plate—on his hands! He collected the $70. I was happy to pay him, just impressed that he could pull it off.

We may have not played in front of large crowds, but I do think we played on the finest grass field in the big leagues. Kansas City's George Toma was the best groundskeeper in baseball. There were no bad hops on his field, because he treated it like his baby, nurturing every inch of it.

One night, the Athletics held a golf promotion before the game, in which six local pros competed against six of us players in a closest-to-the-pin contest. They stuck a flag in center field. I thought George was about to cry that night, watching us hitting wedges and creating huge divots behind home plate.

Pitcher Moe Drabowsky was my roommate and he soon became one of my favorite teammates. Moe was old-school in his regard for all the traditions of the game, just like I was. He had a brilliant mind, too, and used it as a stockbroker during the off-season. He was one of the few guys in the game I ever heard talk about stocks, portfolios, or investments.

We were in Chicago when Dave Nicholson, a bonus boy for the White Sox who used a peek-a-boo stance with his elbow held high, happened to hit one over the roof off Moe at old Comiskey Park.

Moe stormed back to the dugout and sat down next to me.

"Roomy," he said, "the next time I see him, I will show you what big-league baseball is all about."

Sure enough, Moe kept his promise.

We were in Kansas City a few weeks later when Nicholson dug in against Moe, who hadn't forgotten that home run in his previous meeting. After he tossed two slow curveballs off the plate, wasted just to set Nicholson up, Moe threw a fastball that hit Nicholson right in the forehead. Nicholson fell just as if he had been shot, blood spurting out of his head.

As he lay there bleeding, Moe looked in defiantly at him and spit a big wad of tobacco juice toward the plate. I think Nicholson had to get 20 stitches in his face after the game.

Another time, Moe and I were headed back to the hotel in a cab in Seattle after having a few drinks. Well, Moe could get downright nasty if he had been drinking. I could tell that this taxi driver was taking us for a longer ride than necessary, surely in order to get a bigger fare. Unfortunately, Moe noticed it, too, at about the same time.

Our cab reached about 40 miles per hour when Moe reached over the front seat and grabbed that cabbie by the neck, pulling him into the back seat with us.

"Moe, you're going to kill us all!" I screamed. "Let the guy drive!"

He started beating the cabbie.

"Moe!" I screamed, "You're going to wreck us!"

Moe didn't care. Finally, I had to punch him a few times to get him to release the cabbie, who fell back into the driver's seat and promptly punched the brakes. He then pulled the cab to the curb and kicked us out. We had to walk back to the hotel.

On July 13, we were facing the Cleveland Indians at home and Early Wynn was looking for his 300th career win. They called him "Gus," and at 43 years old, he was the oldest player in big-league baseball at the time. He had notched his 299th win near the end of the '62 season with the White Sox and then had been released. He had been out of baseball for a few months before the Indians signed him.

I realized I was facing a legend.

In my first at-bat, I hit a rocket up through the box that just missed his head. I came back to the dugout when Bobby Del Greco, one of our backup outfielders, walked over to me.

"Next time up, you had better hang loose," he said.

"Why's that?" I asked.

"There are two things you don't do on Gus," Bobby told me. "You don't bunt on him and you don't hit the ball back up the middle. He's going to drill you."

"That old fart ain't going to do anything!" I replied.

In my next at-bat, Wynn's first pitch was a fastball right behind my ear. I went straight up in the air and came down hard. I was just a rookie, but in my entire career, that was still the greatest knockdown pitch I ever saw.

Gus got his 300th win that day against us—and he never won another game.

I was learning the customs of big-league ball on the fly, and I was fortunate to have some mentors along the way, such as Rocky Colavito.

He taught me something very, very important one day.

I happened to hit a home run off Whitey Ford in the first game of a series against New York and I was anxious to get to a party. After games, fans stood no more than 10 feet from the back of our clubhouse, hoping to get a few autographs, and we had to walk through them to get to our cars. And since we had played the Yankees, we had a bigger crowd than usual that day.

I bolted from the clubhouse and started to fight my way through the crowd, walking quickly toward my car. I had momentarily forgotten how I felt as a kid when Mickey Mantle had snubbed me.

All of a sudden, I felt somebody grab me by the back of the neck. It was Rocky, tugging at me from behind.

"You have a chance to be a good player, but those people pay our salaries. If you ever walk by them again without stopping to sign for them, I will kick your butt!" he screamed.

Rocky always claimed signing autographs "was like being pregnant."

"You either do or you don't—there is no middle ground," he said. "You can't do it sometimes. You should do it every time you have the chance."

Lesson learned. From that day, I remembered his words always. Rocky was tough enough, too, that he would have kicked my butt. Rocky just happened to be Mama's favorite player.

Mama always wanted to see me play in the big leagues, so she drove that Pontiac I had bought her when I signed—1,050 miles from Savannah to Kansas City—to see me play one series. I had been in a real slump by the time she arrived, but I hit a home run against the Tigers in the first game she attended. The next night I hit another one. She drove back home to Savannah a few days later as a happy, proud mother.

Then I promptly fell into another slump as Lopat continued platooning me.

I didn't know this at the time, but Finley told me years later that when I was not playing every day, Mama had written him a letter. It read: "If you are not going to play my son, send him back home to me!"

Charlie loved her for that letter. He knew she was just a mother looking out for her only son. I mean, how many moms would do that?

I hated platooning anyway. Lopat was a real nice guy, but he had no business managing a big-league club. He was in his second season with the Athletics and he seemed to think I could hit only left-handed pitching, so I went into his office one day hoping to set the record straight.

"Mister Lopat, I hit 38 home runs last year to break the Eastern League record," I explained. "I am not trying to be a smart-aleck, but how many of those do you think were against left-handers?"

The answer was very few. I told him if he planned to continue platooning me, I should be hitting against right-handers. Heck, I hated to face left-handers more than right-handers anyway.

I always blamed Casey Stengel for the proliferation of platooning. He was the first manager to regularly platoon hitters, starting in the late 1930s with the Boston Braves and later with the Yankees, depending on who the other team had pitching.

Then every manager started doing it.

Because of it, after coming up from Portland, I finished my first season in the big leagues with only 226 at-bats. I hit six home runs, 23 RBIs and batted .230.

My rookie salary was a whopping $6,000.

I knew that Norm Seibern, our first baseman, was being paid $25,000.

I remember thinking that if I ever made that much money, I'd be in hog heaven.

One of the highlights of my rookie season came on a trip to Los Angeles. Several of us were invited to the set of the movie *Seven Days in May*, starring Kirk Douglas and Burt Lancaster. We sat on bleachers, watching them film a few scenes, before a director brought Kirk over to meet us. The actor shook our hands, asked a few questions about baseball, and was as nice as he could be.

Someone asked for Burt to come over, too, but he just waved at us and walked away.

When you are playing on a team that finishes 73–89 and 31½ games out of first place, you grab any slice of fun you can off the field.

In spring training the following year, I knew I was ready to break out. I had a taste of what Major League Baseball was all about. I had spent the winter in the Venezuelan League, honing my skills, and hitting pretty well.

Then I did the unthinkable again. I popped a ligament in my ankle for the second straight spring. And once again, I did it on the basepaths.

The organization sent me to Class AAA Dallas, where the Portland club had moved during the off-season, to rehab. John McNamara managed Dallas and he worked constantly to rebuild my arm, which was never the same after I injured it while winning that silly long-throw contest at Elmira in the minors, the night I learned to smoke with Lew Krausse Jr.

John got me to lower my arm a bit, taking the strain off of my shoulder, and I eventually regained my strength. I started throwing rockets again from the outfield. I was hitting well, too. Three months and 271 at-bats later, I had hit 18 home runs—tied with San Diego's Tony Perez for the league lead—and I had driven in 52.

The Athletics called me back up to the big leagues. It was July 8, 1964. I would never play another game in the minors.

I recently looked up my minor league numbers: 2,094 at-bats, 548 hits, 103 home runs, and 415 RBIs. I finished parts of six seasons with a cumulative .262 average.

In the minors, I had learned to smoke and how to enjoy a drink or two, taken part in more than a few dustups, swore like a sailor at times, endured more bus rides and bouts with hemorrhoids than I could count, and slept in dozens of boarding houses.

And now I was more than ready to be a big-leaguer for good.

By the time I arrived back in Kansas City, Finley had fired Lopat after the Athletics started 17–35. He was replaced by Mel McGaha, the guy who chewed me out after I made a fool of myself against the Yankees in spring training a year earlier.

In my first game back, I had two hits off Minnesota's Jim Kaat, the same pitcher against whom I got my first big-league hit a year earlier.

It's been said that necessity is the mother of all invention.

I know that first-"hand," literally.

I was still platooning when the Yankees came to town in early September, hitting against left-handers and riding the bench against righties. McGaha picked up right where Lopat had left off.

On September 4, the Yankees had scheduled right-hander Jim Coates to pitch that night, so I knew I wouldn't be in the lineup. We were 36 games under .500 and the season was coming to a close.

A golf game was always calling my name anyway, especially when the weather was good.

On this Friday morning, it was a beautiful day, and it was my 23rd birthday, so I arranged to play a round of golf with teammates Sammy Esposito, Ted Bowsfield, and Gino Cimoli. Ted and I matched up against Gino and Sammy with $25 Nassaus and automatic presses on the line at Stayton Meadows Golf Club, just a short drive east of downtown Kansas City. (The course is called Royal Meadows today.)

After 18 holes, Ted and I had beaten them out of some money. None of us was scheduled to play that night, so somebody asked, "Nine more?"

Nine? I would have played 18 more if we didn't risk a fine for arriving late to the ballpark.

We played nine more and then I headed to the stadium, barely arriving on time. I glanced at the lineup and was shocked to see my name listed at first base, hitting fourth behind Rocky. It turned out the Yankees had scratched Coates and decided to start Whitey Ford, a left-hander who was surely headed to the Hall of Fame once he retired.

After batting practice, I had a horrible blister developing on my left ring finger, largely because of 27 holes of golf. I walked back into the clubhouse, where I noticed my bright-red golf glove sticking out of the back of my pants' pocket hanging in my locker.

I slipped it over my left hand to protect that blister, walked up to the plate in the bottom of the first, and immediately heard all of the Yankees yelling at me from the dugout.

"You big sissy," was one insult I heard.

The others were a touch more vulgar.

Whitey walked me and as I jogged to first, I could still hear them hollering at me.

In the bottom of the third, Wayne Causey had walked, right before Whitey hung me a curveball. Well, the big sissy hit it over the left-field wall. In the bottom of the fifth, I walked again and the Yankees took Whitey out of the game.

In the bottom of the ninth, we trailed 5–4 with two outs when I came up to face Pete Mikkelsen. Mikkelsen hung a curveball and I hit this one even farther than I did the one against Whitey. My second homer sent the game into extra innings.

We ended up losing 9–7 in 10 innings in front of only 9,900 fans that night, but I celebrated my birthday by playing 27 holes of golf, winning a few bucks, and then hitting two home runs—in the very game in which I became the first big-leaguer ever to wear a batting glove.

Or, more accurately, a golf glove.

I never went to the plate again without wearing one.

The following day, every member of the Yankees took batting practice while wearing red golf gloves. Mantle had sent the clubhouse boy out to buy about 20 of them. They didn't wear them in the game that night, however. Knowing Mickey, I know he did it as a joke, but within weeks, most of my teammates not only wore one while batting, but they also wore them under their fielding gloves as well.

Within a season or two, it seemed every hitter in baseball wore a golf glove on his lead hand. (Sporting goods companies later developed a batting glove specifically made for baseball in the early 1980s.)

I finished the '64 season with only 139 at-bats, almost 100 fewer than I had as a rookie, due to my ankle injury. I hit a paltry .194 with 7 home runs and only 12 RBIs, but at least I can say I brought something important to the game.

One of my goals when I signed with the Athletics organization, if I ever made the big leagues, was to play in the annual Baseball Players Golf Tournament in Miami. I knew it was an event that I could win, but only big-leaguers were eligible to play.

The event, which started in 1956, was a big deal and offered big prizes for the top finishers. Most of the top baseball players who regularly played golf, like Mickey, Don Drysdale, Whitey Ford, Yogi Berra, Jimmy Piersall, Jimmie Foxx, Don Newcombe, and many others, competed every year.

Players had to pay their own expenses to get to Miami, and following my rookie season, I didn't have the money I needed to make the trip. After I returned to Savannah from my first winter ball season in Venezuela, I stumbled into an old buddy by the name of Corky O'Neill.

Corky was a firefighter and he always seemed to carry a wad of cash. I was killing time at a pool hall when he walked in just two nights before the tournament was to start in Miami.

"You want to shoot some 9-ball?" he asked.

"For money?" I asked.

"Five dollars a game?"

Those words were music to my ears. By the time we were finished that night, I had $600 of Corky's money in my pocket.

The next day, I called the LeJeune Country Club in Miami and I got one of the tournament organizers on the phone.

"This is Ken Harrelson of the Athletics," I started.

"Who?" he asked.

"Harrelson. Ken Harrelson. I am with Kansas City. I want to play in the tournament. Is it too late to enter?"

It wasn't. He entered my name and I threw some clothes into the car and took off driving for Miami. I had just driven through Jacksonville when I had a horrible thought.

I had left my clubs on the front porch.

I realized I would have to rent unfamiliar clubs for my first appearance at this event I so badly wanted to win. I arrived in Miami at about 3:00 AM, checked into the Green Mansions Motel and requested a wake-up call for 7:00. I climbed out of bed after four hours and discovered my tee time was only an hour away.

It also was the first time I ever played in front of a gallery.

I shot 75-75-78 (the tournament had been shortened to three rounds when it rained all day on Saturday) to finish second, several shots behind Albie Pearson, who shot a 70 in the final round on a windy day.

Albie, an outfielder with the Los Angeles Angels, put on a remarkable performance considering he was the smallest man in the big leagues at 5-foot-4, 140 pounds. He hit line drives off the tee which sliced through the wind. I don't think a PGA Tour player could have shot any lower that day.

That tournament, however, was special for me in another way. It was there that I met Alvin Dark, who was managing the Giants at the time. Alvin was a golf nut just like me. He had been in contention until the final round, when he shot in the 80s.

The following year, the organizers moved the tournament to the Miami Springs Country Club and I couldn't wait to get there. I still was making baseball's minimum salary, so I needed any prize money I could win.

This time when I arrived, people knew who I was from the year before. A few writers covering the tournament asked, "You finished second a year ago; how will you do this year?" It was four years before

"Broadway" Joe Namath made his famous guarantee in Miami, but I had one of my own.

"I'll win it," I predicted. "Nobody can beat me this year."

The headline in the *Miami News* the following day read, "Nobody Can Beat Me," Says the Hawk.

When I arrived at the course for the first round, a few of the other players ribbed me about my prediction, which led to several $100 bets among the favorites. I had been playing well coming into the tournament and I knew I could win the thing my second time around.

A guy by the name of Alfred Kaskel owned the Doral Country Club at the time. He must have read the newspaper that day, because he sent the director of golf at Doral, Frank Strafaci, to watch me play. He introduced himself before I teed off.

I played really well that first day and grabbed the lead. After the round, Frank then walked up to me and said, "Mister Kaskel would like to sponsor you on the PGA Tour."

"I am still playing baseball," I told him.

"He knows that," the guy said, "but he thinks you can make it in professional golf and he would like you to represent Doral."

Before the second round, another guy introduced himself and asked if he could follow me around the course that day.

"I would be honored," I told him.

It was the great Tony Lema, a regular winner on the PGA Tour at the time and one of the most popular golfers in the world, next to Arnold Palmer. Tony rode a cart that day and followed my round of 73. I hit the ball real well, but I didn't make many putts. Afterward, we had a beer together.

"I would give anything to have your golf swing," Tony told me.

I was flabbergasted when he said that.

I played in a foursome with Alvin during the first two rounds and with Ralph Terry and Albie, the defending champ, during the final two rounds. At times, I could hear some catcalls from the gallery about my bold prediction.

By the time we teed off for the final round, I had a two-stroke lead on Albie. There was a pretty large gallery, adding to the pressure of the money and prizes riding on it as well as my boastful prediction. I eagled the par-5 14th hole and overcame some late jitters to win the tournament by one stroke over Albie.

The win and Kaskel's offer to sponsor me in professional golf really made me wonder if I could really make a living playing golf instead of baseball.

It was not the first tournament championship I had ever won, but the highlight may have been one of my practice rounds the day before the event started. I was taking my clubs out of the trunk when I heard a voice behind me call my name.

"You got a game today?" he asked.

"Not really," I said.

"Well, can I play with you?"

"Jackie, I would be honored," I said.

I am so glad we didn't add anyone to our twosome that day. It was just me and the great Jackie Robinson. We didn't talk much baseball, but we did talk a lot about golf that day. We laughed our butts off for the entire round, because Jackie really had a great sense of humor. I had heard so many terrible stories about him, how many of his teammates had hated him. I had heard he wasn't very likable at all.

By the end of our round, I had a hard time figuring out how anyone could have any hatred toward him. It was the only time I ever met Jackie, but he seemed very humble to me. I realized even then what a historic figure he was, instrumental in changing the culture of the game I played.

He wasn't much of a golfer, so the least I could do was give him some tips that day to improve his game.

"Keep your feet wider, so you have better balance," I told him.

His personality, however, was captivating.

Later in my life, I would play with Arnold Palmer countless times, and with Jack Nicklaus and Sam Snead and many other greats, but playing 18 holes with Jackie will always remain a special moment in my life.

The following year, when I checked into the tournament, I asked what the tournament record was. They told me 295.

"Forget it," I said. "I'll break it."

A writer must have been nearby because the headline the next day in the local paper read HAWK PREDICTS NEW RECORD.

The night before the tournament started, they held a large party with players and sponsors. There were always bets flying among the players, and I bet a lot of money on myself that night.

The next day, I opened with a 76, good for second place behind Albie. We played in a constant drizzle during the second and third rounds and I shot 72 in both, while no other player broke 80. During the final round on a perfectly sunny day, I shot a 70 to beat the tournament record by five strokes. Whoever was in second place finished 17 shots behind me.

I also won the tournament again two years later, finishing my career at the Baseball Players Tournament with three victories in six attempts.

Golf had become my full-time mistress and I squeezed her in whenever I could find time away from baseball.

I even loved just watching golf. Tom Watson and his family were from Kansas City. He was a well-known child golfing prodigy by the time he was 13 and he had been featured in local newspapers as the "next Arnold Palmer."

I blame him for me receiving the first fine of my baseball career.

Because he was so famous at such an early age, Arnold came to town to play Tom in an exhibition match at Brookridge Country Club in the summer of '65. Tom was only 15 at the time.

Being the golf addict I was, I drove out to the course, which I had played often, just to watch them play. I remember Tom was wearing

Bermudas that day. They teed off later than scheduled, at about 1:00 PM, because the match had attracted a lot of media and fans.

On the first hole, a short par-4, Tom drove it over the green. Arnold left his tee-shot in the front bunker. I could tell that the kid had a great game. After the first four or five holes, I checked my watch. It was after 2:00 and I had a 30-minute drive to the ballpark. We had to be in the clubhouse by 3:00 for a game that started at 6:00.

Sure enough, I walked in late that day and the club hit me with a $25 fine, which was a lot of money for me then. I never did find out who won that match and I never thought to ask Arnold years later once we became buddies.

In what I learned would be the usual revolving-door circus of managers under Finley, Haywood Sullivan was next up to manage the Athletics. He took over just 26 games into the 1965 season, replacing McGaha. Our 5–21 record was one of the worst starts in American League history.

After getting to know Finley, I was shocked he waited that long to make the change.

Sully was a great guy who I would get to know well in the coming years. But he wouldn't last, either. We finished 59–103 and Finley fired Sully. The best thing that happened to me was the club traded first baseman Jim Gentile to Houston, so I could play every day.

Once I stopped platooning, I felt much more comfortable at the plate, and I broke out with 23 homers and 66 RBIs to lead the club.

Finley rewarded me with a new contract, if you want to call it that.

He mailed it to my address in Savannah during the off-season, offering a whopping $500 raise. I tore it up. Ten days later, he sent me a second letter, with the same raise, adding a note: "Sign it or quit."

Typical Charlie.

This was the perfect example of how players had absolutely no leverage in those days. There were no agents. There was no free agency. A player had to either take what the owner wanted to pay him or do something else for a living.

I had no choice, so I signed the deal, which boosted my salary to a whopping $6,500.

Finley hired Alvin Dark to replace Sully.

All the players knew Alvin had been a great player himself, so he had instant respect when he first entered our clubhouse. Being a former player always carried a lot of weight with current players.

In one of our first meetings, Alvin told us something I never forgot about being a team player.

"Whether you are happy or not happy should depend on one thing and one thing only: Your ability to read the scoreboard after a game," he said. "One of the secrets to being a good big-league player and team-mate is to become a good actor. If you go 0-for-4 and we win, you had better make yourself look happy. If you go 4-for-4 and we lose, you had better do something to make yourself look angry..."

Like Rocky Colavito's advice on autographs, I carried Alvin's words with me throughout my career. He was right. As the years went by, if I heard a guy who had three hits whistling in the shower after we had lost a one-run game, I was ticked off at that guy.

Alvin also taught me how to read a scoreboard, and I don't just mean read the score of the game. He believed that if every player knew the current situation at any point in the game—such as outs, runners on base, or how each inning dictated certain reactions—we would be much better players for it. If I was playing right field and I have checked the scoreboard, when the ball was hit to me, I knew that I could not miss the cutoff man. Alvin stressed that if we read the score-board constantly, we would never have to ask anybody any question at any time.

Alvin had a great demeanor and he knew the game as well as anybody I had been around. As I said, he was an avid golfer, playing almost every day, and he was a pretty good player, too, another thing we had in common.

It didn't take long for me to grow to love Alvin Dark, and I think he loved me back. We got along very well. He was one of the few people in baseball who never referred to me as Hawk.

He always called me Kenneth.

"Now, Kenneth, you can become a great player in this game if you…" he would say.

"Now, Kenneth, you sure got into that pitch."

Within months of knowing Alvin, I wanted to bust my butt to win games for him. He was like the father I never had.

But I had no idea how big a part of my future he would become.

6 HOT DAYS AND WILD NIGHTS
IN WINTER BALL

IT WAS COMMON FOR MAJOR LEAGUE TEAMS IN THE 1950S AND '60s to allow their best up-and-coming young players to play winter ball in Venezuela. In fact, most clubs encouraged it, realizing a young player would gain more experience and return the following season as a better player.

The Athletics were no different and they wanted me to play in Venezuela following my rookie season.

Playing baseball in a foreign country sounded great to me and I had heard other guys had enjoyed their time in Venezuela, so Kansas City made the arrangements and placed me on the team in Valencia, Venezuela, following the '63 season.

In the weeks before I left home, I received all the typical warnings from baseball officials about how to avoid danger and to stay out of certain areas of the country. There was constant trouble between the police and the radicals, and crime lurked around the corner if a tourist ventured into the wrong areas, just as it does in most countries.

I witnessed that up close just minutes after my arrival.

My flight landed in Caracas and I had to catch a cab to Valencia, about 80 miles to the east. As the cab driver took off like Mario Andretti on this winding road through the mountains, I started to notice all of these crosses along the road where I guessed people must have died in crashes.

I began to wonder if I would ever live to see my first pitch in winter ball.

"Slow this thing down!" I yelled at him.

He had no idea what I was saying, since he didn't speak a word of English. By the time we arrived in Valencia, I was somewhat carsick. The cabbie dropped me off about 100 feet from the front door where I had to report to the club.

I climbed out of the cab, my legs wobbly and just thankful to be alive, and suddenly I heard a commotion. I turned to see this man running around the corner toward me. He must have been 60 feet away.

All of a sudden, a policeman came chasing after him. Then...*Pop!* The cop shot this guy in the back of the head right in front of me!

The guy fell dead in the street.

What had I gotten myself into?

What I had gotten myself into was a faraway place where few people spoke English, a place where I would get into several fights, spend a night in jail, punch an umpire, hit some home runs, fight a bull, and make some money.

And I had a blast while doing it all.

I had so much fun and made so much money off the baseball field that I decided to return following the 1964 and '65 seasons to play for the featured team in the league, Caracas, managed by Reggie Orturo.

The money we earned in Venezuela for three months of winter ball was pretty good for that time—$6,000, plus performance bonuses—and I hit well enough to dip into a few bonuses. I broke the league's single-season records for home runs (14) and RBIs (55) in my final season, both of which have been broken several times since.

But where I really padded my pockets was on the Lagunita Country Club golf course, taking money from the locals who figured they could beat a brash American baseball player easily, and I also won money playing dice.

The team only played three games each week, so I had plenty of time for golf and dice games.

The baseball fans there were knowledgeable, too, and I soon had two nicknames in Spanish.

Since I wore a black golf glove at the plate in Venezuela, some fans and the media dubbed me *El Mano Negro*—"the black hand." Nobody else wore batting gloves there at the time.

And, of course, others called me *El Gavilán*.

I wasn't the only one in Venezuela with a nickname. I really liked Al Ferrara, a young outfielder with the Dodgers whom everybody called "The Bull." Well, the Bull and I had a lot in common. He was very competitive, strong as an ox, and loved to have fun. Believe it or not, the Bull was an accomplished piano player and even performed at Carnegie Hall.

El Gavilán became buddies with the Bull, in more ways than one.

The Bull and I had heard about this little open-air bistro in the mountains where the Russians and flight attendants hung out when they were in town. We decided to give it a try one night. This joint had a jukebox everybody danced to, but the majority of the songs were in either Russian or Spanish. There was only one American song: Elvis Presley's "Don't Be Cruel."

After a little while, I grew tired of hearing all of that Russian or Spanish music, so I walked over to the jukebox, stuck in six Bolivars, and hit the reject button on whatever was programmed to play next. I hit the button for "Don't Be Cruel" six times, meaning Elvis would be entertaining the crowd for about the next 20 minutes or so.

After I walked away, this big Russian guy stuck in some coins and rejected all of my Elvis requests, pushing buttons for more Russian music.

That act offended my patriotism as well as my love for Elvis' music and it was worth a confrontation.

"Get out of here!" I said.

He took a swing at me but I ducked and caught him square, knocking him down. Suddenly, four of his buddies came after me, but the Bull had my back. A few minutes later, three Russians were lying on the dance floor and the other two had run out the door. Growing up in Brooklyn, the Bull obviously had used those digits for more than caressing the piano keys.

"Come on, Bull!" I yelled. "Let's get out of here."

We ran out the door, grabbed a cab, and left before the police arrived.

Another time I was not so lucky.

Near the end of the '65 season, a bunch of the guys threw a teammate a farewell party at a local bar. Our shortstop, Tommy Helms, a great guy but not very big, got into an argument with this big local. I saw this guy hit Tommy and he was getting ready to jump on him again, so I ran over and dove on top of him in the middle of the dance floor. I hit him with a couple of good shots, prompting a huge brawl all over that dance floor. The next thing I knew, I felt something sharp sticking in my ribs.

I looked down to see it was a gun.

I shouted one of the few Spanish terms I knew: "*Tiempo! Tiempo! Tiempo!*"

The guy holding the gun against my ribs was a little Venezuelan guy wearing some sort of hat. Fortunately, he turned out to be a plainclothes cop and was about to take me to jail. At least I knew I wasn't about to get shot right there on the dance floor.

We arrived at the police station and I tried my best to talk my way out of an arrest.

"I am a ballplayer," I said. "I am a ballplayer."

The arresting cop made me turn and face the sergeant, who sat behind this huge desk at the police station.

"Ballplayer," I said.

Nothing.

"*El Hawko.*"

Nothing.

"*El Mano Negro.*"

Still, nothing.

I knew then that I was not getting anywhere, other than straight to a jail cell. Now here it was 1:00 in the morning, and the local law declared that if you were put in jail after 1:00 you had to spend the night.

Reggie Orturo soon walked in.

"Get me out of here, Reggie," I pleaded.

"I can't," he said. "It's after 1:00 in the morning. Sorry, Hawk. I'll get you out first thing in the morning."

They ushered me to that cell and what hit me next carried more punch than anything that big man had thrown at me. It was pure stench. You want to talk about an indescribable smell? It had to be the worst combination of urine, feces, and body odor you could ever imagine. I sat there wondering how my nose would survive until the next morning. It brought back memories of the night I had got caught drag-racing in Savannah.

Fifteen minutes later, the big guy I had just popped a few times walked in.

"You want to go again?" I asked him.

"No," he said.

As it turned out, he spoke a little English and worked for Sears and Roebuck. He explained to me that Tommy had slapped a girl on the dance floor and he had to hit Tommy to defend this girl. That was his version, anyway, and if it were true, I know I probably would have done the same thing. So we sat there and talked the night away, trying our best to ignore the stench.

Good ol' Tommy. He was a scrappy shortstop for us and I grew to really like the guy. One night, he and I, Pete Rose, our second baseman, Bill Bryan, our catcher that season, and a few other guys were having dinner and a few beers downtown at a restaurant next to the hotel where Pete stayed. We soon got into a heated discussion about baserunning and who among us was the fastest.

"Well, I know one thing," I said to Tommy. "I can outrun you."

"That's it!" Tommy declared, staring straight at me. "I will bet you $100 that I am faster than you!"

"Let's go!" I said.

"Right now—out in the street," he shot back.

We walked outside as Bill and Pete stood with their hands up, blocking traffic. Somebody marked off 60 yards. Horns honked and frustrated drivers, now forming a parking lot in the middle of the street, screamed at us. I took off and beat him badly. I slowly walked back to the starting line.

"I'll race you for a hundred," Pete said.

As everybody in baseball knew, Pete could fly. He blew by me and easily beat me.

By then, the fumes from the hundreds of cars not moving anywhere had filled the air.

I had just eaten a full meal, washed it down with several beers, and then ran two 60-yard sprints. That wave of gas fumes got to me, too. I walked over to the curb and threw up everything. Then Tommy burped and I could tell his time was coming. He followed me and barfed up all of his meal.

Pete and Bill just stood there laughing at us.

Pete and I never got along that well, even back then. He didn't like me much and I didn't like him much. We were just two different guys who had nothing in common, other than baseball and wanting to win every game. And none of those feelings have changed much over the years.

To his credit, I will state that Pete is one of the few guys I ever knew who never thought we were out of a game, no matter the score, no matter the inning. If there were two outs in the ninth and we trailed 7–1, Pete thought we had a chance to come back and win. For that belief and his never-say-die attitude, I admired him.

For all that other stuff that came later, like his betting on baseball, you can put me in the camp which claims he should *never* be inducted into the Hall of Fame. He did the one thing that we all knew, even way back then, that a baseball player can't do. He bet on baseball. Then he lied about it repeatedly over the years. I will never change my mind on that issue. I do admire the guy's memory: it seems like Pete can tell you what pitch he hit, on what count, and how many men were on base and what the score was of any game in which he ever played.

To start that season, I shared an apartment with Bill and Carl Greene, but that would be short-lived. Bill was about 6-foot-4 and 225 pounds. Carl was about 6-foot-3 and 235. I never could cook—I still can't—so we had an agreement that those two would do the cooking and I would do the dishes.

They were great guys and I liked both of them. That arrangement worked out well for a few weeks until I grew tired of doing the dishes every night. I sort of went on strike for whatever reason, refusing to fulfill my end of the bargain. Maybe it was hard to grip a bat with dishpan hands, but I don't know to this day the real reason I stopped.

During my dishwashing strike, I think Bill had received one of those "Dear John" letters from his girlfriend and he suddenly became irritable. I was a bit homesick at times, too, and perhaps not in the best of moods on this one particular night.

Finally, after we finished our meal that night on one of our off days, Bill snapped. I sat there playing solitaire, just minding my own business.

"Hawk, get up and get those dishes washed!" he ordered.

"Listen," I said, "you do the cooking and I will do the dishes when I get around to it."

Bill glared at me, threatening to kick my butt unless I got over to that sink in a hurry.

"Bill, I ain't washing the dishes right now," I declared.

We both stood up, nose-to-nose. Carl, who was always chipper and trying to keep the peace and harmony among the three of us, knew trouble was brewing.

"Listen, we got a sweet deal here with this apartment," he pleaded. "If you guys fight and break stuff, we are going to get thrown out of here. If you make a ton of noise, that landlord will be up here right away."

I took off my watch and laid it on the table. Bill swung at me and hit me with the flat of his hand. We traded a few blows and I noticed Carl pulling out his suitcase.

"You guys had better stop fighting and better start packing," he said.

Bill and I swung away on each other a little more until a chair, the table, a full-length mirror, a lamp, and a few other things were broken into pieces. When we finished, we took Carl's advice and started packing, too. Sure enough, there was a knock on the door within minutes. It was the apartment manager, ordering us in Spanish to vacate the premises by 9:00 the next morning, or he would call the police.

We finished packing when Bill said, "You guys wanna go go-kart racing?"

"Good idea," I said. "Let's go."

We raced go-karts and then we headed out for a few beers. We came home for our final night in that apartment and then vacated as ordered first thing the next morning. We checked into the local hotel where most of the players stayed and we had to eat all of our meals out.

At least there would be no more dishwashing disputes.

The cop's shooting of that guy in front of me on my first day in Venezuela was not the only time I heard or saw gunfire.

One night, Bill, Carl, and I rode in the backseat of a cab and we heard the unmistakable rat-tat-tat of a machine gun. As the cabbie drove on, the gunfire seemed to get closer and closer. As I said, all three of us were well over 6-feet tall, so you can imagine how it looked for three of us to see who could get the closest to the floor of that cab. Finally, the cabbie took a turn and drove away from the trouble, as we slowly climbed back into our seats.

In my time in Venezuela, I had made some friends among the locals who frequented the bullfights. They explained to me that fighting a bull was easy since they used baby bulls with bulbs on their horns and nobody got hurt. So one day they picked me up and we drove 30 miles out into the country to this large ranch. The tradition called for the man to fight a bull in honor of the girl he was with at the time. I just happened to be with the daughter of the impresario of the bullfighting venue, so they asked me if I wanted to honor her by fighting a bull.

I looked down into the ring and saw this baby bull with bulbs on his horns. He didn't look too intimidating to me. Heck, the Washington Senators' Frank Howard was much bigger than him.

"Sure, why not?" I said.

I walked out through the gate into the ring, wearing tennis shoes, as they handed me a big cape. All of a sudden, someone opened that gate and what must have been that baby bull's father trotted out, snorting loudly and looking straight at me. I could tell he wanted a piece of me, too. His horns were wider than a Cadillac. His balls looked like things I had bowled with.

Then snot flew out of his nose and he started to move toward me.

Let me tell you, they never saw a guy in jeans and tennis shoes scramble so fast to high-jump a fence. I learned later that it was a common gag they pulled on first-timers who thought bullfighting looked easy.

It wasn't all brawls, street races, and bullfights, however.

There were disputes with umpires, too.

One night, this home-plate umpire was having a terrible game. He was a horrible umpire to begin with, one of the worst I had ever seen at any level. He called me out on a pitch way outside and I grumbled as I headed back to the dugout. Then my temper got the best of me and I started yelling at him. I continued screaming at him when I reached the dugout, so naturally, he threw me out of the game.

I charged out of the dugout at him just as he ripped off his mask. I must have been three feet from him when he raised that mask and bopped me on the top of the head with it. It was obviously done on purpose.

Calling me out on a bad pitch was one thing, but hitting me in the head with that hard mask was another. I reared back and swung at him. It was a good thing for me that this was the one time I didn't land a solid punch.

Making headlines back in the U.S. for decking an umpire wouldn't have been good for my major league career.

Fortunately, my fist had glanced off the side of his head and shoulder. I looked over at our dugout and all of my teammates were laughing their butts off.

Popping an umpire was taboo and I always realized that. My idol in high school was a player by the name of Carlos Mobley, who had been adopted from an orphanage in Savannah. He was a senior when I was a freshman. Carlos was about 6-foot-3 and he was just a tremendous athlete, one of the first in town to letter in four sports. He played a great centerfield and the Yankees signed him out of high school. He was one of the best athletes I ever saw, someone the scouts label a "can't miss."

That is, until he hit an umpire in the minor leagues.

Carlos had reached AAA in his third season in the minors when he hit an umpire. It ruined his career and he never made it to the big leagues. His plight always stuck in the back of my mind when it came to umpires, even though I momentarily forgot it that moment in Venezuela.

The league suspended me 15 games, which they eventually reduced to five, and I also was fined 2,000 Bolivars (about $440). Good thing I was hitting well, because the club picked up the fine and helped get the suspension reduced to five games. I think the only reason I was not suspended by Major League Baseball for that stupid act was because the umpire had hit me first.

Anyway, I usually got along great with umpires from the time I learned to play the game and that was the only time in my baseball career I ever tried to hit one.

But I still maintain he had it coming.

As I said, Mama always told me if somebody hit me first, I was allowed to hit them back.

And I figured that applied to Venezuelan umpires, too.

It's a wonder I survived any of it. But by the end of those three winters, I had more money—and plenty more at-bats—in my pocket. I learned a little Spanish. I learned Pete Rose was one fast son of a gun, even on a full stomach. I learned how to run from a bull.

And most of all, I learned that you don't want to spend any more than one night in a Venezuelan jail if you can help it.

7 CHARLIE O.'S MADNESS

I HAD TALKED TO HIM ON THE TELEPHONE, BUT I HAD NEVER met the notorious owner of the Kansas City Athletics until we returned home after my first road trip as a big-leaguer.

I say notorious only because I had heard all of the veterans bash him like a drum over the previous few weeks. They griped among themselves about what a jerk he was, how cheap he was, and just how petty he could be on any given day.

No player I know of really liked Charles Oscar Finley, better known to baseball fans simply as Charlie O.

Finley grew up near Gary, Indiana, but made his fortune in the medical insurance business in Chicago. He had purchased the Athletics in 1960, during my second season in the minor leagues, and he quickly gained a reputation for being kooky and eccentric. He also acted as his own general manager, rather than hiring someone with a baseball background for the job.

Despite our paltry home attendance, Charlie considered himself a marketing genius. And his pride and joy was a big mule he named after himself to serve as the team's mascot. He arranged for that mule to travel everywhere we did, including hotels, press rooms, and cocktail parties.

That big-toothed mule became a big part of my life with the Athletics. The players sometimes were forced to act as caretakers for that big mule on the road. We had to load him on and off the elevator of the team hotel when Finley wanted to show him off. We had to get him onto the field, whenever Finley wanted him paraded in front of the fans.

On one trip to Cleveland, Finley even organized an autograph session on the street for us, featuring the mule as the big attraction. We were required to show up and sign autographs for fans at 7:30 AM, as they gathered around to pet the famous mule.

Another time at the Cadillac Sheraton in Detroit, Finley ordered the hotel workers to knock down a wall so the mule could have his own suite. They layered the room with straw and hay to make him feel at home. Meanwhile, we were sleeping *three* to a room while the mule rested in style in his suite.

Sometimes, I really believed Finley loved that mule more than he liked people, especially his own players.

At old Comiskey Park in Chicago one day before we played the White Sox, they brought in this huge crate and placed it in the middle of the clubhouse. A few clubhouse workers pried it open and out walked a tiny mule. Charlie had shipped us a smaller version of Charlie O.

This smaller mule, however, wouldn't budge when it came time to getting him onto the field.

And I happened to be standing nearby.

"Get him out on the field!" Finley screamed at me. "Get him out on the field! Hawk! Get him out there!"

Two of my teammates were in front of this mule, pulling on his harness. I stood behind it, pushing it in the butt. We were making a little progress when it stepped on my right foot. I let out a scream, but did Finley care? Not a bit.

He wanted that mule on the field ASAP and didn't care one bit if one of his starting ballplayers was put on the disabled list in the process.

But the capper came at Yankee Stadium when Finley wanted a volunteer from the Athletics to ride the original Charlie O. one day before a game. Of course, there were no takers. What big-league ballplayer would make a fool of himself by doing such a thing?

Then Finley upped the ante by asking, "Anybody do it for $25?"

"I will," I answered.

We received $10 a day for meal money in those days and that didn't buy a cup of coffee, toast, and eggs in New York City. Any little bit of extra cash helped.

I thought I would have some fun with it, too, so I turned the bill of my hat upwards to look just like a jockey.

Without a saddle, I climbed aboard that big beautiful animal and headed toward the outfield. I got him trotting along pretty good around the warning track toward right field and then I turned him down the line toward first base. Then I just happened to notice Mickey Mantle and Roger Maris sitting on the corner of the dugout, laughing at me. I also saw that Roger was holding a Fungo bat, used specifically to hit balls to infielders during practice.

Just as I guided that mule past them, Roger threw that bat and hit Charlie O. right in the butt. He bucked way up with his front two legs and I had nothing to hang onto, and I slid around his neck underneath him.

We ended up staring at each other face-to-face.

I swear to God that the mule's teeth were a foot long. I was trying to hold on for dear life, as I noticed the mule's personal trainer running onto the field to rescue me.

Finally, I let go and dropped onto the ground, but I had another problem: I had swallowed my chewing tobacco. I got up and slowly wobbled to the dugout. Then I threw up for a few minutes.

Still, I had an extra $25 in my pocket for spending money in the Big Apple.

You think that experience would have been enough humiliation for me, but when we arrived in Los Angeles, Finley offered $25 for me to do it again.

"Sure, why not?" I said. "It can't go any worse than the first time."

We were at Dodger Stadium, where the Angels played their home games that season. This time, I got the mule going pretty good on the warning track and headed toward the left-field stands. That is when a fan happened to stick a box of popcorn in front of Charlie O.'s face.

It stopped suddenly, as though it had hit a brick wall. Again with no harness or saddle, I went flying right over its head and landed on the warning track. My knees were all skinned up.

Did Finley care?

Of course he didn't. He was laughing so hard, watching his namesake munch on that popcorn. The fans were laughing, too. I laid there hurting. But I had another $25 in my pocket to spend in Los Angeles.

It's really a wonder that Finley gave me that money to ride the mule, because he was famous for his cheapness. He was so tight with money, he squeaked.

Most teams used spanking new white baseballs for batting practice. The Athletics? Finley ordered the team's equipment workers to dump milk into the washing machines to make old balls look like new ones. We would hit what would normally be bombs during BP and those balls would land 30 feet short of the warning track.

Also, if a player intentionally slammed his bat on the ground or broke it, he had to pay for it. Those bats cost anywhere from $6 to $10 back then. (Today, they cost more than $100.)

Charlie wasn't always cheap, however.

He did loan me $5,000 to buy my first house in Kansas City. Of course, he took chunks out of my weekly paycheck to pay him back.

In my third season, I was really killing the ball. So, I asked our manager, Haywood Sullivan, if he'd talk to Charlie about getting me a raise.

He checked into it and then told me Finley would see me when we returned from a long road trip, in which I had five home runs and about 14 RBIs. I couldn't wait to get home to Kansas City to see him, figuring I had a big salary boost coming. Finely told me to come to his suite at the Muehlebach Hotel.

I walked in just as he was having breakfast, as excited as I could be, anticipating how much money he would pay me.

"Son, I followed you on that road trip and I have watched you on TV," he started. "Now, let me show you what you are doing wrong..."

He laid a towel on the carpet as if it were home plate, then he grabbed a cardboard tube as if it were a bat. He stood there like a hitting instructor, going through the mechanics. I had just hit the cover off the ball on that road trip and now I had to listen to him explain what I was supposedly doing wrong at the plate.

And about that raise—I got a big fat zero. He never even mentioned it.

But I did get an unpaid hitting lesson from the craziest owner in baseball.

He was impetuous and known for his knee-jerk reactions when it came to players, too.

During the latter part of my rookie season, he once told Lopat to send me back to Portland. I had been struggling a bit, so Eddie told me before a game at Detroit that I was going back down to Class AAA.

"Do you want to play today or sit out this last game before you leave?" he said.

I chose to play. I noticed Finley sitting in the first row behind our dugout at Tiger Stadium. Fortunately, the Tigers' Frank Lary hung me a slider and I hit it into the upper deck in center field. After we won the game, I started to pack my gear when Eddie called me back into his office.

"You are not going down," he said. "Charlie changed his mind. He said, 'Anybody who can hit a ball that far is not going down to the minor leagues.'"

That's just how he was.

One day, John Wojcik, a good-looking left-handed hitter, struck out four times. Finley just happened to be at the game and John was sent down. It broke John's heart and he never made it back to the big leagues. Nobody could afford to have a bad day when Finley was at the ballpark, because he was so impulsive.

In July 1965, while we were in Chicago to play the White Sox, Finley hosted the entire team at his large farm in La Porte, Indiana, about 50 miles outside of town. He had just signed a young pitcher out of North Carolina and he wanted to introduce him to the other players. His name was Jim Hunter.

It was an extremely hot day. We played basketball and drank beer and had a barbeque and a great time together. Charlie showed us he could be a gracious host when he wanted to be. In fact, we all got pretty drunk that day.

When we returned to the Sheraton on Michigan Avenue in downtown Chicago, I ripped off my clothes and slid into bed. I woke up the next morning to the sound of giggles and to bright lights. As I opened my eyes, a few ladies walked by my bed.

It turned out that Drabowsky had pulled my bed out into the hallway during the night. I had so much to drink, I slept right through it. I jumped out of that bed and pounded on the door, planning on knocking Moe out, but he had locked me out. I found a phone somewhere down the hall to have a key sent up to me.

Moe always was pulling practical jokes. When we went to Minneapolis to play the Twins, our team hotel was located next to a novelty shop, where he would stock up on stink bombs and fart-noise apparatuses. We would get onto a crowded elevator and within 15 seconds, everyone smelled Moe's handiwork.

Like many guys, Moe absolutely hated Finley.

And Moe, like the time he pounded on that cab driver while the cab was in motion, could be crazy at times. He would run and slide in the outfield before games on days he was not pitching, just to tear his uniform, which ticked off Finley.

Moe would look at me, smile and say, "Oops. Tore my pants again. Screw Charlie!"

Charlie apparently knew that Hunter would become a superstar pitcher, because he wanted to give him a nickname. Somehow, he came up with "Catfish" and invented some story about how he had landed a record catfish as a kid. I heard he paid him $50,000 to go along with the story. I often asked Jim if it were true, and he always just smiled and never once answered.

All the guys in Kansas City got along well, but Cat became my favorite teammate. I am telling you right now there was no better teammate in the history of baseball. Cat was funny, a real practical joker like Moe. He was just a wonderful all-around person. He was the heart and soul of our ballclub in Kansas City.

One story will tell you everything about Catfish Hunter.

I was playing first base with Catfish on the mound in Baltimore one night when Boog Powell hit me a one-hopper. It was the perfect double-play ball, but I booted it. Because of my error, the bases were loaded. I will never, ever forget this: Cat walked over to me and said, "Hawk, don't worry about a thing. I will bail you out of this jam."

He struck out the next batter and got the next guy to hit a weak grounder for the third out. Over the years, I saw Cat say something similar to all of his infielders and then he would follow through and work his way out of the jam every time. He would never blame a teammate for his problems on the mound.

When an opposing pitcher knocked one of us down, nobody had to say a word to Cat. He went back to the mound and promptly drilled one of theirs, usually the pitcher. He knew how the game was played and he always had our backs.

By the time Cat hung it up, he had five World Series rings and had won 224 games.

When I heard he was suffering from Lou Gehrig's disease in 1999, I called his house in North Carolina. His wife, Helen, answered.

"How's he doing, Helen?" I asked her.

"Let me put him on the phone," she said.

"Cat, I would love to see you. Why don't you and Helen come down and spend a long weekend with us in Orlando?" I asked.

"Hawk, I would love nothing more than that," he said. "But I can't even button my shirt."

That was the last time I ever spoke to him. He died a few months later at the age of 53.

When I think back to my time with the Athletics, I can't help but think of Cat and all the good times we had together.

The Athletics also wore the most colorful uniforms in the big leagues, during an era when white and grays dominated. One time, Finley had us wear all-gold uniforms from head to toe. We looked ridiculous. We also wore white spikes, while every other team wore black.

Finley lied often and embellished so many stories that we had no idea what to believe. We once read a newspaper story about those white spikes. He was quoted as saying, "We got our white shoes specially made in Australia, about 100 miles south of Melbourne."

He obviously never looked at a map and had invented the entire story. One hundred miles south of Melbourne would put you in the middle of the ocean.

Besides the mule, Finley was always searching for new marketing ideas or publicity stunts to increase our usual tiny crowds. Who else would sign a pitcher who may have been in his sixties?

The great Satchel Paige joined us for the final month of my third season. Satchel claimed to the media that he was 59 years old at the time, but he had once confided in me he didn't know his exact date of birth. I figured he had to be a few years older than 59. He hadn't pitched in the big leagues in 12 years, when he won three games for the 1953 St. Louis Browns.

No matter his age, Satch was a living legend from the Negro Leagues, a piece of walking, talking baseball history. And I loved him.

I would pull up a stool next to his locker and ask him, "Satch, tell me about..." finishing it by picking a famous name from the Negro Leagues. I was fascinated by him. He took a liking to me, too, and he was a great storyteller.

Satchel usually spent our games in the bullpen for the first month, rocking back and forth on a big rocking chair for all the fans to see. Then Charlie decided it was time to see if he had anything left in his aging arm.

On September 25, 1965, Satchel got his start against the Boston Red Sox in Kansas City and a near-miracle happened. All old Satchel did was shut out the powerful Red Sox lineup for three innings, allowing only one hit (Carl Yastrzemski rocketed a double off the wall on a 3-0 count).

I don't think Satch threw one pitch over those three innings that would have broken a pane of glass. It was unbelievable.

Satch left the game with a 1–0 lead, but our bullpen gave up five runs in the seventh and eighth innings in a 5–2 loss.

After the game, I went over to Satch's locker.

"Satch, can I have your glove?" I asked him.

"Sure," he said, handing me his Wilson A2000.

At the time, I didn't realize how valuable the piece of baseball history I held in my hands actually was. Fast forward about 25 years when a man named Kenny Smith called me. He was the curator for the Hall of Fame in Cooperstown.

"Hawk, we understand that Satchel Paige gave you the glove he wore during his last appearance," he said.

"Yes, he did," I told him.

"We would love to have that glove in Cooperstown," he said. "Can you send it to us?"

"Sure, Cooperstown would be the best place for it," I told him.

I started to look for it, but I couldn't find it anywhere. I had moved so many times since 1965, I had no idea where that glove was located. I must have searched for three or four days, before I had to call Kenny back with the bad news. Not finding that glove literally made me sick to my stomach.

I have always considered myself a baseball historian and I wanted to hear first-person stories from the days gone by.

Just as I peppered my minor league manager Lloyd Brown about stories of rooming with the Babe, and Satch about the Negro Leagues, I pestered my coaches in the big leagues, too. Luke Appling, Gabby Hartnett, and Jimmy Dykes each coached the Athletics while I played in Kansas City.

Luke had played shortstop for the White Sox for 20 years and was inducted into the Hall of Fame during my second season in Kansas City. Gabby caught for the Cubs for 19 seasons and was behind the plate when Babe supposedly called his shot during the 1932 World Series. Prior to Johnny Bench, he was considered the greatest catcher in baseball history. I would quiz him about the art of catching and what he thought of all the current-day catchers.

"The first responsibility of a catcher is to get your pitcher into a rhythm and keep him in it," he once told me. "It might take a few innings. But you get the ball and get it back to him quickly. You put your signs down quickly."

Gabby became famous for hitting a game-winning home run as darkness fell at Wrigley Field, leading the Cubs over the Pirates for the 1938 NL pennant.

He was so popular that Al Capone once requested his autograph. The picture of him signing for Al appeared in all the Chicago newspapers the following day. He then received a telegram from the commissioner of baseball, requesting he never allow himself to be photographed with Capone again.

Gabby wrote back to the commissioner, "Okay, but if you don't want my picture taken with Al Capone, then you be the one to tell him."

Dykes had spent more than 55 years in the game as a player, manager, and then a coach. He would always seek me out on the airplane and sit down next to me, just about killing me with his cigar smoke.

The stories those three told were priceless to me. I would have given anything to have a tape recorder with me in those days. Those three guys were the essence of baseball in my eyes. They were living legends. I not only picked their brains in the clubhouse or dugout, I often played golf with each of them.

In regard to Finley's constant circus, I started to realize what a real threat he was when he started to mess with Alvin Dark, who had guided us to a 74–86 record in 1966. That was more than 17 games better than the club he had taken over from Sully.

Alvin and I had just started playing a round of golf one day at Millburn Country Club with two other guys when an assistant pro rode out on a golf cart to see us.

"Mister Dark, Mister Finley is on the phone for you in the clubhouse," he said.

"I'll go take this call," he told me. "You guys go ahead and play on and I will catch up with you."

He came back a little later and didn't say a word.

"What was that all about?" I asked him.

"Finley just fired me," he said.

We played a few more holes and he didn't say much else. When we arrived at the 16th hole, the assistant pro came out again.

"Mister Finley is on the phone again," he told Alvin.

Alvin headed to the clubhouse and we finished the round. We were drinking a beer in the clubhouse when he re-emerged. Alvin never drank alcohol, so he ordered an ice tea and sat down with us.

"Well, he just rehired me," he told us. "When he talked to me the second time, he asked me what kind of manager he should hire. So I went through a list and we talked for about an hour. Finally, he said, 'You know what? I am rehiring you!'"

It was the typical, impulsive Charlie.

Years later, after I retired, Charlie showed what a real jerk he was with his treatment of second baseman Mike Andrews during the 1973 World Series against the New York Mets.

In the second game of the series, Mike committed two errors that helped the Mets win the game 10–7. Finley then made him sign a false affidavit stating that he was injured, so they could replace him on the roster with another player for the remainder of the series. Commissioner Bowie Kuhn overruled Finley, forcing him to reinstate Andrews, but Mike never started again and only got to pinch-hit in Game 4.

Even though the A's won the series in seven, Mike was absolutely crushed by it and he never played again after that season.

What Finley did to him was absolutely terrible.

He eventually sold the team in 1980, I believe in part because he knew free agency was about to force players' salaries to explode.

When he died in 1996, he was 77 years old.

The day I heard the news, I couldn't help but think back to those days in the mid-1960s, the times I rode his mule, wore his white shoes and his silly uniforms, and grew frustrated with all of his cheapness and foolishness.

Today, thinking of those crazy times all these years later, it is hard not to laugh.

8 HONDO, HODGES, AND THE SENATORS

I COULDN'T HIT A LICK THROUGH THE FIRST HALF OF THE 1966 season and I started to get down on myself and my ability. Three years into my big-league career, I was not progressing at the plate and my numbers showed it.

I had been scuffling along through my first three seasons, hitting a cumulative .229 and striking out 204 times in 848 at-bats. I had some power surges here and there, hitting 23 home runs once I finally started playing regularly in 1965, but I still wasn't as consistent as I wanted to be.

For whatever reason, I had no idea what I was doing wrong.

To reach the left-field fence at Kansas City's Municipal Stadium took quite a poke and I was hitting plenty of warning-track outs that would have resulted in my circling the bases at most any ballpark, other than Yankee Stadium or Cleveland's cavernous football stadium.

That in itself was especially frustrating.

"Don't let this ballpark beat you, Kenneth," Alvin Dark told me over and over.

Off the field, I was not doing much better. Charlie Finley continued dipping into my meager paychecks as reimbursement for that home loan. My frustration on the field and debts off it were mounting quickly.

One day in the batting cage, one of our outfielders, Deron Johnson, could tell I was frustrated.

"Hawk, just try something *different*," he told me.

"Like what?" I asked him.

"I don't care what it is, just try something different," he repeated.

So I started to experiment with my stance. I raised my left heel off the ground and kept my toe to the ground and took a few swings. I started to hit one line drive after another.

I stayed with it, although it may have appeared as if I was off-balance with my left heel raised off the ground. Suddenly, I felt great at the plate.

Then on June 23, I was stunned: the Athletics traded me to the Washington Senators for Jim Duckworth, a right-handed pitcher who had great stuff.

Even though I was no longer under his thumb, Cheapskate Charlie wanted the Senators to deduct money from each of my paychecks and then send the money to him, since I hadn't fully repaid him the money I owed.

Fortunately, Washington general manager George Selkirk was having none of it.

I loved George. He was very reasonable and he and I got along very well. He happened to be the answer to a great trivia question: who succeeded Babe Ruth in right field for the Yankees, and also wore No. 3 (which was later retired when the Babe died in 1948)?

I hated leaving Alvin, because we had grown so close. But aside from that, the trade didn't bother me much, simply because I was getting away from Finley's shenanigans. I witnessed his meddling, pettiness, cheapness, lying, and mistreatment of people for three years and I had had enough of it.

When I arrived in our nation's capital to start a new life with a new team, the first thing I noticed was the heat. It was a hot summer to begin with, but the Senators operated on a shoestring budget much like the team I had just come from. There was no air conditioning in the clubhouse, only a couple of old fans to push the hot air around.

Just like my old team, the Senators also didn't draw many fans. The only big crowd of the season seemed to be on opening day when most of the Washington dignitaries, politicians, and perhaps even the president came out to the ballpark.

It wasn't long before one of my new teammates took me to the Walter Reed Medical Center, filled at the time with veterans severely injured in the Vietnam War.

During my first visit there, I sat down with a good-looking Italian guy, who was a quadruple amputee, and his wife.

"Hawk, you wouldn't know it now by looking at this body," he said, smiling, "but I once was just about 6-foot-5."

His wife told me he had been a pretty good football player and she thanked me for visiting. I walked out of there thinking just how lucky I was. I had all of my limbs and I was headed to the ballpark that night to play the game of baseball for a living. Walter Reed really got to me, and I never once took for granted how lucky I was because of brave men like those I had just visited. Whenever I could squeeze in a visit to cheer them up, I did.

Another time, I walked out of the clubhouse and somebody grabbed my arm.

"Hawk, there's a man over here who wants to meet you," the guy said. "His name is Roger Donlon."

Roger had been an officer from the U.S. Army Special Forces and was the first Congressional Medal of Honor recipient from the Vietnam War. He had been seriously wounded from first a mortar attack and then a grenade and small arms fire as he continued to fight to save several of his fellow soldiers.

After just a few minutes of small talk, I really admired this guy, so I invited him over to our apartment complex where several of the ballplayers lived. We got a few of the players together and listened to Roger tell his war stories from Vietnam, how he killed so many enemy soldiers advancing on a foxhole in which he and several other members from his special forces' unit lay wounded. The details of war were gory and gruesome.

"The bottom line is we did what we had to do to survive," Roger explained. "We had to fight fire with fire and do what was necessary to protect each other and come home."

All of us were fascinated by Roger's stories as we drank into the early morning. Finally, sometime after 2:00 AM, he passed out on my couch. I never saw him after that, but I will never forget him.

The memories of these two brave men and others I visited stuck with me throughout my lifetime. I always considered myself patriotic and always appreciated the freedoms we enjoy living in the United States. And it was because of thousands of men just like those two guys.

But my time with the Senators was defined largely by my interactions with two other men. One was a teammate I would grow to love and admire like a brother. The other was the manager, a baseball legend of sorts, who I grew to despise and resent.

Let me introduce you to Frank Howard and Gil Hodges, respectively.

I will start by saying I have never in all my years met a nicer man than Frank, whom everybody called "Hondo." He was 6-foot-8 and 280 pounds of pure muscle, but he was the Jolly Green Giant to me. He was so much fun to be around, a wonderful, caring, kind man who happened to scare opposing pitchers to death at the same time.

And he was my roommate.

It's safe to say I loved Hondo, who always called me "Fab," which was short for "Fabulous Hawk," from the start.

His size alone would frighten anybody who didn't know him. Hondo had a 36-inch waist to go with his giant arms, giant neck, and giant personality.

Frank, who came up with the Dodgers and was part of their 1963 World Series championship team, was a heck of a player, too. I still say he is one of the most underrated players in baseball history.

He hit for average (.273 in his lifetime), had big-time power (382 home runs), and was great in the clutch (1,119 RBIs).

And he could hit a golf ball a country mile, too.

One time he and I were playing with Willie Mays at the LaCosta Country Club in California.

Hondo didn't pack his clubs on that trip, so he had to rent this itty-bitty set of clubs. He was forced to lean that giant frame at almost a 45-degree angle to address the ball before hitting it. We went to the range before our round and Hondo still consistently belted his drives over the range fence about 360 yards away.

I can still hear Willie in that high-pitched voice of his, saying, "Hondo, how far could you hit it with your regular set of clubs?"

What I loved about Hondo was that nobody who played the game ever hustled more consistently, no matter the score, including Charlie Hustle himself. If Hondo hit a one-hopper to the mound, when other players may have jogged down the line expecting an easy out, he would bust his butt like his life depended on it. He always gave 100 percent.

That's another reason he was so popular with teammates and fans. When I came up to the big leagues, most veterans didn't put up with selfishness or a lack of hustle, and a team-first attitude usually rubbed off on almost everyone. But there would always be one or two guys who didn't always play the game the right way, and they had to be reminded.

I remember several times when a teammate would hit a two-hopper and then jog down to first base, almost conceding the out. I made it a point to be on the top step of the dugout, awaiting his arrival and greeting him with something similar to, "If you do that again, we are going to fight!"

I meant it, too.

The good thing was, I usually had two or three teammates standing behind me ready to back me up. That's just the way it was. (I don't believe those conversations happen often in today's game.) That's why

I always admired guys like Hondo, Robin Yount, George Brett, and players of their ilk.

Robin once told me, "The way I want to be remembered is simply how I ran to first base."

Think about that for a minute.

When George hit a single, he rounded first like it was a double—until he saw it wasn't. When he hit a double, he rounded second base thinking triple—until he saw it wasn't. Guys like Yount and Rose and many others did the same thing.

Hondo, for all his size and power, was built in the same mold.

He was always positive, too, even when he was slumping. The same way Rose had been in Venezuela, Hondo never thought we were out of a game, even if we trailed 8–1 in the eighth inning. One time he was going badly and had struck out about 8 times in his last 10 at-bats. Most guys would have been moping around, consumed by their own troubles. Hondo walked around the dugout encouraging everyone else: "Come on guys…come on guys…we're not out of this."

I learned so much about how to play the game from him. I always said I learned how to compete by watching two players: Hondo and the Tigers' Al Kaline. There were no better competitors on this earth than those two guys.

Hondo wasn't quite as vocal about the game as Kaline was, as I learned when he cussed me out when I tried to run on him as a rookie, but he was always Mister Positive.

Let me tell you, nobody messed with Big Frank without regretting it. And I mean nobody.

The Tigers' Willie Horton and Frank were regarded as the toughest guys in baseball during my era. A few guys may have messed with Willie once or twice, but nobody really messed with Frank. And ironically, they were two of the most mild-mannered guys in the game off the field, unless their buttons were pushed.

I really don't know when his transformation took place, but I learned years later through a golfing buddy's wife that Hondo had been an incorrigible youth while growing up in Columbus, Ohio. The informant was none other than Barbara Nicklaus.

She once told me that Frank had a troubled upbringing and got into a lot of fights, until her father, the superintendent of schools, took Hondo under his wing and straightened him out.

Thank God, because he was the strongest man I ever met.

I think I saw Frank ticked off only three or four times.

One time, we had just ordered room service and he paid for it as he always did after it arrived. He also was one of the most generous men I ever knew. Frank's order was a dozen scrambled eggs, a quart of orange juice, and about a loaf of toast. His appetite was as big as the rest of him.

We were eating breakfast when a sports show on TV discussed a possible fight being arranged between Muhammad Ali and Wilt Chamberlain.

They interviewed Ali and then they interviewed Wilt. Both talked about what they would do to each other in the ring. It had to be nothing but a money-making exhibition, since an experienced and great fighter like Ali would have destroyed even the biggest football or basketball player.

For some reason, this proposed fight didn't sit too well with Hondo, who stood up, threw his fork down, and screamed, "I will fight both of them at the same time and I will kick both of their butts!"

I believe at that moment that huge man standing there in our room meant it, too. My money would have been on him.

I happened to be there when "Wilt the Stilt" actually met Hondo. One night we went to Gino Cappelletti's bar, The Point After, in downtown Boston. It was the most popular joint in town and there must have been 200 people waiting outside to get in.

We joined Gino at a huge booth. A little while later, a doorman walked over to me and said, "Wilt Chamberlain is outside and he wants to come in and join you guys."

Within minutes, the 7-foot-1 star of the Philadelphia 76ers walked over to our table as I got up to greet him. Frank couldn't stand up from the middle of the booth, but he reached across the table to shake Wilt's hand.

Later, when Hondo stood up to go to the bathroom, I noticed Wilt staring at him. Before he came back, Wilt whispered to me, "Hawk, that's the biggest man I have ever seen!"

Once on a road trip to Minnesota, I saw Frank's protective side. His sister had arrived from Green Bay to visit him, so the three of us headed over to Duff's, the hotspot in downtown Minneapolis. We had a few drinks at the bar, minding our own business, when I heard somebody say, "He doesn't look so big to me!"

The voice came from a nearby table, where three Minnesota Viking players sat staring at us. Two of the three were obviously linemen, judging from their size. One of those linemen soon walked over and asked Frank's sister to dance.

"I'm sorry but I don't dance," she told him.

"Come on, honey," he said, grabbing her arm.

If the guy wanted to provoke Hondo, that would be the way to do it. He had laid a hand on his sister.

Hondo stood up, grabbed this Viking lineman by the shirt, and picked him up. He then slammed him down into the chair. The veins on his neck bulged like they were about to explode and his face was as red as the inside of a cherry pie.

"I will give all three of you a choice," he yelled. "You can get out of here right now or I will break all three of your necks!"

They looked at each other, stood up, and quietly walked out the door.

I sure could have used his brawn one night at a bar called Sonny's in D.C., just before spring training of my second season with the Senators.

I was sitting at a table with a couple of Washington Redskins players when I heard glass breaking at the table next to mine. I noticed a woman had spilled her drink on her boyfriend, and the glass had broken, so I grabbed my handkerchief and offered it to her.

"You need this?" I asked her.

She took it, used it, and then handed it back to me.

"That's okay. You can keep it," I said.

"Screw you!" she told me.

"What? I was just trying to help you," I told her.

"Shut up!" the boyfriend told me.

"Let's go!" I told him.

I got up and landed one good punch just as she hit me over the head with a beer bottle. The bouncer ran over to us, screaming, "Take it outside!"

Then, as I walked out the door, one of his buddies hit me over the head with a second beer bottle. I had taken two beer bottles to the head and was bleeding profusely. It took 10 stitches to sew up my wounds, and I showed up at Pompano Beach for spring training sporting my latest bar-fight wounds.

I am sure that didn't put me in good standing with Senators manager Gil Hodges. From the beginning, I didn't like Gil and he didn't like me.

It didn't matter if I hit two home runs in one day, or threw a potential game-winning runner out at home, he cared more about my appearance. He took one look at my long hair and instantly disliked me.

"Get a haircut" was one of the first things he said to me.

All the Senators disliked his two-faced approach. He treated us like dogs and yet he loved being around the media.

It was common knowledge among the Senators that Hodges' goal was to somehow get back to New York to manage the Mets or the Yankees. He had played for the Brooklyn Dodgers and for the expansion Mets. He loved nothing more than talking to the media when we were in New York.

One day at Yankee Stadium before a game, Hodges walked around the clubhouse, demeaning player after player.

"Hondo, you stink…Brinkman, what are you doing here? You can't play this game…Hawk, who signed you?"

Nobody escaped his senseless wrath. Johnny Orsino, a catcher, spent the season on the disabled list. He happened to limp into the clubhouse on crutches in the middle of Hodges' tirade.

"Orsino! You can't play this game either!" he yelled.

Here was a guy who was injured, not even in uniform, hobbling on crutches, and Hodges was screaming at him.

The clubhouse guy then walked over to Hodges and told him some media members were outside waiting to talk to him.

As soon as the door opened, six or seven writers walked in and Hodges flipped his personality switch.

"Hey, guys!" he said, smiling. "We were just having a little family meeting in here. How's everybody doing today?"

We all looked at each other and just shook our heads. What a hypocrite, I thought. He never turned down a chance to talk to, or be nice to, the media in New York.

Hodges was especially tough on Eddie Brinkman, our shortstop. Eddie lockered next to me and was hitting about .140, really struggling at the plate at the time. He was distraught and needed help, as well as some encouragement.

"Hawk, should I go see the man and talk to him about hitting?" he asked. "He can probably help me, right?"

"Sure, Eddie," I said. "Go in there and ask him what he thinks."

Eddie walked out of Hodges' office about two minutes later. He sat down next to me, tears filling his eyes.

"Brinky?" I asked. "What'd he say?"

"I asked him if he could help me with my hitting and he told me, 'Nobody can help you with your hitting! Now get out of my office!'" he said.

That's the type of cold-hearted man Hodges was. He was uncaring and vicious to his own players.

One time, he picked on the wrong man.

Hondo was the team's highest-paid player at $50,000 and rightfully so. He always put up big numbers. He hit tape-measure home runs on a regular basis as the rest of us watched his mammoth moonshots in awe. And like I said, he was the team leader and he always hustled. He earned his money.

As we started a long road trip on a flight to Minneapolis to play the Twins, he had been struggling, however.

We flew on one of those old Constellation airplanes, and Hodges' flight routine was to sit in front with his coaches, Rube Walker and Joe "Piggy" Pignatano, playing cribbage. Hondo and I happened to sit one row behind them, on the other side of the aisle.

Out of nowhere on this particular flight, Hodges looked over at Hondo and exclaimed, "Big-league hitter, my butt!"

Hondo didn't say a word, but for the second time, I saw the veins on his neck bulging. He was getting red in the face again, too. A little bit later into the flight, Hodges looked at him again and uttered, "Fifty-thousand-dollar player, my butt!"

Again, Hondo didn't say a word.

A few hours later, as we stood in line at a downtown Minneapolis hotel to receive our room keys, Hodges grabbed his key and noticed Hondo.

Again, he said, "Big-league hitter, my butt!"

Hondo couldn't hold back any longer. He grabbed Hodges with those massive arms and lifted him up against one of the large pillars in the hotel lobby.

"Gil, I have had enough of your crap!" he said, holding our 220-pound manager up in the air against this pillar as if Hodges was the Scarecrow from *The Wizard of Oz*.

I jumped on Hondo's back, as did Piggy and then Phil Ortega. The three of us were trying our best to get Hondo to let go of Hodges. To Hondo, we must have felt like three fleas on the back of a bear. I really thought he was going to rear back and throw one of those large paws at Hodges' head and I knew that wouldn't be good for anybody.

As much as I despised Hodges, I didn't want him dead and I surely didn't want Hondo to go to jail.

Finally, Hondo just let go, as Hodges dropped to the floor like a box of rocks. I really don't remember Hodges riding him any more after that day.

That episode revealed quite a bit about both men. Hondo was a patient, caring man until pushed too far. And Hodges was a tyrant who bullied even his best players for no apparent reason.

Hodges usually tormented Hondo about his weight.

There was little doubt in my mind that Hondo hit better, played better, and felt better at about 280 to 285 pounds. Hodges wanted him to report to spring training in 1967 weighing only 255. So Hondo complied, and when I first saw him that spring, he looked gaunt and weak. He had been frustrated with dieting.

He struck out four times in that first spring training game in Pompano Beach.

"Roomy, come with me," he told me after that game. "I am getting some real food."

We went over to the All-Star Lounge, which had the biggest and best burgers anywhere. I swear those hamburgers were the size of waffles. I tried to eat one, but couldn't finish it. Hondo ate two. We went back to the team hotel, where a buffet was arranged in the restaurant.

Hondo walked down the line of the buffet and noticed the large salad bowl.

"Honey, you don't mind if I take this back to our table, do you?" he asked the waitress.

Hondo picked up the large bowl, tossed some salad dressing on it, and then devoured the entire thing.

It was always amusing to watch that man eat.

Anyway, when we returned home from that road trip in which he wanted to kill Hodges, we had to face the Indians' Sam McDowell one night. As I said, Sam had the best stuff I had ever seen.

Sam had walked the bases loaded with fastballs with one out by the time I got to the plate. He threw five fastballs to me as I worked the count to full. So what was I looking for? Of course another fastball. Then I heard the zip of his curveball. I was frozen. Strike three!

As I reached the top step of the dugout, I heard Gil again with the "Big-league hitter, my butt!" comment.

But this time, it was directed my way.

I snapped. I went after Gil but Rube Walker, who was a pretty big guy, got between us.

"Calm down, Hawk," Rube said. "I think the man forgets he used to strike out 140 times each season."

Things just grew worse between me and Hodges.

One night after a game, he told me to get a haircut, as he often did. At the particular time, I was the only guy in the lineup hitting worth a crap. Even Hondo was slumping.

But I didn't get a haircut as he ordered by the time I arrived at the ballpark the next day. I put on my uniform and walked over to look at the lineup card. I wasn't on it.

"What the heck is this?" I asked Hodges. "I am swinging the bat pretty well."

"I told you to get a haircut!" he said.

I knew that Bob Humphreys, one of our relief pitchers, had cut some of the guys' hair in the past, so I walked over to his locker.

Bob wrapped a towel around my neck just like a professional barber and started clipping away. By the time he had finished, there was a ton of hair on that floor. He had cut my hair really short. I then folded my hat into my back pocket, so Hodges could get a good look at me, and headed out to shag some flies during batting practice.

When batting practice finished, I walked back into the clubhouse and glanced at the lineup again. My name was now listed.

Another time we were boarding a flight for a road trip and I was wearing this beautiful Madras sport coat to go with my white loafers. I always took pride in being one of the best dressers in the big leagues, even though I wasn't making much money.

Hodges looked me up and down like a drill sergeant examining a buck private.

"Don't ever wear that sport coat again," he ordered.

"What's wrong with it?" I asked.

"I said don't ever wear it again!"

Ironically, I got to know his wife, Joan, a little bit and there couldn't have been a sweeter woman. She was nothing like Gil.

The team held a bowling outing once and I noticed Hodges was acting differently when she was around. Some guys maintained it was because he was away from baseball, away from the clubhouse and the pressures of the game. But I wondered if it was because of Joan's presence.

It was strange, because he was the nicest guy in the world that night.

Most guys had off-season jobs then and I spent the winter after my first season with the Senators trying to sell Pontiacs. I would drive from a D.C. suburb in Maryland, where I lived, about 20 miles to the car dealership. Traffic in Washington even then was as bad as anywhere in the country.

The only money I made that winter was by shooting pool during my lunch hour at a joint near the dealership. I always walked out of there with an extra $30 or $40 in my pocket. It took about three weeks until I realized people in D.C. don't buy cars during the winter.

That following spring, as Hondo tried to shake off the effects of his diet, I tore the cover off the baseball heading into the 1967 season. I had hit .360 with 9 home runs and more than 25 RBIs, leading the club in every offensive category that spring.

On opening day, I was excited because a huge crowd was expected. Everybody got excited on opening day, even in places like Washington. There were always U.S. senators in attendance and sometimes even the president showed up.

And to boot, we were playing the Yankees. Whatever team I played for always got fired up to face the Yankees.

I looked at the lineup to see where I was hitting…and my name was missing. Hodges had listed Dick Nen at first base. I couldn't believe it. Nobody could. Hondo had noticed how upset I was and came over to my locker.

He put his hand on my shoulder and told me, "Don't get upset, Fab. Just relax."

I stormed into Hodges' office.

"Gil, why am I not in the lineup?" I asked.

"Because [Mel] Stottlemyre is pitching today," he said.

"Do you know that I have always hit him pretty good?" I asked.

It was obvious to me that he never bothered to check our history, because he didn't respond.

"This is bullcrap!" I said.

"I made out the lineup and that's the way it is," he replied.

I walked out of that office and my hatred for him intensified by the minute.

We headed to New York a few weeks later, and when it was Stottlemyre's turn to pitch, sure enough, Hodges didn't have me in the lineup again.

Nen, who was playing in my place, walked over to me.

"Hawk, I am sorry," he said. "I can't believe it, either."

I knew it wasn't Dick's fault. He was a great guy and had nothing to do with Hodges' decisions.

I stormed into his office again.

"Okay, let's get this thing out in the open," I demanded. "I can't stand you and you can't stand me. We need to settle this right here and now!"

Hodges didn't move a bit, or even look up at me. He just mumbled, "Get out of my office."

"Gil, you had better get rid of me because I am not playing for you," I demanded.

We flew to Boston as Hondo tried to calm me down. Hondo always called Hodges "the man" or the "DI," as in drill instructor.

"Look, Fab, the man is wrong," he said. "He's really not a bad guy. He's just flat-out wrong in this case. But something will happen. You are too good a prospect and you have too much talent not to play every day. Somebody will trade for you. Just hang in there."

The next day, June 9, 1967, the phone rang in my hotel room. It was Selkirk, the Senators' general manager. I think George felt bad for me because he knew Hodges and I disliked each other.

"Hawk, I am going to do something that I shouldn't do," he told me. "I will do this for your future. I am going to get you out of here. You are going back to Kansas City. They made a deal for you."

I was absolutely elated. Who would have ever thought I would feel that way about returning to a club owned by that cheapskate Charlie Finley?

I hated to say good-bye to Hondo, but I was ecstatic to leave Hodges in my rear-view mirror. A year earlier, I had hated to leave Alvin but was excited to leave Finley.

The more I thought about it, one thing became clear: I believed Finley wanted me back in order to continue nipping at my paychecks, as a repayment on that loan.

As for Hodges, the Senators continued their losing ways and he left them after the season. He got his wish—he was named manager of the Mets. Within two seasons, he would manage them to a World Series title.

Following the 1971 season, the Senators and my buddy Hondo moved from Washington to Texas to become the Rangers.

And me?

As I left the Senators, I still was a relatively unknown big-league player hitting a paltry .203.

But I was about to enter a whirlwind time in my life.

9 BASEBALL'S FIRST FREE AGENT

I ARRIVED BACK IN KANSAS CITY ONLY 351 DAYS AFTER I HAD been traded to Washington, and I realized I had been correct about one thing.

Finley had paid the Senators to get me back, only to start nibbling at my paychecks again. He wanted reimbursement for that personal loan for my house and having me on his team was the only way he figured to be repaid.

Sometimes I took home as little as $150 per week after Charlie had taken his cut.

It's a good thing I could make money doing other things, such as shooting pool, playing golf or gin, or arm-wrestling.

One night at the Lindell Athletic Club bar in downtown Detroit, I went through three or four Detroit Lions' players who thought this baseball player would be a quick pushover. Some writer was there that night and wrote about it and then I had football players ail over the country coming up to me, wanting to arm-wrestle me for money.

They would put up $50 or $100.

I never lost, until one night in Kansas City.

Billy Martin was there that night at the Apartment Lounge and he instigated the entire thing, taunting the Chiefs' Curt Merz that he couldn't beat me. Curt was about 6-foot-4 and 270 pounds and had giant arms.

Thirty seconds into the match, we were at a stalemate. Finally, he wore me down and eventually beat me.

For my first four seasons in the big leagues, I made much more money off the field than I did in baseball. I made money by betting on myself.

One weekend I was at LaCosta Country Club to play in the annual football-baseball golf tournament sponsored by American Airlines. The organizers paired a professional football player with a big-leaguer from the same city.

I was sitting around one day with Johnny Unitas of the Baltimore Colts, Merlin Olsen of the Los Angeles Rams, and Lance Alworth of the San Diego Chargers when a member of the club wanted an opponent for a game of 9-ball.

"Here's a man who will play you," Unitas told him, pointing at me. "He's as good as anyone I've ever seen."

The guy wanted to play for $20 per game. He beat me a few games as I was warming up before I offered to increase the stakes to $50. He accepted. I then got hot, running his debt to $650 by the time we had finished. The guy came up with only $250 and promised to send me the rest in the mail.

I never saw it.

After I had flown home, Unitas told me that the guy was a prominent businessman and had told the tournament committee that I was a pool hustler. He said he would resign his membership at LaCosta if they ever invited me back to the tournament.

On the field, I started hitting the heck out of the ball and had raised my season average to .285 by mid-August. The only guy hotter than me in the American League was Boston's Carl Yastrzemski, who was making a run at the Triple Crown as the Red Sox battled the Twins, Tigers, and White Sox atop the AL standings.

Alvin, loving my production at the plate, tried to step in to save more of my paycheck, but Finley wasn't having any of it. I could sense that Finley and Alvin's relationship was getting worse by the day.

Finley was an overbearing owner who meddled in every day-to-day decision a manager should have been allowed to make alone. I really don't know how Alvin dealt with him and still maintained his calm demeanor in front of the players. Alvin always was such a classy guy. We probably never knew what he had to put up with working for a man like Finley.

We ended a long road trip August 3, winning two of three games in Boston to finish the trip with a 6–6 record. I had the game-winning hit in both of those wins against the Red Sox—a homer one night and a double the next.

During the loss to the Red Sox, our pitcher Jack Aker got bombed. I could tell he was feeling down before our flight home, so I told him to sit with me in the back of the airplane.

We were one of the few teams to fly commercial in those days because of Charlie's cheapness, and on this day, we had to fly from Boston to Baltimore to St. Louis to Kansas City. It was a typical travel day for the cost-cutting A's.

Jack was a quiet guy to begin with and I tried my best to cheer him up. Since we had two stops to make, I had plenty of time. Jack and I had only one drink between Boston and Baltimore, but five or six more each by the time we reached Kansas City. Normally, we had to pay for our drinks on flights, but the stewardesses usually took care of us with a few free extras.

Nobody got out of line and nobody raised his voice that entire flight home.

Alvin usually spent his flight time in the front of the plane playing bridge, as he did on this day. He never needed to wander to the back of the plane to check on us, because he knew we were professionals who knew how to behave in public. But for some reason, Alvin did walk to the back of the plane to see how we were doing.

Two weeks went by before we flew to Washington to begin another long road trip when Alvin announced, "We won't be having any drinks on this flight."

By the time we landed, we learned that Finley had suspended Lew Krausse Jr. for being "drunk and disorderly" on our flight home two weeks prior. Nobody had any idea what he was talking about or why he had waited two weeks to make an announcement. I knew Lew didn't have more than two drinks, because he sat directly in front of me the entire flight home.

Soon after we arrived at the stadium in Washington, Aker, our player-representative, had been ordered by Finley to read a six-paragraph statement that alcohol would no longer be served on our flights. It stated that the Kansas City Athletics would no longer tolerate the "shenanigans" of those "who do not appreciate playing in the major leagues." It also labeled our actions as "deplorable."

It was signed, "Charles O. Finley."

The kicker was that Finley had released this letter damning our alleged behavior to the media. Articles about it appeared on the sports pages in Washington and home in Kansas City.

That was the final straw for every player on that team, so Aker decided to draw up our own letter.

It read: "In response to Charlie Finley's statement of August 18, we, the players of the Kansas City Athletics, feel that an unjust amount of pressure has been brought to bear on several members of the club who had no part whatsoever in the so-called incident on the recent plane trip from Boston to Kansas City.

"The overwhelming opinion of the players is that the entire matter was blown out of proportion. Mr. Finley's policy of using certain unauthorized personnel in his organization as go-betweens has led to similar misunderstandings in the past and has tended to undermine the morale of the club. We feel that if Mr. Finley would give his fine coaching staff and excellent manager the authority they deserve, these problems would not exist."

Jack and I showed it to Alvin in his room in the Shoreham Hotel. We wanted to defend Lew, who did absolutely nothing to deserve a suspension. Alvin read it and said, "Alright, but this may get you into trouble."

Now, if you knew Alvin, he was a very religious man who rarely swore and never drank. He didn't believe in either, but he did allow his players the freedom to behave like adults.

Our response appeared in the Kansas City sports pages the following day.

We finished the series' finale at Washington and were preparing to board a bus to Baltimore when we heard the shocking news: Finley had fired Alvin. Apparently, it was because he discovered Alvin had read our letter before it was released to the newspapers.

I just snapped. I was livid. I knew all the guys had to be shocked and disappointed because everybody loved Alvin, especially me, but nobody said much about the firing to the media. When the media finally gathered at my locker, I let it all out.

I am sure the writers knew I would probably say something, because they knew I was close to Alvin. But they had no idea I was about to go off the way I did. I called Finley "a disgrace to baseball." I also said his actions were detrimental to the game. I said he didn't know what he was doing, among other things.

I went on and on.

"Alvin Dark is one of the greatest managers in all of baseball," I declared.

Then we traveled to Baltimore and checked into the Lord Baltimore Hotel. I figured there would be trouble brewing the next morning, so before I went to sleep I called down to the desk and told the hotel clerk, "Under no circumstances do I want any phone calls."

That morning, the newspapers in Kansas City featured my comments below a headline: HAWK CALLS FINLEY A MENACE TO BASEBALL. Somehow, the word "menace" got repeated in many media reports, but I never used that word.

Well, at 8:30, the phone rang. My roommate, Mike Hersberger, handed it to me.

"Son!" the voice on the other line shouted. "What are you trying to do to me? Haven't I been like a father to you?"

"No, sir, Mister Finley, you have not been like a father to me," I stated.

That angered him and he called me a "hippy, long-haired son of a [expletive]" among other things.

"Mister Finley, we both know you wouldn't be calling me these names if you were standing in front of me right now," I told him.

"Do you want your release?" he asked. "I will call you back in 30 minutes."

I really didn't want to be released. We had a losing record but I thought we had the nucleus of what could become a great team. Twenty minutes later the phone rang again.

"Son, as of this very moment, you are no longer a member of the Green and Gold!" Finley barked.

Then he slammed down the phone.

"What'd he say?" Hersberger asked.

"He released me," I told him.

"You lucky son of a gun," Mike said.

Mike may have thought I was lucky, but I realized I was unemployed at the moment, so how lucky could I be? I had bills to pay.

I called Joe Richler in the American League office to learn what my options were. We had no agents in those days to handle those kinds of matters for us.

"Hawk, he put you on irrevocable waivers," he told me.

"What does that mean?" I asked.

"It means this: the only person who can take you off of irrevocable waivers is you," Joe explained. "And I know *you* are not going to do that."

I still wasn't 100 percent clear what that meant. As soon as I hung up the telephone, it rang. It was Ed Short, the general manager of the

White Sox, who introduced himself and then put his manager, Eddie Stanky, on the phone.

"Hawk," Eddie said, "we got the best pitching in the league right now, but we are struggling offensively. We need some hitters. We need some power. If we get you here, we can win this thing."

Short got back on the phone and offered me $100,000 to play for the White Sox. He said they weren't interested in getting into a bidding war, so this was a one-time offer.

For some reason, I don't really know why, I didn't take the deal. I think I just needed a moment to think about what had just happened. Within a minute, my phone rang again. It was Haywood Sullivan, my former manager, who was now in the front office of the Red Sox.

"Hawk, you and Charlie got into it, huh?" he asked. "Well, we want you to come up here and play for the Red Sox."

Bear in mind, I was making $12,000 per season the previous day with the A's. Now some team was offering me an $88,000 raise to play for a contender whose owner was not named Charlie O. Finley. And a big-market team like the Red Sox wanted me, too? Suddenly, I knew what irrevocable waivers meant to me.

It meant I was about to hit the jackpot. I felt like a kid on Christmas morning.

In retrospect, thank god I ripped Finley to the media.

I went to the ballpark to retrieve my gear when Luke Appling, the interim manager Finley had promoted to replace Alvin, called me into his office.

"Listen, Charlie knows he made a mistake and he wants you back," he told me. "He was hot about what you said and he's sorry for it. He will give you a raise to $25,000."

"Luke, I just got offered $100,000 from the White Sox," I told him.

Luke shook my hand and said, "Best of luck, kid!"

A representative of the Tokyo Giants called me, making the highest offer yet. They wanted me to sign a three-year contract for three times what my best offer in the States would be. But there was just no way that I wanted to spend the next three years in Japan, so I didn't seriously consider it.

I called Alvin, who had arrived back in Kansas City, because I trusted his wisdom.

"Kenneth, here's what's going to happen," he said. "Right now, you are a lucky young man the way you are swinging the bat. I think you will end up getting at least $150,000 per year and whatever team you go to will win the pennant."

Then Sullivan called me again, wanting to meet at the airport in Baltimore. I met him in a bar there and he offered me $118,000 to play for the Red Sox. I accepted.

I flew back to Kansas City. That night, the NFL's Chicago Bears were playing the AFL's Chiefs in an exhibition game. Jack Haley, who owned the Apartment Lounge, called me and suggested we go to the game.

To recap my last few days: I had ripped Charlie publicly, been put on waivers by a last-place team, and had accepted more than a 1,000 percent raise to play with a contender. It was safe to say I was feeling pretty good.

As Jack and I walked into the stadium after kickoff that night, I started feeling much, much better, if that was possible. The Kansas City fans noticed me and all stood in unison. I was receiving a standing ovation—at a *football* game. But I understood why I was getting such attention. It was already well known that Finley had plans to move the A's to Oakland the following season. I had just ripped him a good one, so those fans sided with me for being their spokesman.

Jack later told me what his mom said after he had told her of the standing ovation.

"I knew my son would make it big one day," she said.

We both got a kick out of that one.

I went to bed that night feeling pretty good about myself, having no clue things would get even crazier the next day.

I woke up to the telephone ringing. It was Paul Richards, the Atlanta Braves' general manager. The Braves were also in a pennant race and Richards offered me $125,000 to sign with them.

I called Sullivan back and told him about Atlanta's offer. I reminded him that I was a Georgia boy at heart and that playing close to Mama would be a dream come true.

"Hawk, that's a lot of money," he said. "Go take it."

If Sully didn't win the bidding war over me, he was fine as long as I landed in the National League and wasn't playing against his Red Sox.

I called Richards and told him I'd come to Atlanta. I was relieved the entire process was over.

The following morning, Dick O'Connell, the president and general manager of the Red Sox called me. He asked what it would take for me to reconsider.

I really had no prepared answer. I just blurted out, "How about $150,000?"

"Okay, you got it!" he said.

Right then I knew I should have said $200,000. I called Paul back and told him of Boston's new offer.

"Well, I can't go that high," he said. "You go ahead and take it."

Two hours later, Paul called me back.

"I talked to Bill Bartholomay, our owner," he said. "He is ticked off at me. He really wants you down here in Atlanta. We will give you $200,000."

Now I was breaking out in hives. I started thinking about how much I loved hitting in Fenway Park and I also liked Sully. In the end, I decided to eat the $50,000 difference and stuck with Boston's offer.

I caught a flight to Boston the next day while the Red Sox were in New York.

I walked into the club offices and met with Tom Yawkey, the club's owner, and O'Connell. O'Connell then summoned the team's accountant to the room, who cut me a check for $92,000. I walked down the street to Shawmut Bank at Kenmore Square and approached one of the bank's officers sitting behind a desk and said I'd like to make a deposit.

"There's a teller over there," he instructed.

"Sir, maybe you should look at this check and tell me how to go about depositing it," I said.

He took one look at the zeroes on the check and said, "Wow!" That check would be a week's pay for a player today, but this was 1967. He made a phone call, which I presume was to verify the legitimacy of the check. I then opened an account, deposited the check, and took out some cash.

The next morning I flew to New York and walked into Red Sox manager Dick Williams' hotel suite.

"Hawk, you remember that Lonborg incident?" he asked.

He had recalled the time he ordered his pitcher, Jim Lonborg, to drill me.

"Can we just forget about that?" he asked, smiling.

We stood there laughing.

That night, I walked into the visiting clubhouse at Yankee Stadium as a member of the Red Sox for the first time. I knew some of the guys, but not all of them. A few of them walked over to greet me.

Yastrzemski walked over to me, shook my hand and said, "We are glad to have you." He then turned around and walked back to his locker.

As I would learn over the next few years, that was Yaz just being Yaz. He never got too excited about anything. He was a serious guy. Serious about baseball. Serious about life. Serious about everything.

Don't get me wrong. He laughed once in a while, just not very much. I didn't like him much before I got to the Red Sox, mainly because he always beat whatever team I had played for.

I had just beaten the Red Sox two games of the three-game series not two weeks earlier, so I sensed most of the guys were ecstatic to have me in their lineup, especially now that young power hitter Tony Conigliaro was missing. Tony C. had just been hit in the face by a pitch, one of the worst beanings in the history of the game, and he still was in the hospital.

I was somewhat anxious for my first game and fired up to play with a contender, where everything seemed more intense. Suddenly, there was more media coverage, more fans, and more attention paid to everything I did.

The Yankees started Bill Monbouquette that day and Williams put me fourth in the lineup, following Yaz.

And just like in my first-ever start in the big leagues, just like in my first-ever appearance in Yankee Stadium, I was ready. In my first at-bat as a Red Sox player, I hit one of Monbouquette's sliders over the score-board in right-center at Yankee Stadium and we won the game.

(In 2007, when I attended the 40th reunion of that Red Sox team, player after player came up to me and said about the same thing: "Hawk, we were so down after Tony C. got beaned. And when you hit that home run in your first at-bat with us at Yankee Stadium, we knew things were going to be alright.")

That was one of my few highlights that season.

I didn't contribute much down the stretch. I am not sure but I may have been trying too hard. I did have a few big moments, but I wasn't consistent.

Let me be honest: the '67 Red Sox were going to be alright because of one Mister Carl Yastrzemski.

What that man did night after night was simply amazing. It was the greatest offensive season I had ever seen. I always believed the best hitters in the game got their hits in the late innings with the games on the line. Well, Yaz got his hits in the seventh, eighth, and ninth innings with the game on the line. He got hits with men on first and second base. He got hits when we trailed by one or two runs with two outs. To this day, I have never, ever seen a clutch hitter like Yaz.

I have said it over and over and will say it to the day I die: if I had to take one player in baseball history to get a hit with my family's lives on the line, I would pick him—over Ted Williams, Babe Ruth, Mickey Mantle, Willie Mays, or any other great clutch hitter who ever played.

I learned how to compete from watching Frank Howard and Al Kaline, but I learned all about clutch hitting from kneeling in the on-deck circle watching Yaz.

He also was the best hitter I ever saw at getting out of the way of a pitch. He played 23 years, had almost 14,000 plate appearances, and was hit by a pitch only 40 times. That is an amazing statistic. One time, I saw Jim Kaat throw one right behind his ear. Anybody else would have backed straight into it, but not Yaz. He went straight up into the air as the ball whizzed by his head. He stared Kaat down and then hit the next pitch the opposite way over the Green Monster.

He was much like Kaline that way.

We always told our pitchers not to throw at Kaline, because you didn't want to tick him off.

I think opposing players had to feel that way about Yaz, too.

Recently, Bruce Cornblatt, a producer for the Major League Baseball Network, asked me a question during the making of its documentary on the '67 Red Sox.

"Hawk, I don't mean this in a derogatory way," he said, "but you always talk about how great Yaz was down the stretch that year. So why did the other teams continue to pitch to him with you hitting behind him?"

I thought about that often in the on-deck circle back then: why were they pitching to Yaz with me struggling behind him? I would give anything to ask Dick Williams or any other managers from that time the same question, if only they were alive.

One thing was obvious about Yaz: he didn't seek the spotlight, but he thrived in spite of it. He just wanted to help the team win. He led by example. It was definitely his team and a win or a loss usually depended on how he performed at the plate.

Before I got to know Yaz real well, one of the things I heard about him was that he would sometimes take a shot of Seagram's VO whiskey during a game. Well, in the fifth or sixth inning of a real hot day at Fenway soon after I arrived, I walked into the clubhouse for something and saw Carl also walking in there, too. Before I headed back to the dugout, I lingered a bit just to see if it was true.

Sure enough, I saw him grab a VO bottle, then pour a few inches into a glass and down it. I am telling you, that shot would have knocked me on my butt. It didn't affect Yaz one bit.

I don't know what he ate for breakfast at his house, but on the road, he would order pizza and wash it down with a glass of Beaujolais.

And because of his greatness, I suddenly found myself in the midst of what became known as "the greatest pennant race in the history of baseball."

When I reached the Red Sox, only two games separated them from Detroit, Minnesota, and Chicago. Remember, there weren't divisions and playoffs back then as there are today. The AL and NL champions were determined by the best records and those teams met in the World Series.

The difference between playing in Washington or Kansas City and playing in Fenway Park was incredible. The stands were now full, or close to it, since the Red Sox were in a pennant race. There was a large group of reporters covering every game. Red Sox fans loved their team and the players and I couldn't walk down the street without being mobbed for autographs, just because I was a part of their team.

I also learned that they weren't just Boston's team. The Sox were all of New England's team. It seemed that everybody in the entire region from Canada to Hartford loved them.

My new surroundings made me take the game a little more seriously as well, so I basically put one of my passions on hold.

During the 1966 season, I played golf every chance I got. I was addicted to it. I played before night games and especially during off days.

Sometimes after day games, I squeezed in nine or even 18 holes before it got dark.

Sure, I may have been cheating myself on the baseball field, but I was playing for sub .500 teams in Kansas City and Washington. On the golf course, including some of the country's finest championship courses, I had consistently shot in the 60s, with a low of 64 and a half-dozen rounds of 65, and there were days I seriously considered chucking baseball to try professional golf. Especially after winning the baseball players' tournaments in Miami.

But once I signed with the Red Sox, things changed. For starters, I couldn't play in the winter in New England. And now I played for a contender.

Besides Yaz, the Red Sox were full of talent and toughness, including shortstop Rico Petrocelli. After I got to know him, I would have taken him in a fight against just about anybody. One day, a teammate was picking on our clubhouse boy, who was only about 17 or 18 at the time. He shouldn't have been bullying the kid, but nobody stopped him until Rico blew up.

"I have had enough of that crap," he said.

Rico ran over to him and slapped him upside the head about five times before the other guy could raise his hands. It happened so fast, I wasn't sure what I was seeing with my own eyes. Rico could have been a prizefighter if he had wanted to.

Another time, Dick Ellsworth was on the mound when he turned and motioned Rico to move toward second base. Rico didn't move. Dick motioned for him to move again. Rico stood still. The batter then hit the ball back up the middle for a hit.

As we got back to the dugout, Ellsworth asked Rico why he didn't move.

"Don't you ever tell me how to play this game!" Rico shot back. "Now shut up!"

Dick Williams heard the dispute and walked toward them both.

"What's going on here?" he asked.

"You shut up, too!" Rico said.

Williams walked away and didn't say another word.

I thought Dick was a great manager. He had gut instincts and the right temperament. He knew what he was doing. As a player, I always posed questions to managers to try to understand their mind-set and Dick always impressed me with his answers.

One night we were tied 2–2 with Chicago in the bottom of the eighth when the White Sox brought in left-hander Gary Peters. We had right-handed hitters Jerry Adair, Elston Howard, and George Thomas on the bench ready to pinch-hit, but Dick sent up left-handed hitter Jose Tartabull.

We sat on the bench looking at each other, wondering what he was doing. Tartabull then drilled a liner to right field to drive in the game-winning run.

After the game, I asked Dick what his strategy was.

"Well, it wasn't a hard decision," he said. "Jose is a terrific first-ball fastball hitter. I knew if I sent him up there, Peters wasn't going to screw around with him. He was going to try to throw a fastball on the first pitch to get ahead of him. I told Jose to jump on the first pitch."

One afternoon at Fenway, late in the season, I was playing right field when I threw to third, missing the cutoff man and allowing the hitter to go to second on what should have been a single. The next guy followed with a hit to drive in the winning run. We were in the middle of a pennant race and I committed a huge mental error that cost us a game.

I sat in front of my locker with tears in my eyes when Dick walked in. I could hear his spikes on the wooden planks of the clubhouse floor. The clubhouse was dead silent and I just knew I was about to get reamed for the loss, deservedly so.

Dick headed over to the beer cooler, cracked open a cold one and said, "That was a tough game. We'll get 'em tomorrow!"

He walked into his office and did not say another word.

Yaz later told me that very moment was the defining moment in that pennant race for us. Dick was a rookie manager, but if he could take a tough loss like that, we knew we would be fine.

And the rest of us knew we would win because of Yaz.

After I retired and a few years passed, I referred to Yaz as the "Renaissance Man of New England."

As a reference point, the Red Sox drew about 653,000 fans in 1965. That increased to 811,000 in '66, which was the last season they ever drew fewer than 1 million fans. Attendance more than doubled to 1,727,832 the season I arrived. Today, the franchise attracts almost 3 million fans every season to Fenway.

There is no doubt that Yaz and that '67 season was the renaissance of baseball in New England.

We got to the final weekend of the regular season tied with Detroit and one game in front of Minnesota. There wasn't any part of me that thought we had the best team or the most talent in the American League. I really believe the Twins, with Harmon Killebrew, Rod Carew, and Cesar Tovar leading the way, had the best team. All big Harmon did that year was hit 44 home runs and drive in 113 runs.

But we played the best defense. It seemed that nothing hit the ground in the outfield with Yaz in left, Reggie Smith in center, and me in right. Rico was great at short, and George "Boomer" Scott could flash some major leather at first base, too. Boomer was a funny guy. Every time he grounded out, he griped that he couldn't catch a break. He would hit a routine two-hopper to shortstop and come back to the dugout complaining, "Man, I can't catch a break! I scalded that seed!" We would just look at each other and smile.

The race all came down to that final weekend. We had two games left against the Twins at Fenway and we had to sweep them to have a chance to win the pennant. And we also needed the Tigers to lose another game.

Kaat, off whom I got my first big-league hit four years earlier, started for the Twins that Saturday. Jim had a good fastball and a great curveball, but I always hit him pretty well. In my first at-bat, he threw me a good curveball to strike me out, but I heard something pop near the mound.

I walked back to the dugout wondering if he'd just hurt his elbow.

Sure enough, he had done just that. The Twins had to go to their bullpen after only 2⅓ innings. We scored all six of our runs in the fifth, sixth, and seventh innings to win 6–4. Now we had identical 91–70 records.

Detroit had split a doubleheader with the Angels at Tiger Stadium, and were a half-game behind us. They would play another doubleheader on the final day of the season.

It all came down to Sunday, October 1.

We needed to beat the Twins and have the Angels win at least one game of their doubleheader for us to clinch the pennant.

That morning, Yaz told me that he knew Angels manager Bill Rigney and that he'd find a way to win one of those games.

The Twins started Dean Chance, a 20-game winner that season, against us on Sunday.

We fell behind 2–0 heading into the sixth. Lonborg, our ace who started the game, opened the inning with a beautiful bunt single down the third-base line. Then Jerry Adair singled. So did Dalton Jones and Yaz, whose single to center scored Lonborg and Adair to tie the game.

I came up with runners on first and third and I just knew Chance would throw that spitter. Sure enough he did and I hit the crap out of it, but it was a one-hopper right at Twins shortstop Zoilo Versalles. It was a perfect double-play ball.

But for some reason, Versalles, who fielded it only a few steps from second base, threw home to try to get Jones at the plate. His throw was high, Jones was safe, and now we had runners on first and third. By the time the inning was finished, we had scored five runs.

In the newspaper the following day, Twins manager Cal Ermer was quoted as saying, "It was the dumbest play I ever saw in my life. It was the perfect double-play ball. He could have stepped on second base himself and then thrown it to first."

Lonborg did the rest from there, allowing only one run as he cruised into the ninth. He got Carew to hit into a rare double play to put us just one out away. I had come out of the game for a pinch runner, so I stood on the top of the dugout steps, glancing around the stadium trying to soak in the moment as the fans were on the verge of celebration. By now, we had realized the Tigers had won their first game 6–4.

Until the day I die, I will never forget seeing Rico catch that pop-up to end the game. From the moment it touched his glove, fans left the stands and swarmed the field. I fought my way through the crowd to get to Lonborg, who was riding on somebody's shoulders.

By the time we pushed our way through the fans to get to the clubhouse, Mister Yawkey ordered the radio call of the second Tigers-Angels game piped into the clubhouse. If the Tigers won the second game, we had to head directly to the airport to catch a flight to Detroit to play a one-game playoff the following day.

Detroit started its ace, Denny McLain, but he lasted only 2⅔ innings as the Angels built an 8–3 lead.

I didn't find this out until later, but Rigney had three of his starters warming up in the bullpen the entire game, since it was the final day of the season. Even though the Angels weren't headed for anything but a three-month vacation, they were approaching it as if it was Game 7 of the World Series.

The Tigers scored two runs to make it 8–5 and then put runners on first and second with only one out in the ninth.

I looked around the clubhouse and all of us listened as if we were playing the game ourselves. Rigney brought in George Brunet, a big left-handed starter who had great stuff, out of the bullpen to face Dick McAuliffe.

A home run would tie the game. McAuliffe, who had 22 homers that season, had enough power to do it.

What did Brunet get McAuliffe to do? Something he did only *once* the entire season. He hit into a double play.

As we heard the words over the radio—"Ground ball to Bobby Knoop at second, throw to Fregosi for one out, back to first for the double play! The Angels win!"—I turned to see Mister Yawkey hugging Yaz. He had tears in his eyes.

Within minutes, Yaz was covered in shaving cream.

His prediction about Rigney had been spot on.

Somehow, some way, the Red Sox had won the American League pennant and I was part of it.

It has been called the "Impossible Dream Season" in New England ever since.

The events from April through October of 1967 still baffle and mystify me in some ways. I learned you just never know your own fate.

Sometimes, things just happen. I went from being a relatively unknown, $12,000-a year ballplayer for the Kansas City A's, playing in front of a few thousand people each night, to a guy making $150,000 a year for the AL champion Boston Red Sox.

And I was about to play in a World Series.

I thought back to what Alvin had predicted four months earlier: I would end up with a $150,000 contract and whoever I played with would win the pennant. I always knew that he had one of the great minds in baseball, and he hit it right on the money.

As the national anthem played before Game 1 of the World Series against the St. Louis Cardinals, I stood in right field at Fenway Park and I had tears rolling down my cheeks.

Then Bob Gibson dominated us that night as the Cardinals won 2–1.

In Game 2, Yaz had belted two home runs and Lonborg was brilliant, pitching a shutout as we won 5–0.

I hadn't felt comfortable at the plate, and Dick must have noticed because he asked me about it. I couldn't lie to him with the World Series on the line. I wasn't seeing the ball well. Like anything to do with pressure or failure, I figured it had to be self-induced.

My only real contribution during the series was making what was probably the greatest catch of my career. Lou Brock hit a liner to right-center and I ran as hard as I could to make a full-layout diving catch. It was only possible because of how Yaz had positioned me moments earlier. I never would have come close to reaching that ball otherwise.

The next day, Brock was quoted in the local papers saying it was the greatest catch anybody ever made against him.

Yaz continued being Yaz. He was awesome in the series, but we gave him little help.

When I claim that nobody was more prepared than Yaz, I mean it. The Cardinals brought Joe Hoerner in relief one game. Of course, being in the American League, none of us had seen him before.

Yaz asked Sal Maglie, who handled all of our scouting reports, about Hoerner.

"He starts all left-handed hitters off with a low fastball to get ahead," Sal told Yaz.

Yaz got that first-pitch fastball and hit it about 15 rows over the bullpen.

After we won 8–4 in Boston to force a Game 7, we realized we had to face Gibson for the third time. He had been just dominating, having beaten us twice already, allowing only one run in 18 innings. But we had our ace, Lonborg, pitching for us, too.

I arrived at Fenway thinking we would have to play a perfect game to beat Gibson. We couldn't make any mistakes or give the Cardinals any extra outs. I glanced at the lineup card and saw I was in right field, hitting fourth behind Yaz. I got dressed and looked in my locker to grab my glove before I headed to the dugout.

It was gone.

I searched everywhere and couldn't find it. I couldn't believe it: somebody had actually stolen my glove out of my locker before the seventh game of the World Series. It was a nightmare. I asked around and nobody could find it. I went locker to locker to locker, frantically searching for it. It was a long and narrow glove and very pliable and I hadn't made an error all season with it.

Finally, relief pitcher Danny Osinski offered me his backup glove. He handed me a glove which looked just like mine, but when I put it on, it was as stiff as a board. It hadn't been broken in.

The Cardinals had built a 4–1 lead after five innings and we had to keep them at four runs if we had any chance at coming back, simply because of the way Gibson was pitching.

I learned that night just how mentally tough he was. In my third at-bat, he started me off with a sinker. I backed out of the box, wondering if he had lost his fastball. Gibson never threw sinkers. But then he threw another one. Now he had me 0-2, and then he threw a slider to strike me out.

As I walked to the dugout, I told Rico that Gibson had lost his fastball.

Gibson was coming back for Game 7 on only three days' rest. He couldn't throw as hard as he normally did and yet he was battling us with a sinker and a slider. No other pitcher could have lost his fastball in the most important game of the season and not been bothered by it one bit.

Tim McCarver led off the sixth with a line drive between me and Reggie. I took off running. I knew I had a shot at it as I dove and reached out, just like I did on Brock's liner a few days earlier. I had caught the baseball in Osinski's backup glove.

Then just as I hit the ground, the ball slowly popped out onto the grass.

The official scorer credited McCarver with a double, but I knew I should have made the catch. I *would* have for sure, if I only had my regular glove. I just couldn't squeeze it with that stiff glove.

Mike Shannon then reached on an error before Julian Javier hit a three-run homer to make it 7–1, putting the game—and the series—out of reach.

Many players didn't like Gibson. He was moody, cantankerous, and he often threw at hitters. That was no secret. After I grounded into a double play in the ninth to complete my 1-for-13 series, he had backed up first and we crossed paths after the play.

"Gibby, you're the greatest," I told him.

I had to pay my respect to the man because of what he did in that series.

We lost 7–2, but I always wondered if I had made that catch, would it have made any difference in the later innings?

To this day, I have no clue who took my glove or what happened to it.

I would hate to ever claim "The Case of the Missing Glove" cost the Red Sox the '67 World Series, but in my mind it was a factor in allowing the Cardinals to put the game away after they built a three-run lead.

When the game was over, everybody in the clubhouse was down, naturally. But I didn't let that feeling stick with me, perhaps because of how far I had come that season. I was disappointed of course, but most of my disappointment was for Mister Yawkey, Dick O'Connell, and the fans of New England. I liked those two guys and I knew the fans had suffered a long, long time.

In fact, after I received my World Series ring (the winner's ring included diamonds; the loser's, rubies), I had a jeweler swap my rubies for diamonds. I figured we were just as good as the Cardinals, but the difference was that they had Gibson and we didn't.

But you know what I learned from the chain of events of 1967, resulting in me becoming baseball's first free agent and climbing from the outhouse to the penthouse?

Some of your greatest moves and moments in life aren't premeditated. They aren't even planned at all. They just happen spontaneously.

And you have to thank your lucky stars when they do.

10 A YEAR LIKE NO OTHER

THE WORLD SERIES LOSS WAS BEHIND US, PHYSICALLY AT least if not mentally, and I couldn't wait for my first spring training with the Red Sox.

The previous season had been the Year of Yaz, no doubt. I witnessed the tail end of his Triple Crown season while mostly kneeling in the on-deck circle, as he led the Red Sox to one crucial win after another down the stretch.

But he needed help in the lineup. I contributed only three home runs and 14 RBIs to go with a lowly .200 batting average once I arrived in Boston, and I knew I had to improve my production.

One day before spring training, Joe Cronin invited me to his office on Boylston Street in downtown Boston.

Joe had been a Hall of Fame shortstop with the Red Sox and a player-manager back when such a thing existed. He had 15 big-league seasons under his belt as a manager and 11 more as Boston's general manager before he became the president of the American League for 15 years.

Let me put it this way: Joe's baseball knowledge matched that impressive résumé.

More importantly for me, he knew hitting. So when I walked into his office, I knew he'd have some good advice for me.

When I walked into his office he immediately asked, "Are you dumb or what?"

"What are you talking about?" I asked.

"Well, you stand in the same place in the box against a hard-throwing right-hander as you do against a slow-throwing left-hander," he said. "Where is the sense in that? You do realize that you can go anywhere in that box you want, right? That is *your* box. That's why they call it the batter's box. It's not the pitcher's box."

Joe forced me to think about my approach at the plate as spring training grew closer.

One of the best things about spring training with the Red Sox was hanging around a certain baseball legend who wore No. 9.

Ted Williams, probably the greatest left-handed hitter who ever lived, served as special hitting instructor and also had the title of vice-president of the club.

Nobody had more charisma than Ted and I loved being in his presence. Immediately, he taught me two things.

"The big-league season is a grind, so take a nap every day before a game," he told me. "And don't read the newspaper. If you do read it, don't read the sports pages."

When I was younger and I had a big day at the plate or hit a home run, I couldn't wait to read the next day's newspaper. But from that moment on, I took Ted's advice to heart. I told the clubhouse guy, "If there's something in the sports pages that I need to know, put it in my locker."

Ted had a reputation for being able to talk about the art of hitting for hours at a time. He also would talk fishing. He had become quite the fisherman, but I never fished with him. I got to know Bobby Doerr, one of Ted's Red Sox teammates, and he told me to thank my lucky stars I didn't get the chance.

Ted had invited Bobby to the Florida Keys once to fish for bonefish with him.

"It was the worst weekend of my entire life," Bobby told me. "For two days, I had to sit completely still in the bow of the boat. Every time I flinched, Ted snapped, 'Don't move! Don't move!' For two days, I couldn't talk or move a muscle. I just sat in the bow of that boat, like a statue."

I did see Ted's fishing talent once. There was a sportsmen's display at the Prudential Center in Boston, which included this huge water tank about 30 feet in diameter, and we had been invited to a fly-casting contest, where contestants tried to cast into a tiny target in the middle of the tank.

I got one in. Ted never missed. He was perfect.

One of the most-amusing aspects of being a Red Sox player was watching the dynamic between Yaz and Ted.

Yaz would get Ted so riled up on just about any subject, but especially about hitting. He spent much of his free time just pulling Ted's chain. It was hilarious to see. I also heard their tennis matches were legendary. Ted was obsessed with trying to beat Yaz on the tennis court, but I don't think he ever did.

The slider had come along in the latter part of Ted's career and he absolutely hated that pitch. He maintained it was the hardest pitch to hit—and he was probably right. But Ted knew hitting as well as anyone who ever wore a pair of spikes.

But Ted wasn't always right, even when he thought he was. He could be a stubborn mule about new ideas. It was his way or no way. I argued with him one time about the specifics of hitting a slider one day when I finally snapped, "Ted, you are full of it!"

He would take that if he liked you. If he didn't, you had to watch out, but I disagreed with Ted plenty of times.

One time we had lunch together to talk about my hitting. For one thing, he wanted me to go to a lighter bat, maybe a 33-ounce bat, since I always swung one of the heaviest bats in the game, anywhere from 35 to 40 ounces. He also told me to back off the plate more if I was in a slump, in order to start seeing the ball better.

"Heard you had lunch with Ted today," Mister Yawkey told me. "Forget everything he told you."

Dick O'Connell then saw me.

"Have lunch with Ted?" he asked. "Well, forget everything he told you."

I had all these new ideas and approaches from Cronin and Ted in my head by the time I arrived in Winter Haven, Florida, in February 1968.

I also was somewhat confused and anxious, because I found myself the subject of trade rumors.

I had bounced from Kansas City to Washington back to Kansas City before I found myself with a contender in Boston, happy as I could be. I had quickly grown to love the city. I loved the ballpark, loved hitting behind Yaz, and loved the New England fans.

The last thing I wanted to do was move on to yet *another* team.

Tony C. was back in right field that spring, but probably not fully recovered from his serious eye injury. There weren't any worse beanings in baseball history than the one he had taken the previous season. The club hoped he would return to his previous self, but as opening day grew near, it became obvious he wouldn't.

Instead of Tony, I could tell that Dick Williams wanted to give Joe Lahoud every chance to win the right-field job. Joe was hitting the cover off the ball in spring training.

So where did that leave me?

I went to Williams' office and made it clear that while I wasn't one of those players who demands, "Play me or trade me," I was only 26 years old and I did want to play every day. He agreed, telling me I was "too good of a ballplayer to sit on the bench." He said that if there wasn't room for me in Boston, he would trade me to a team which would play me regularly.

On one very hot day in spring training, Yaz and I were taking extra batting practice. Jackie Moore was throwing to us and he wanted a catcher, so this big, young kid volunteered. I had never seen him before.

Yaz hit for 25 minutes. Then I hit for another 20 minutes. This big kid had been catching in that heat for about 45 minutes, not complaining once.

Yaz and I grabbed a Coke and went to sit down as the young catcher took a few swings.

After a few minutes, Carl looked at me and said, "It's a shame that kid will never make it, because he's got such great desire."

That was my introduction to Carlton Fisk, although he didn't make the big-league club that season.

Nineteen sixty-eight will go down as one of the most turbulent years in United States history.

And by the time it ended, it would be my greatest year in any sport.

However, it sure didn't start that way.

On April 4, Martin Luther King Jr. was shot and killed in Memphis when we were preparing to fly to Detroit to begin the regular season. We watched the TV as riots broke out in several major cities. President Lyndon Johnson, who I didn't care for at all, sent the National Guard into Chicago.

What I recall most about that opening series is how the Tigers' Willie Horton, a terrific hitter who happened to become a good buddy of mine, went out into the streets of Detroit pleading for peace and quiet in the wake of MLK's assassination. All the players were proud of him.

I had been battling a flu bug that had zapped my energy, so Lahoud played right field regularly and won the job to start the season. I also was battling my old nemesis—another case of hemorrhoids.

I wasn't healthy enough to play regularly until the 10th game of the season, in which the Indians' Sam McDowell shut us out. Three games later, I finally got a couple of hits to snap out of a 1-for-10 start. I didn't hit my first home run until the 18th game of the season, on May 2.

The next day, I faced my old buddy Catfish and my old team, the Athletics, whom Charlie Finley had relocated to Oakland.

The wind was blowing out at Fenway and Cat threw a great pitch, a fastball inside. I somehow fisted it up into the air and the wind carried it just over the Green Monster. As I rounded first, I looked at the mound and said, "Cat, I'm sorry." We both knew it was a cheap home run.

Most of the A's approached me before our first game of the series, happy that I finally landed a big paycheck and was playing for a contender with the Red Sox. That A's team really was a close-knit group, bonding largely for their common disdain of Finley. I knew then that they would be in for bigger things in the near future, because they were loaded with talent, despite Finley's cheapness.

During the first week of May, I finally started to feel comfortable at the plate. I used that lighter bat Ted had recommended and immediately hit one of the Twins' Jim Perry's sliders into a light tower beyond the Monster.

Good pitchers like the Orioles' Jim Palmer and McDowell had no trouble wearing me out in the past. Palmer was a high-fastball pitcher with a great curveball and Sam's stuff was awesome. I had virtually little chance against pitchers like those two.

In addition to Ted's and Joe's advice on hitting, Al Vincent had said some things to make me *think* differently. Al had been hired as the Athletics' hitting coach when Alvin arrived in 1966 and he didn't change my mechanics or my swing at all. He just worked on my mind.

My thought process when it came to hitting had been "behind the plate," as I like to say. I constantly thought about where my feet and my hands were. I also stood off the plate. Eventually, I called those areas "the house of demons."

Al made me realize that I had to visualize what was out in front of the plate, mostly the baseball, and where it was headed once I hit it, as well as my follow through. He also convinced me to stand closer to the plate, as if I controlled the area above it.

I also used Cronin's advice to move either toward the pitcher, or to the back of the batter's box, depending on who was on the mound.

Palmer, who had an excellent memory when it came to hitters, noticed the change during my first at-bat against him after Al had changed my way of thinking. I came to the plate one night in Baltimore and I was practically standing on top of it.

"Hawk, you had better get off the plate," he yelled from the mound.

I glanced at Orioles catcher Andy Etchebarren and said, "Andy, if he hits me, I am going out there to break his pitching arm."

Palmer's first pitch was way over my head but I didn't flinch. From that time on, I hit pretty well off of him. I stood on top of the plate and hit almost everything he threw to me, whether it was that high fastball or that great curve of his.

It was all about a sense of control, and suddenly, I had it and he didn't.

As the '68 season progressed, I approached hitting differently. I moved around in the batter's box. Sometimes, I grabbed a lighter bat. And often, I stepped up closer to the plate. I felt different. I felt *dangerous*.

And it showed.

I hit 10 home runs that May.

America was in the midst of turbulent times, and an upcoming presidential election.

Bobby Kennedy was the heavy favorite to win the Democratic nomination for president that spring. I knew Bobby and liked him very much. Most Red Sox fans loved the Kennedys, at least the fans who were Democrats, because of their proximity to Boston. Bobby oozed charisma, just as his brother Jack had. Bobby came into the clubhouse a couple of times, and like most of the Kennedys, he was a big Red Sox fan.

He was visiting our clubhouse one day that May when my hair was long, and surprisingly, so was his—much longer than he usually wore it.

He sat down next to my locker and told me, "You're the reason I am growing my hair long."

I laughed at that one. Imagine, my hairstyle influencing a presidential candidate.

We talked a bit about Jack and his other older brother, Joe, who had died in an airplane crash in World War II.

I never got involved much in politics, but for some reason it seemed candidates often tried to pull me in their direction.

A representative of George Wallace once called me and asked if I would introduce him before one of his appearances in Boston before a primary. I guess it was because I was a registered Democrat at the time and gaining popularity in New England, so I agreed to do it, until I informed my agent Bob Woolf about it.

"Hawk, you had better rethink that idea," he told me.

I learned to trust Bob soon after I had hired him. I was one of the few players to even have an agent then. Yaz had recommended Bob to me. Bob had been a successful attorney in Boston, but he had dipped his toe into the new business of representing athletes. Tigers pitcher Earl Wilson, who came up with the Red Sox years earlier, was his first client; I was his second.

I did some research on Wallace and called his people to back out of my commitment.

The worst encounter I ever had with a politician involved Bobby's younger brother, Ted, then a young senator from Massachusetts. I attended a political fund-raiser one night, wearing a gold lamé suit accompanied by a very pretty date.

Despite my outfit, everybody was staring at my date. At one point, Ted reached out and grabbed her butt as he walked by her. I just happened to see it.

Immediately, I wanted to walk over to him and punch him, but he had two giant state troopers serving as his bodyguards that night. A few of my friends saw what he did, too, and had to talk me out of trying to get by those two troopers to reach him. That was right before the Chappaquiddick incident.

Other than Bobby's remarks about my hair, wanting to punch his obnoxious little brother, and then backing out of introducing Wallace, that was about it for my involvement in politics. I strictly regarded it as a spectator sport from that time on. I always believed athletes should never use their popularity to influence voters in any way about a candidate. I believed voters should read, watch, and form their own opinions.

On June 4, Don Drysdale was looking for his record sixth straight shutout in Los Angeles, facing the Pirates in a National League game. Everybody in both leagues was talking about it.

Bobby was scheduled to speak at the Ambassador Hotel that night, anticipating he would clinch the Democratic nomination. Just before the game started, he began his speech by wishing Drysdale good luck at nearby Dodger Stadium.

Drysdale did get his sixth straight shutout that night, as he stretched his record scoreless streak to a remarkable 58⅔ innings.

By the time we arrived at Fenway the next day to play the Tigers, we had heard the terrible news: Bobby had been shot moments after he delivered his speech. He was hanging on for dear life at a Los Angeles hospital. We felt terrible about Bobby and I think most of us went through the motions that day in a 5–4 loss to Detroit. He had just been in our clubhouse weeks earlier, commenting about my hairstyle.

Bobby's death was just the latest shocker in a year of shocking events.

Like many Americans, I was saddened by the thousands of lives we were losing in Vietnam. It was nothing but a political war.

When I was young, one of my favorite older cousins, Travis Johnson, played with me all the time. He would always hand me a dime, which was worth something in the 1940s. Then he died in the Korean War, which was very, very tough for a little kid like me. It was something that stuck with me, so knowing families were losing loved ones in Vietnam saddened me to no end.

On the field, I continued to hit like I had never hit before in the big leagues. My popularity in Boston grew by the day.

And because Yaz was reluctant to grab the spotlight that was due him because of his greatness, it was left for me. Red Sox fans treated me like a star. I couldn't walk into a restaurant without getting a standing ovation. I really believed I just filled a gap that existed before I arrived. Red Sox fans needed a personality on their team to celebrate.

And I was that guy.

Fans did some crazy things to get an autograph or to just shake my hand.

One time when I was downtown, a guy ran across traffic to get my autograph and was hit by a car right in front of me. Fortunately, he lived.

Jerry Fineberg, a real estate mogul and a good buddy of mine, was driving me home one night on the freeway on the north side of Boston when some guy whizzed by us going about 85 miles per hour in a Mercedes coupe. Suddenly, the car crashed violently into the guardrail which divided the exit ramp from the freeway.

I figured the driver had to be dead. We pulled over and I hopped out and ran to the car. The Mercedes' engine was smoking and the front end had been crushed. I opened the driver's door to see the driver slumped over the wheel. He was dazed but somehow not seriously injured. A woman was sitting in the passenger seat.

He slowly came to and glanced over at me.

Then he reached over and grabbed his wife's arm.

"Honey! Honey!" he said. "It's the Hawk!"

I always accommodated the media, too, which had raised my profile. Reporters usually swarmed my locker after a game, realizing they could rely on me for a colorful quote or two. My locker was about 25 feet from Yaz's locker. He knew he had to talk to the press so he did, but I knew he didn't enjoy it at all. It was his obligation. I watched him fulfill it, and then he normally retreated to the trainers' room.

Back then, there was plenty of mutual respect between players and the sportswriters. I enjoyed entertaining them and talking to them was never something I dreaded. And since I was having the season of my life, hitting over .300 and near the top of the league in home runs and RBIs, the writers flocked to my locker.

Off the field, I was the only guy in baseball at the time who needed a bodyguard. I constantly had guys confronting me when I went out to clubs or restaurants. They would approach me and say something smart, just hoping for a fight.

So I hired a guy by the name of Randy Lamattina, a Boston policeman who worked for me in his off-duty hours.

Whenever trouble brewed, Randy would jump right in and either defuse it or take care of it himself. He was a young, tough guy. He also made national news the hard way years later. He had worked on the bomb-defusing team for the Boston PD. One day a bomb blew up in his face on live television. It was a miracle he lived.

I frequently accompanied Derek Sanderson and Bobby Orr of the Boston Bruins to talk to high school students about the dangers of doing drugs. One day we were talking to about 600 kids at a high school when a kid stood up and asked me if I'd ever tried marijuana. When I told him I hadn't, he asked how I knew it was bad for him.

"Well, I have never jumped off a 10-story building, either, but I know if I did, I would probably get hurt or killed," I said.

The students all laughed, but I started thinking about that kid's question. I went home and told Randy, "Go find me a marijuana cigarette."

He came back a little while later and handed me a joint.

I lit it, smoked about a third of it, and started to get dizzy. Then I grew sleepy, so I put it out and went to bed. That's the only illegal drug I ever tried in my lifetime. I have never even laid my eyes on cocaine.

One reason I never tried hard-core drugs is that I knew I had an addictive personality. If I tried something, I could have become the poster child for an addiction to it.

I became good friends with many of the Bruins, but none better than Sanderson. Nicknamed "Turk," Derek was the original Dennis the Menace. There's not a bad bone in his body, but he was always stirring up trouble. Once I got to Boston, I couldn't help but notice how close the Bruins, Celtics, and Red Sox players were. Many of them buddied around together. They were much closer than any athletes in any other city I ever knew of.

I had the perfect apartment for partying, too, with my white shag carpet and a huge round bed in the bedroom. Several Boston athletes wanted to go to the Hawk's pad to party whenever they got the chance.

On Saturday, September 28, the second-to-last day of the season, I jogged out to right field in the top of the first at Fenway against the Yankees, realizing I was about to witness baseball history.

Mickey Mantle, who had earlier announced his retirement, would take his final at-bat. I had tears running down my cheeks. I looked over and saw Yaz in left field and knew he was emotional, too.

Mickey took his final swing in the second inning, popping up to Rico Petrocelli at shortstop. He jogged to the Yankees' dugout and headed toward the clubhouse. The Yankees had planned to lift him after his first at-bat and we had known it ahead of time.

I went 1-for-3 that day, a 4–3 loss to the Yankees, in Mickey's final game.

I thought back to that day in Savannah when he snubbed my autograph request, and now I was standing on the field in his final game. That was unbelievable.

By the end of the season, I thought I had this hitting thing figured out. The previous season was the Year of Yaz, and this one became the Year of the Hawk.

People may not believe you should talk about yourself in the third person, but I realized the Hawk had become my alter ego. I admit there were times in the on-deck circle and I would talk to myself.

"Okay, Kenny, this is a big at-bat," I would say. "Just get out of the Hawk's way and let him do his thing."

It may sound strange, but I did it often that season.

Relying on the Hawk was my way of dealing with pressure, I learned. It was as if I had someone else there to help me deal with it. I had completely adopted the name and had it embroidered on just about everything I owned—shirts, coats, hats, slacks, my baseball gear, and stationery.

The Hawk finished off my coming-out season with 35 home runs and a league-leading 109 RBIs, but my average dropped from .336 to .275 over the final few months. My ex-roomy Hondo led the league with 44 homers, and the guy who batted in front of me, Yaz, led the league with a .301 average.

The reason my average plummeted late in the season was those cursed hemorrhoids. People would ask how what seemed like a minor nuisance could affect performance that much. The truth was, it was due to a lack of sleep. I was in so much pain that I was only getting two or three solid hours each night. Mine were so big that a product like Preparation H wouldn't do anything for them. Surgery would have worked, but I didn't want to miss games during the recovery.

Some days, I couldn't even drive, so Yaz would swing by and pick me up for the 35-minute drive to the ballpark, which I spent squatting on the floorboard of the passenger seat of his car.

Nevertheless, I still had the season of my life.

I was 26 years old and I hadn't gotten any stronger. I hadn't changed my swing. The only way for me to explain it was that the awe factor was gone for me. I had a sense of control at the plate. If I got a 2-0 count, I was confident enough to think that guy on the mound was now in a lot of trouble.

The science of hitting a baseball is a mysterious thing. A fraction of an inch is the difference between hitting a pop-up and a line drive, swinging a rounded bat at a round object coming at you more than 95 miles per hour.

Looking back, it's amazing I had my best season given my health issues and the fact that 1968 also was known as the "Year of the Pitcher."

The Tigers' Denny McLain won 31 games, the last time any pitcher has won 30 or more, and Drysdale set the consecutive score-less inning streak with the Dodgers in the National League. McLain beat me and his catcher, Bill Freehan, out for AL MVP honors. The guy had 28 complete games, so he deserved the award and I had no problem with it.

I did have problems with what he did to me two years later, however. He called me up, asking to borrow $1,500.

I knew he was a gambler, and I figured he was betting on baseball. But I sent Sharon McLain the money, just as Denny requested. And to this day, I have not received a penny of it back.

The Indians' Luis Tiant won 21 games with a 1.60 ERA that season. Normally, that would be good enough to win the Cy Young, if not for McLain's unbelievable season. Luis threw as hard as anybody in the game at that time for just a little guy.

I loved Luis, who had four 20-plus win seasons and ended his career with 229 victories. I had hit two home runs off him in a game at Cleveland. When the Indians returned to Boston two weeks later, I noticed him watching our batting practice.

Back then, it was acceptable for pitchers to sometimes watch BP before a start. However, it was taboo for them to talk to the hitters they would be facing an hour or so later. That never bothered Luis, who had trouble pronouncing my name through his thick Cuban accent.

"Honk," he said, "I am going to you away four times today."

I just laughed. Nobody who knew Luis could get mad at him.

He blew me away the first three times up. When I came up for my fourth at-bat, he looked in and asked, "Where do you want it?"

"Right here," I told him, holding my hand waist-high in the middle of the plate.

He threw it directly to that spot and I hit a little three-hopper to the shortstop. I was 0-for-4 with three strikeouts.

The number of runs scored that season was an all-time low in Major League Baseball, so they decided to lower the mound from 15 inches to 10 beginning in 1969, where it remains today.

Also, the seams on the ball were much higher than they are today. Higher seams make it much easier for pitchers to throw any type of breaking ball. I swear I could hear the buzz of a sharp curveball from guys like McDowell in those days. Higher seams also restrict the flight of the ball once it is hit.

Nevertheless, my big power numbers didn't lead the Red Sox to another pennant. We finished with an 86–76 record, 17 games behind the Tigers, who finished 103–59. They seemed unbeatable that season and it was their chance to face the Cardinals in the World Series, so I sent a telegram to Kaline. It read: "Al, it's been an honor and a privilege to play on the same field with you and I want you to know that I learned about how to compete at the major league level from watching you play. I wish you the best of luck in the World Series. Good luck, Hawk Harrelson."

It's the only telegram I ever sent to another athlete in my life.

That's how much I respected that man.

Even though we didn't contend, I couldn't go anywhere in Boston without being mobbed by fans by the time the season came to a close. I think I came along at the right time, because the town needed a colorful character.

A group called the Val Perry Trio even wrote a song about me, "Don't Walk the Hawk."

They performed at a restaurant across the street from where the Red Sox stayed during spring training in Winter Haven. Every time I walked in there, they played that song. It was a cute little song and when I first heard it on the radio I laughed my butt off. It was flattering, but I don't think it broke any sales records.

I also had increased my wardrobe with the extra money I was making with the Red Sox. I soon became known as the wildest—I would say the best—dresser in the big leagues. I wore many color combinations, like pink and gray, or purple and black. Woolf and I worked a deal with a clothing-design company, which planned to release an entire line of clothes in my name.

After the season, I was invited to Los Angeles for the first-ever Academy of Professional Sports Awards, held at the Beverly Wilshire Hotel, to accept the American League's Player of the Year award, which had been voted on by the players. The MVP, which McLain had won, was voted on by the media. Drysdale and Willie McCovey represented the National League. There were also two award winners from the AFL, two from the NFL, and two more from the NBA.

Joe Namath, one of the AFL's honorees, and I had always gotten along pretty well. We had hung out together at times in New York and in Boston. But Joe had some hangers-on around him on this night. Two of them were real jerks and I almost got into a fight with one at the hotel.

The best part of that night was talking to McCovey about hitting for a few hours at a party after the awards ceremony.

Anyway, Joe and I smoothed things over, and a day after Christmas, he invited me to New York to watch his Jets face the Oakland Raiders in the AFL Championship Game.

"After we beat Oakland, we are all going to my place for a party, so come on over," he told me.

I took the shuttle from Boston to New York and wrapped myself in a big fur coat. It was absolutely freezing that day at Shea Stadium. My seats were in the end zone, and I spent much of the game cussing out Joe. That vantage point did give me a chance to see Joe's brilliance, however.

The wind was blowing sideways at about 30 miles per hour that day. I watched Jets receiver Don Maynard running a fly pattern down the right sideline, as Joe lofted a pass toward the middle of the field.

I was a high school quarterback, so I knew a little about how to lead a receiver, but when Joe released the pass, I thought he'd missed Maynard by a country mile.

But as Maynard approached midfield, he turned around and the football fell right into his hands. Joe had played that wind perfectly. I really believed that for about six seasons he was as good as any quarterback who ever lived.

After the Jets won the game 27–23, I headed over to his apartment for the postgame party. Joe spent most of that night sitting on top of his stereo, just rubbing his sore knees.

Two weeks later, I flew to Miami to see Super Bowl III. Nobody gave the Jets, a 17-point underdog, a chance to upset the NFL's Baltimore Colts that day, but Joe sure seemed confident to me.

The night before the game, we went to the Palm Bay Club in Miami. This was just a few days after he made his now-famous guarantee that the Jets would upset the Colts. Let me say upfront that Joe didn't have one alcoholic drink that night, but I had a few gin and tonics. His date's name was Susie and she owned a condo there, where we escaped just after midnight.

Now that we were in the quiet where we could talk more easily, I asked him if he really thought the Jets would beat the Colts.

"I will tell you exactly what will happen," he said. "The Colts will sit back in that zone and keep everything underneath them and we will six- and eight-yard them to death. I will throw underneath them all day long. Just watch."

That's exactly what happened. Joe and the Jets shocked the football world with their 16–7 upset of Baltimore.

I realized I was in the midst of a jet-set lifestyle at this point, enjoying all the benefits of being a popular big-league ballplayer. I had friends on the Dodgers in Sandy Koufax and Drysdale, with whom I had been invited to play in a golf tournament in Palm Springs after the Super Bowl. Actors such as David Janssen, Clint Eastwood, and Chuck Connors played in it, too.

Chuck, who was very close with Sandy and Don, had played in the big leagues with the Cubs and Dodgers before turning to acting and starring in *The Rifleman* years earlier.

After a round of golf one day, Don, Sandy, and I were having a few drinks at Canyon Golf Resort with Ron Santo of the Cubs and a few other players. We were just sitting around, telling lies and having a great time. I got to meet Frank Sinatra, who was kind enough to introduce himself to the guys who had never met him. Then Yul Brynner walked up to us. It was amazing to see everybody stop talking all at once to stare at Yul. He had that deep voice and instantly captivated everyone at the table.

Just when I thought it couldn't get any better, Sinatra told us, "Hey fellas, I have to fly back to Los Angeles, but you are welcome to go over to my house. There is plenty of food and drinks over there. After a while, I'll send you a little something." I was in heaven.

He walked out and within minutes, his private jet buzzed the club-house on his way back to Los Angeles. We headed over to Frank's house, and about two hours later, he delivered on his promise—five or six of the most beautiful women I had ever seen walked in the door.

There is no way to put into words how my life changed in 1968.

I went from being a relatively unknown baseball player struggling at the plate, watching Yaz handle the heavy lifting, to finishing near the top of the American League in almost every offensive category.

Suddenly, I was the toast of New England. I hung out with the top quarterback in pro football. I was golfing in Palm Springs and I had plenty of money in my pocket.

Could life get any better?

11 I AM NOT LEAVING BEANTOWN!

JUST TWO WEEKS INTO THE 1969 SEASON, I AWAKENED ON a Saturday morning to be hit in the face with a big story in the newspaper: the Red Sox and Cleveland Indians were talking about making a trade.

We needed a right-handed starter, a reliever, and a catcher. The Indians? Well, the Indians needed just about everything. The story, written by Larry Claflin, mentioned my name and George Scott as possibly going to Cleveland.

I called Boston general manager Dick O'Connell that morning and asked him if the story had merit. He assured me I had nothing to worry about. I felt better immediately.

Luis Tiant was on the mound for the Indians that day and I hit one of his first pitches into the light tower beyond the Green Monster. Later in the game, I hit another home run.

As I jogged around first base the second time, I figured I'd put an end to any possible trade rumors.

We won that day and I went home to take a shower.

I was feeling great, having hit two bombs and headed out on the town to celebrate. Wendell, an elderly black man I had hired to shop and cook for me, was cooking something in the kitchen when the telephone rang.

It was my old manager, Alvin Dark, who happened to now be managing the Indians.

"Kenneth, come over to our clubhouse tomorrow and put the red hat on," he said. "I just traded for you."

I was stunned and didn't know what to say. Was Alvin joking around with me?

He wasn't.

"Alvin, I am not going—"

"Kenneth, you will play for me. You know me," he said.

I stood there holding the phone, not knowing what to say or what to do next. O'Connell had just told me I was not part of the trade talks. I don't remember what else I said to Alvin before I hung up. Wendell saw the look on my face.

"I just got traded to the Indians," I told him.

Wendell didn't say a word. He slumped against the wall and collapsed. I thought he was having a heart attack. I caught him before he hit the floor and dragged him into a chair. After I gave him a glass of water, he seemed much better. He told me there was no need to call an ambulance.

He was no more shocked than I was.

Mike Andrews, our second baseman, somehow found out about the trade and arrived at my apartment within a few hours. I had no plans to go out and celebrate now. We started to drink, even though Mike wasn't a big drinker, and it didn't take him long to get hammered. He eventually fell asleep on my white shag carpet in the living room as the phone continued to ring.

Finally, I took it off the hook and went to bed.

I got up the next morning to see Mike, hungover, trying to get his head on straight. He had a game to play in a few hours, but I didn't—I had made up my mind that I wasn't reporting to the Indians.

There was a knock at the door and I looked through the peephole to see Yaz. He stormed inside and started pacing with his hands on his hips, as he always did when he was frustrated or angry.

"How can they trade you?" he said.

For a moment I was touched that he was concerned about my well being. Then he said, "Now who's going to hit behind me?"

Mike and Yaz soon left for Fenway as I pondered my next move. The trade was all over the front page of the sports page. The Red Sox got starter Sonny Siebert, catcher Joe Azcue, and reliever Vincente Romo in exchange for me and pitchers Juan Pizarro and Dick Ellsworth. Sonny had pitched a no-hitter a year or two earlier and still had good stuff, Romo was a good reliever, and they got the catcher they needed, so I knew right away it was a good trade for the Red Sox.

The Indians gave up plenty to get me.

Problem was, I made up my mind I didn't want to leave Boston. I was making plenty of money with some endorsements, and I knew they would disappear with this trade. I had that new clothing line coming out. I also owned two sub shops. And the Red Sox were contenders while the Indians usually fought just to get out of last place.

I decided to drive to Fenway but I didn't want to be seen, so I wore a fake mustache and these huge sunglasses. The security guy recognized me and escorted me up to O'Connell's office.

I walked in and Dick was sitting at his desk.

"Hawk, what I told you yesterday morning was the truth," he said. "Your name didn't come up until later."

I knew he wouldn't lie to me. But I told him I didn't want to leave Boston.

I then went to Mister Yawkey's office.

"I will always love you and I loved playing here," I told him. "I want you to know I understand the trade. But I don't want to leave."

"That means a lot to me, Hawk," he said. "But will you do me a favor?"

He wanted me to call some corporate leaders who had threatened to cancel their season tickets. I called each one of them and told them that the trade would make the club better. Then I shook Mister Yawkey's hand and I walked out.

I snuck out of the ballpark in my disguise, but not before I noticed dozens of signs held by fans supporting me.

Once the shock wore off, I had to come to grips with the fact there wasn't much I could do at this point. I could retire and never play again, or I could report to Cleveland.

Word hit the newspapers about my not wanting to leave Boston. The following day, baseball commissioner Bowie Kuhn called my agent and requested we fly to New York for a meeting in his office.

My actual salary with the Red Sox was $50,000, not counting that huge bonus I got when I originally signed with Boston. I told Bob, "Let's use a $100,000 bonus as a tool, knowing they won't give us that."

Over the previous few days, each of the Indians who had been traded to the Red Sox had told the media how much they were looking forward to playing in Boston. But they could not report to the Red Sox until I agreed to the trade and reported to Cleveland.

Bob and I agreed that their comments helped give us leverage. How in the world could the Indians take them back after what they had said about Cleveland and about wanting to play in Boston?

When Bob and I walked into Kuhn's office that day, O'Connell and Gabe Paul were already there. We all shook hands.

Kuhn couldn't be involved in any salary discussions, so he walked out and Bob started talking on my behalf. I noticed that Gabe held a handkerchief in his hand. As Bob talked, detailing my demands and how much I didn't want to leave Boston, Gabe started to dab his forehead with it. He was sweating. I wasn't a great poker player, but that was his tell. He knew we had all the leverage.

I said I was willing to retire if necessary, but that I would consider accepting the trade if I got a two-year contract for $100,000 per year and another $100,000 up front as a bonus.

That didn't go over too well with Gabe, and by the time we walked out of the room that day, there was no deal.

We flew back to Boston.

The next day, Gabe called us. He wanted us to return to New York to continue to negotiate.

I was taking a shower that morning and *Sesame Street* was on TV. One of the characters was trying to teach the children viewers how to save money.

"Put one penny in the bank today," the voice said. "Put two pennies in the bank tomorrow. Put four pennies in the bank the day after tomorrow...If you do this, you will save a lot of money."

On the flight back to New York, I started thinking about that show. I got a piece of paper and started figuring statistics and money. Maybe this was something I could use to renegotiate with the Indians.

We had agreed to meet Gabe at the 21 Club. Bob walked in and put his briefcase on the table.

"Gabe, this thing is full of offers for Hawk," he said, referring to my off-the-field income and endorsements. "He really doesn't need to play baseball."

The briefcase, of course, was empty aside from some pens and notepads. There were no additional offers, but Gabe must have bought it. He never asked to see the supposed offers.

Finally, I gave Gabe my *Sesame Street*–inspired offer: I would play for the minimum salary if the Indians gave me a penny-doubled for every home run I hit.

I could tell Gabe was trying to do the math in his head. I already had done it on the airplane. Twenty-five home runs would amount to more than $167,772.60. I knew I could accomplish that, even in Cleveland's cavernous ballpark. Thirty home runs would have paid me more than $5.3 million. And if I hit 35 home runs, like I did the previous season, it would have paid me more than $171 million.

Of course, the entire club was probably worth only a few million dollars at the time.

I thought it was an ingenious proposal, but it would be a gamble. What if I got hurt? But I always liked to gamble, as long as I was betting on myself.

Gabe took out a handkerchief and dabbed his forehead some more. He was now sweating profusely.

After all that back and forth, we agreed on a $75,000 salary with another $25,000 for promotional appearances in Cleveland, such as one with the May Company.

At that time, baseball's rules made the team that traded a player responsible for making the traded player report to the new team. My situation and refusal to report to Cleveland immediately resulted in a rule change. The new rule made the particular team that traded for the player in question responsible for getting him to report.

Some writers called it "The Harrelson Rule."

And some writers hated me for it.

Jimmy Cannon was a little short guy from New York who always smoked a big cigar. When our deal was announced, he walked up to me and said, "Hawk, do you know what you did today? You just changed the salary structure in all of baseball. They should build a statue of you in Cooperstown..."

Just when I thought he was complimenting me, he added, "And you ought to be ashamed of yourself!"

So much for flattery.

Our flight from New York back to Boston wasn't so pleasant. We hit some terrible turbulence, flying through the rain and lightning. I looked at Bob, who was gripping his armrests so tightly his knuckles were white.

For a minute or two, as the plane shook, I thought that maybe I wouldn't have to report to Cleveland after all.

Eventually, we landed safely.

I had no choice but to report to Cleveland.

My brief time of hitting behind Yaz, playing at Fenway, and being the toast of Beantown was history.

12 "SUDDEN SAM" AND LIFE IN CLEVELAND

THE INDIANS, WHO FOR THE MOST PART HAD TOILED NEAR the bottom of the American League standings since last appearing in the World Series in 1954, had not won a championship since three years after World War II had concluded. Worse, they rarely contended for one.

It's not that I didn't want to play baseball in Cleveland, but I had fallen in love with Boston and playing for the Red Sox. While Fenway Park was a great place to play—and hit—for me, the Indians' old stadium had been designed for football. It was the worst in big-league baseball and everybody who played in the American League knew it.

But it was about to be my new home, like it or not.

Before I reported to the Indians a week after the trade was announced, I visited Alvin in his hotel suite in downtown Cleveland. In those days, it was very common for a manager to tell a player what he wanted from him.

And Alvin had always been honest with me.

"Look, Kenneth, we both know this is the biggest ballpark in baseball," he said. "I really don't care about your average. I don't care if you only hit .200. Just give me 20 home runs and 75 RBIs. If you do that, I think we can be competitive."

I gave a press conference my first day there and smiled for cameras, talking the club's chances up to the writers and generally pretending that I was happy to be there. All the while, my heart was broken.

Still, I always had the ability to adjust to new surroundings. I had adapted to new cities, new situations, and new teams well in the past and I planned on doing the same this time around.

In times like those, I always referred to that small newspaper clipping Mama had attached to our bathroom mirror, about yesterday, today, and tomorrow.

I rented a penthouse at the Winton Place west of downtown, right on the shores of Lake Erie. Indians owner Vernon Stouffer lived next to me and Browns owner Art Modell lived in the apartment below me.

I asked my sister, who was a great interior decorator in addition to everything else she had accomplished, to fly in and redecorate it for me. Stouffer also told me I could use his helicopter, which had its own landing pad on top of the building, to avoid the traffic and to commute to the stadium. The club had really rolled out the red carpet for me.

Sports Illustrated soon called, wanting to do a big story on me and my new situation in Cleveland. So I let them come photograph my new pad as part of the story.

Their photographer wanted to get a shot of me in the helicopter flying above the stadium, so he flopped himself out the door and put his feet on the helicopter's railing. He wanted to take the picture with the helicopter about 1,000 feet in the air. I thought he was nuts.

"Get back in here!" I screamed at the guy. I was sure he was about to fall to his death.

"I'm good," he said. "Just act natural."

It didn't take long for me to call the helicopter operators to shuttle me to the ballpark. That big whirly-bird would land in center field three hours before the game started, drop me off, and then fly back out of there. The writers in the press box loved that scene.

The best trip I ever took on that thing, however, was to and from a long-driving contest I had been invited to.

It was being held in Conneaut, Ohio, about 70 miles east of Cleveland on the Pennsylvania border. I had a very tight schedule that day, so

I called the helicopter pilot to make the arrangements. He picked me up and landed right next to the tee box. I climbed out wearing a pair of cowboy boots and didn't even take the time to put on a pair of golf spikes. I grabbed somebody's driver, took a few practice swings, and then ripped one about 350 yards, winning the contest easily. I flashed the peace sign to the fans there and hopped back on the helicopter. The entire appearance lasted about 10 minutes. I don't even know what first prize was, because I didn't stay around to collect it.

I patterned that appearance after my golf idol, Hobart Manley, who did something similar years before in Savannah. Hobart sat in the clubhouse enjoying a drink one day, when all these contestants were on the first tee swinging away during a long-drive contest. When he was called to the tee box, he put down his drink, walked out there with street shoes on, took a couple of practice swings, and ripped one down the middle of the fairway beyond everybody else's ball.

He calmly walked back into the clubhouse, picked up his drink, and continued doing what he was doing. Hobart was some sort of cool.

It's not that the Indians didn't have some tradition, either. I realized some real baseball legends had passed through Cleveland over the years, such as Bob Feller, Herb Score, and Mama's favorite player and my old buddy, Rocky Colavito. Herb was a flame-throwing left-hander who took a line drive from the Yankees' Gil McDougald off his left eye in 1957. The impact broke several bones in his face and was one of the worst baseball injuries ever sustained by a pitcher.

Ted Williams once told me that Herb had the best stuff he ever saw. Mickey Mantle also told me Herb was the toughest left-hander he ever faced. By the time I arrived, Herb was the Indians' radio announcer. One day he and I were talking about his injury when he admitted he tried to come back too early from it in the spring of '58. After that, he wasn't the same pitcher, but he became a legendary radio broadcaster. He was just a wonderful person to be around and one of my all-time favorites.

The Indians still had their ace left-hander, "Sudden" Sam McDowell, a 6-foot-6, 240-pounder, whom I was plenty familiar with. We had come up through the minors together and I had faced him often over the years. Sam was a strikeout machine, recording 279 in '69, and a perennial 20-game winner. By the time I joined the Indians, he was a three-time All-Star.

Once when I had just come up with Kansas City and faced Sam for the first time, he threw me a pitch that I didn't really see, so I turned to the umpire and asked, "Did you see that?"

"I think I did, so I just called it a strike," he answered.

He was just like a Randy Johnson, but he threw much harder than Randy. His curveball was so good that I could hear it spinning through the air.

But Sam had a problem—and it came in a bottle, or a can, or a glass, depending on where he chose to drink.

The first time I saw him out on the town, I was with the Red Sox. Yaz and I went to this late-night joint in downtown Cleveland. We were in a bad mood after a tough loss to the Indians and we also were very hungry. The postgame spread in Cleveland was just a bunch of bologna, literally, and some bread anyway.

It was almost 1:00 in the morning when we noticed this big guy sitting in the back of the place, but we couldn't tell who it was because it was so dark inside. Pretty soon, the guy got up and walked over to us. He was hammered.

"I am going to blow you away tomorrow with fastballs!" he told me, slurring his speech.

It was Sam, completely drunk, out late on the night before he was scheduled to pitch. I hit his first fastball the next night a mile down the left-field line, but it stayed foul. That was the last fastball I saw. He struck me out four times that night with breaking balls.

As I learned as a teammate, Sam's only problem on the mound was his mind. He frequently tried to trick people instead of relying on his awesome stuff. And sometimes, he said things that left me shaking my head.

We were playing at Oakland on a cold night and Sam was hooked up in a pitcher's duel with Catfish. Two of my favorite people in the world were just blowing hitters away that night.

Heading into the ninth, the A's had a 1–0 lead when I hit a run-scoring double to tie the game. Sam had about 11 or 12 strikeouts to that point when the shortstop booted one on the leadoff hitter in the bottom of the ninth. Then Sam walked the second batter and we committed another error to load the bases.

Alvin walked to the mound. I was playing first, so I joined the meeting. The A's had announced Tommy Davis as a pinch hitter. It was late in his career and we all knew that he couldn't catch up to a good fastball. Alvin reminded Sam of that fact and headed back to the dugout.

Alvin no sooner had one foot back on the top of the dugout steps when Sam threw a high changeup straight down the middle of the plate. Tommy hit it off the left-field wall to win the game for the A's. I couldn't believe what I had just seen after listening to that conversation.

Sam didn't even shower. He ripped off his uniform and talked a clubhouse guy into driving him back to the Edgewater Inn. I got a ride there after I grabbed a shower and knowing where Sam would be, I walked into the hotel bar.

By the time I arrived, Sam already had a few empty bottles in front of him. I asked him what he was thinking throwing that changeup.

"Well, Tommy knows that I know that he can't hit a fastball anymore, and I knew that he was looking for it," he explained. "So I wanted to fool him. And I think he may have overheard our conversation…"

That was Sam's rationale.

It wasn't the only time he'd done something like that, either. We were often ticked off at Sam for getting beat on that changeup. He had one of the best fastballs in the history of the game. His curveball was one of the best in baseball. He had a great slider. And yet, he relied on that changeup to get him out of trouble.

Once before one of his starts, Alvin told him he'd be fined $100 every time he shook off the catcher that night, Duke Sims.

That got Sam's attention. He went out and struck out 15 and threw a two-hitter and didn't shake off Duke once.

Another time, Sam had about 13 or 14 strikeouts in the top of the ninth against the Tigers in Cleveland. Aurelio Rodriguez hit a low fast-ball into the middle of the seats beyond the left-field wall. When he hit it, our left fielder, Roy Foster, turned around to run after it and flipped over the inner-field fence the Indians had installed to shorten the playing field by about 20 feet.

Sam and I were smokers who usually enjoyed a cigarette between innings in the dugout. I came into the dugout and lit one up while Sam pulled out one of his Kools. He then said something that made me almost choke on my smoke.

"Hawk, I got to get out of here," he told me, meaning he wanted to be traded. "I got outfielders who can't catch a routine fly ball."

Sam had seemed to ignore the fact that the routine fly ball landed in the left-field seats.

But the granddaddy of them all happened when I went to pick him up one morning to play a round of golf at Firestone Country Club. He lived at the old Cleveland Hotel. I pulled up to the curb and there was no Sam out front, where I told him to be. I waited a couple of minutes and there was no sight of him.

I beat on his door for a few minutes before he finally opened it. He had dried blood all over his face and his lips were swollen.

"I was walking home last night and I had a girl with me when two guys said something to me and started a fight," he explained. "Evidently, I beat the crap out of both of them."

I left him in his room and went downstairs. On my way out, I asked the bellman if he'd seen Sam come home the night before.

"Yeah, I did," he said. "Sam was drunk and he saw this little guy walking down the street with a girl. I think Sam grabbed her butt and this little guy just beat the crap out of him."

That was Sam. I loved him, but when he drank, he sometimes lost his grip on reality.

Still, Sam was one of those guys who would literally give you the shirt off his back. He would give you his last dollar if you needed it. There was not a bad bone in his body. And he could hit the golf ball a mile, too.

On one particularly hot summer day in Cleveland, the producers of a local Saturday night movie-comedy show called *Big Chuck and Hoolihan* talked Sam and me into performing the "Who's on First?" routine on the dugout steps. We had no script. We just improvised. And Sam was great at it. That clip can still be found on YouTube.

Remember *Cheers* and Sam Malone, played by Ted Danson? That character was based on Sam. And just like Sam Malone, Sam McDowell also quit drinking once he retired from baseball. He moved to Clermont, Florida, and spent decades touring the country, speaking about the dangers of alcohol abuse. He has counseled hundreds of baseball players over the years. And he hasn't had a drink in more than 30 years.

That routine Sam and I did for TV was so good the producers gave me my own variety show, called *The Hawk's Nest*. I did my best to play Merv Griffin, and introduced guests such as Wayne Newton or Vic Damone. We had some big-name stars and great ratings, but for some reason the show lasted only one year.

There wasn't such a thing as interleague play back then, but the Indians and Cincinnati Reds always got together for a one-game "battle of Ohio" every summer that didn't count in the standings. It was nothing but an exhibition game played for the fans.

It also was my introduction to the great Johnny Bench.

It was played in the middle of August, on a hot day in Cleveland, and the first thing I did when I arrived at the ballpark was to tell Alvin I didn't want to play that day. The game didn't count and I wasn't too fired up about it. But Alvin said if I got a hit in my first at-bat, he'd take me out.

I walked up to the plate and told Johnny that if I got on base, I was stealing second on the first pitch to the next batter.

"Okay, no problem," Johnny said, smiling.

I led off with a rocket to left and headed down to first. The Reds' pitcher, Camilo Pascual, had a huge leg kick and I thought I could steal second off him easily, no matter who was behind the plate. On the first pitch, just as he started that high kick, I got a great jump and took off toward second. I still had about 10 feet to go when the ball beat me there and I was tagged out easily.

I headed across the field toward our dugout and winked at Johnny. He smiled back. I guess I didn't need to tip him off that I was going. The guys in the dugout told me he threw me out from his knees, never even bothering to stand up. I have seen a lot of baseball in my time, but no catcher had a better arm than Johnny.

As the years passed, he and I played some golf together. Doctors had found a growth on Johnny's lung and he underwent major surgery to remove it following the 1972 season. He said he was never the same after that.

One time, I played Mario Lemieux's charity golf tournament in Pittsburgh, but my wrists were just killing me. I went out before the tournament to hit a bucket of balls, but I couldn't stand the pain. I headed back to the hotel just as Johnny was walking down from his room. When I told him how much pain I was in, he told me to follow him back to his room.

We went up to Johnny's room and he placed magnets all over my wrists and my knees. I felt better almost instantly and headed back to the course. I hit balls for about 30 minutes and then played the tournament pain-free. From that moment on, I became a huge fan of magnets. I already was a big fan of Johnny's.

My teammates in Cleveland, just like the guys in Kansas City, Washington, and Boston, were a good group of people. The only teammate who was somewhat moody and distant was a talented young infielder by the name of Tony Horton, but I still liked him very much. He was about 6-foot-3 and 220 pounds, just strong as a bull. We hung out together some on the road.

When we arrived in Chicago in late August to begin a three-game series against the White Sox, we went to the restaurant at the Continental Hotel.

Within minutes, the maître d' approached me and said Rocky Marciano, the legendary boxer, had invited us up to his suite.

I had met Rocky before and he had heard about my brief boxing career. He had been retired from the ring for about 10 years and was promoting fights. He told me he was always in search of the next big box-office draw.

"If we arranged a fight between you and Sonny Liston at Fenway Park, we could sell it out," he told me. "How much would it take to get you to fight him?"

I thought about it a minute and told him, "One-hundred thousand."

I thought it was a great idea.

"Sonny may knock me on my butt, but you never know. I might land a shot and surprise him," I said.

"Let's do it!" Rocky said.

We didn't spend time rehashing many details, but I walked out of his suite that night actually thinking I had a chance to fight the great Sonny Liston in the ring during the upcoming off-season, and I would be receiving a nice chunk of cash to do it.

A few days later, on August 31, Rocky was headed to Des Moines, Iowa, in a small private airplane when it crashed into a field short of the airport runway. He and two other people died instantly. I read about it in the newspaper the next morning and I was in utter shock.

It was a sad day, one of the saddest of my life, to think that Rocky was gone forever after I had just talked to him, laughed with him, and discussed me possibly participating in a fight he would promote. It brought back memories of Bobby Kennedy dying soon after sitting next to me in the Red Sox clubhouse.

Baseball always has had its superstitions, more than any other sport. I didn't create them, but I believed in many of them. Some are too crude to detail. (Some struggling ballplayers would try anything to get out of a funk.) Another was, "If you are going badly at the plate, get into a fight to change your luck."

We were in Oakland and I was in a major funk at the plate. Lew Krausse Jr., my old buddy from the Athletics, was still playing for the A's and we had made arrangements to meet after the game. I told him I was going to look for the biggest guy I could find and start a fight.

Lew and I headed to a nightclub and it wasn't long before he spotted one for me. The guy was about 6-foot-5 and walked right by our table. Lew elbowed me, saying, "There he is."

I noticed the big guy went out to dance with his girl, so I grabbed another girl and headed to the dance floor. I bumped into the big guy "accidentally."

"Don't do that again!" he screamed at me.

"Well, let's go!" I shot back.

I happened to be wearing a new pair of cowboy boots. We headed out of the club and as I walked down three steps toward the street, I turned around to swing at him when my feet came out from under me. I hadn't broken in those boots and it was as if I was standing on ice. He landed a good shot to my eye and I swung again and missed. We started to fight before the police arrived to break it up.

The police recognized him as soon as they arrived, cuffed his hands behind his back, and loaded him up in the back of a paddy wagon. I noticed he had blood all over his shirt.

Just before they closed the door, he looked at me and said, "I know who you are!"

That was unsettling to hear, to say the least.

I headed back to the Edgewater Inn and went to Sam's room. Sam always carried a gun in his bag. Back then, you could stick one right in your luggage wherever you traveled. I explained what happened and asked him if I could borrow his gun. Sam went over to his bed and reached underneath his pillow. He pulled out his pistol and handed it to me. He was sleeping with a gun under his pillow!

The next day I showed up at the ballpark, wearing a big pair of sunglasses to hide the damage. I had to convince Alvin to let me play. When I went out to the field in the bottom of the first, I heard a loud *Boom!* The guy had come for me, I was sure of it. It turned out that some kid had popped a popcorn bag in one of the first rows.

Jim Nash, a big right-hander, started for Oakland that day. My first time up, I doubled off the wall. I later hit another double. Not bad for a guy hitting with one eye open. That night, Lew took me back to his place and pulled a big steak out of the refrigerator. He laid it across my swollen eye.

Before we left Oakland, the other guy's lawyer came over to the Edgewater Inn to see me. After I told him there was no way I would be pressing charges, he said his client's clothes were ruined in the fight and he wanted to be reimbursed to the tune of $700.

I couldn't get $700 out of my pocket fast enough. I paid the lawyer, gave Sam back his gun, and that was the end of it.

As the 1969 season neared its conclusion, the Indians were going nowhere as usual, but the Mets were steaming toward the National League pennant behind pitchers Tom Seaver and Jerry Koosman. Guess who managed the Mets? That's right, my old nemesis Gil Hodges.

I had thought a lot in the previous two years about why we hadn't gotten along in Washington. Every December, Joan Hodges still sent me a Christmas card and I often wondered how grumpy old Gil had ever married such a wonderful, caring person as Joan.

Hodges had suffered a heart attack during the '68 season and according to his players, he suddenly became a changed man.

"You wouldn't believe the difference," outfielder Don Clendenon once told me. "He became the nicest guy in the world."

Many of the Mets told me the same thing. Apparently, that heart attack triggered Gil to act more civil to people.

That and the fact that I liked Joan were on my mind when I walked into Alvin's office in Cleveland one day late that September. Every player in baseball received the option to buy World Series tickets. I figured the Mets players and coaches would be in short supply if they ended up beating the Braves for the NL pennant. So I told Alvin I was thinking of offering my tickets to Hodges.

"Kenneth, I think that would be a great gesture on your part," he said.

I got on the telephone within minutes, calling Shea Stadium. I reached Hodges' office.

"Gil, this is Hawk," I started.

Dead silence. No "hello," no "how are you?" Nothing.

"I wanted to offer you my World Series tickets if you get there," I said.

"Thanks, but I don't need them," he responded.

Then he hung up. That was it. Not another word.

It was the last time I ever spoke to Gil Hodges.

As a side note, there was a little guy outside Alvin's office listening to our conversation. Apparently, he was a correspondent or runner for a Cleveland columnist by the name of Hal Lebovitz, who wrote a column in the next day's newspaper with the headline, HAWK HARRELSON ASKS GIL HODGES FOR WORLD SERIES TICKETS.

The little guy had gotten his story backward. But when Lebovitz discovered the truth, he never wrote a retraction. It was my first real time being burned by a sportswriter. From that day on, Alvin, who knew the real story, didn't get along with him, either.

Hodges and the Mets did reach the World Series that season by beating the Braves. I was an American League guy and I never rooted for the National League in the All-Star Game or in the World Series anyway. So you can imagine who I pulled for when the Orioles, who had won 109 games, faced the Mets that October.

But the Mets shocked everyone by winning the series in five games.

Hodges had the World Series championship he desperately wanted. And he won it in New York, where he had always wanted to manage.

Less than three years later, after playing a round of golf during spring training with the two long-time coaches who were so loyal to him, Rube Walker and Joe Pignatano, he collapsed with another heart attack. He died in Piggy's arms on a sidewalk outside of a Ramada Inn in West Palm Beach on April 2, 1972, two days shy of his 48th birthday.

I finished my first season in Cleveland surpassing Alvin's requests. I had hit 30 home runs (27 with the Indians) and I had 92 RBIs. I really believe, all things considered, that I had a better year than the previous season, for which I was named the AL Player of the Year.

In the spring of 1970, I headed to Tucson for what would be my first full season with the Indians.

One night, I grabbed a cab and headed to a nice restaurant up in the mountains to grab a drink and some dinner. The hostess put me at a table behind a partition and I ordered a Smirnoff and tonic and a big steak.

Just after I had received my meal, the hostess seated a guy on the other side of the partition. I recognized him right away—it was Robert Mitchum. I remember reading that he had once been arrested for vagrancy in Savannah, so I thought that would be my icebreaker with him. I walked around the partition and introduced myself.

"I know who you are, Hawk," he said. "Sit down and have a drink with me."

I hadn't yet finished my steak, but how many chances would I get to have a drink with Robert Mitchum?

We sat there, talking and laughing for about 20 minutes. He was a terrific guy.

Ironically, I had almost been cast in a movie starring Mitchum a year or so earlier, but I didn't think to bring it up at the time. When I participated in the baseball players' celebrity golf tournament in Palm Springs and was talking with Drysdale, a movie producer approached us out of nowhere about being in a film.

We gave him our contact information but that was the last any of us ever heard from him. The guy made the movie *El Dorado*, a Western with three huge stars—Mitchum, John Wayne, and James Caan—while three certain baseball players missed their big breaks in Hollywood.

Now that I had come out of my shell as a power hitter, I considered myself a pretty decent baseball player by the age of 28. I had a great arm and could put it on display if I played right field. I was a good first baseman, much improved defensively after learning the nuances of the position from the guy who seemed to hate me, Gil Hodges. I had decent speed. I considered myself a good teammate, always encouraging the guys around me.

But there was one thing I never could do—slide.

I was the worst slider in the baseball world. (I met another guy who would challenge me for that title many years later: Ozzie Guillen.)

Before my second season in Cleveland, I had ordered some special spikes, which were about a quarter-inch longer than normal, to deal with the notoriously bad outfield grass. The Browns played football on it from September through December and just chewed it up.

Near the end of the spring, we were riding on the bus to Mesa for a game against my old team, the Athletics, when Alvin delivered a little speech.

"Guys, we are getting close to the season and I want you to run hard on the bases," he told us. "If you are on first, there will be no more peeling off at second base. I want you sliding into second. We are going to get game-ready beginning today."

After listening to him, I decided to wear my new spikes to break them in before we headed to Cleveland.

That day, Rollie Fingers had an 0-2 count on me, but he screwed around and walked me. Max Alvis then hit a ground ball to Sal Bando at third base. Sal bobbled it, which gave me a chance to make it to second safely. Normally I would not have thought to slide, but I suddenly remembered what Alvin had told us on the bus, so I decided late to slide. Then my new longer cleats got caught in the infield dirt.

Then I heard a loud *Pow! Pow!* Immediately, I knew my leg and my ankle were broken.

I looked down to see my right foot pointing about 45 degrees to the right of my leg. I reached down with both hands, grabbed it, and turned it back to the left, lining it up the way God had made it 28 years earlier. I got sick to my stomach and almost vomited.

Wally Bock, our trainer, came running out to me, and all the Athletics' infielders gathered around me.

Within a few minutes, my ankle swelled to the size of a coconut.

I had always trusted Alvin's wisdom on just about any subject. He had been spot-on when he predicted what salary I would make and whatever team I signed with a few years earlier would win the AL pennant. So when he told me not to take any pain pills, I listened.

I guess Alvin had been worried about players getting addicted to pain pills.

They rushed me to the hospital in Mesa and placed me in the Barry Goldwater Suite. At the opposite end of my bed in this huge suite was a bar. It didn't take long for several of my teammates to visit me. I had taken Alvin's advice, lying there in extreme pain, as my teammates held an impromptu party, standing around the bar, drinking and eating and laughing. I suffered for two days and nights, watching those guys eat and drink and flirt with all the pretty nurses. After a while I couldn't take

it any longer. I decided I had enough of their partying. I started screaming at those guys to get out of my suite.

When Indians officials came to see me, I asked if it would be okay if I
flew to Boston to let Dr. John McGillicuddy, an orthopedic surgeon for
the Red Sox, operate on me. They agreed.

Gabe Paul did have one request, however. Knowing I would not play
in one game that season, he asked me if I would take a pay cut, since I
was the Indians' highest-paid player at the time. Alvin happened to be
in my room when Gabe walked in.

"He will not take a pay cut!" Alvin said, speaking for me.

I told them both I would try my best to return that season.

The flight from Phoenix to Boston before the surgery was pure agony.

When I arrived at Boston's Sancta Maria Nursing Facility, I told my
nurse what Alvin had told me about taking pain pills. She didn't seem to
respect his medical expertise, so she gave me a big black pill and within
minutes, I felt much better.

Dr. McGillicuddy put my ankle back together using tweezers and epoxy,
re-assembling it piece by piece. He also inserted several screws and pins.
He later told me it was a good thing I turned my foot back into place on
the field when it happened. That reaction made the surgery and my reha-
bilitation easier. He also said it was the worst ankle injury he had ever seen,
but that his work would last me about 20 years. (Today, I am in my mid-
seventies and the ankle has held up fine for the most part, other than having
trouble with my first few steps when I get out of bed in the morning.)

When I left the hospital, I sported a plaster cast from my foot all the
way up to my butt. It wasn't exactly stylish. It included laces for me to tie,
just like a shoe. I took it off to shower, but I had to sleep wearing that bulky
thing.

As the weeks passed, more than that heavy cast was wearing me
down. Day by day, I was losing my enthusiasm for rehabbing. I just
didn't want to do the work and I honestly didn't really care if I ever
played baseball again.

When the doctors finally removed the cast, one of them had given me some unusual advice to break down my adhesions.

"Get yourself a thermos and fill it half with orange juice and half with vodka, on ice," he instructed. "Go to the ballpark and then drink as much of that as you can. Let it kick in. Then before the game, go down the right-field line and run sprints as hard as you can."

This was advanced medicine at its finest: I ran up and down the right-field line, half drunk after drinking a bunch of screwdrivers on a doctor's orders, listening as my adhesions popped one by one. Nowadays, they would have taken me into a room and popped them out in 10 minutes and I would have walked out of there to take batting practice.

My buddy Tony Horton was in the middle of a contract dispute with the Indians that spring, but he gave in and accepted the club's offer the day before I broke my ankle. He grew unhappier by the day when the season began. He finally had a nervous breakdown and left the club in August.

When he returned to the clubhouse a few weeks later, his father was with him. I happened to be sitting at my locker listening to the game on the radio.

"This is your fault, Hawk," Tony said, pointing at me.

Tony cleaned out his locker and walked out of the clubhouse. I sat at my locker crying, feeling terrible for him. I never saw him again. I can only guess he was referring to my broken ankle, which came a day after he signed for less money than he had demanded. If I had broken it two days earlier, I can only guess, he would have received a better contract. Tony never played baseball again.

I also wasn't the only Indian to suffer a serious injury that season.

At the age of 23, Ray Fosse was one of the best-looking young catchers in baseball.

He could hit for average and power and he had a great arm. He was a great teammate and a really tough guy, and he was having a great season, good enough to make the AL All-Star team. That's where his future collided with a guy from my past, the one and only Pete Rose, my former teammate during winter ball in Venezuela.

Rose ran over Ray at home plate during the All-Star Game, fracturing the catcher's shoulder. Ray never was the same player after that.

Here's something few people ever knew: Rose and Fosse had dinner together the night before the game. The next day, Pete treated it like Game 7 of the World Series and Fosse was never the same. Even though I loved Ray and didn't care much for Pete, I never blamed Rose for what happened.

Would I have done the same thing? You bet your life I would have.

Furthermore, I think Ray would have knocked Pete into the seats if the situation was reversed. You have to understand the culture of the All-Star Game in those days. The focus was on winning the game first and foremost. It wasn't to get every player in the game like it is today, or just to put on a spectacle for the fans.

The AL players and NL players didn't like each other much once they crossed the lines in those days and they badly wanted to beat the other team.

When I played in my lone All-Star Game in '68 in Houston at the Astrodome, Dick Williams was our manager because the Red Sox had won the pennant the year before. Before the game, he warned us that not everyone was going to get to play because he was there to kick the NL team's butt.

Some of our starters, like Yaz, got four at-bats that night. Willie McCovey, Willie Mays, Ron Santo, Tommy Helms, and Hank Aaron played the entire game for the NL, too. Each manager played to win. I pinch-hit in the third inning, and flew out to left field off of Drysdale. We ended up losing 1–0 to the National League.

The important thing was, I remember being ticked off, just as if it were a regular season game that counted in the standings.

In July, right after the All-Star Game and Fosse's injury, I started to play golf and was hitting the ball really well even with that big cast on my leg.

The golf bug was biting me again. I went out to Firestone Country Club to watch the PGA Tour event there and to see my buddy Kenny Still, who was in contention on the final day of the tournament. I watched the final round from a golf cart.

Kenny was a real character. I spotted him walking down the fairway holding two small transistor radios. I immediately knew what he was listening to. He loved to gamble on NFL games and it was a Sunday in the fall. He was in contention to win a professional tournament, yet he was listening to the games he had wagered on at the same time.

Anyway, watching the final round of the tournament got me to thinking more and more about my golf game.

When I finished my rehab, I knew it was time to do something other than play baseball. I guess I had done what I wanted to do in the game, and now it was time for another challenge. I returned in September for the last few weeks of the season, getting 11 hits and one home run in 39 at-bats.

But mentally, I had checked out. My enthusiasm for playing baseball was completely gone.

At the same time, I knew deep down that if I had stayed with the Red Sox, I may have wanted to play eight or nine more years, barring injury. I had hit 65 home runs and drove in more than 200 runs during my last two full seasons when I was healthy, so I had little doubt in my ability to be very productive. The most fun I ever had were the parts of the three seasons I played in Boston.

After the season, I went down to Miami, where Alvin had a townhouse, and called him to break the news. He asked me to meet him at a restaurant near the Miami airport. By then, Alvin was both the general manager and the manager, so he had the ability to negotiate contracts. Gabe Paul had become vice-president of the club.

"Look, Kenneth, we just lost Tony Horton," he said. "We can't lose both of you. Give me one more year."

I loved Alvin and I felt loyalty to him. He had done so much for me over the years, going back to our crazy times under Finley's rule with the Athletics. When he could tell I was wavering, he slid a blank contract across the table.

"But how much is it for?" I asked.

"Don't worry about it," he said. "I will take care of you."

I signed it.

By signing, I accomplished something I always wanted to do. I wanted to become the only player in history to play a season in which he had no idea how much money he was making. I knew that was a strange goal, but it was one of mine.

All of my paychecks were sent to Bob Woolf, so I never saw them. He paid my bills and then deposited money into an account I could access. I never asked Bob what the Indians were paying me and he never told me.

The first few months of the 1971 season were pure drudgery for me. It really was nothing against Cleveland or the Indians, although we weren't very good. We were five games under .500 and I was hitting .199. I had only five homers and 14 RBIs through the first 52 games.

I was just ready for a change.

I was ready to play golf for a living.

Bob Toski, a legendary golf instructor, had tried to talk me into retiring a year earlier, to try the golf tour. He offered to sponsor me up to $100,000 a year and then split any winnings thereafter.

I was done and I knew it. I was ready to have Bob get me ready for the PGA Tour.

I went to Alvin and told him how I felt.

He tried to talk me out of it again. Then when he realized he was getting nowhere, he called Cubs manager Leo Durocher. Apparently, the two already had talked about a trade.

"Hawk, you will hit 50 home runs at Wrigley if you come here," Leo said.

I told him, "I don't want to come there. I don't want to play baseball anymore."

I had given Alvin a 10-day notice, but he asked me to call Gabe. This time, I didn't want to negotiate or request any more money. I just wanted out.

As the days passed, the media got wind of my plans. Gabe sure didn't try to talk me out of it, knowing he would save a lot of money by not paying me to play for a team going nowhere anyway. Everybody in baseball knew I was leaving to play golf. So did all the people on the PGA Tour. Finally, the Indians accepted it, too.

I told Alvin that I wanted my final at-bat to be at Fenway Park, so we agreed my final game would be Monday, June 21, against the Red Sox in Boston, where I enjoyed the finest moments of my career.

A day earlier, I went 0-for-3 with a walk in our 7–6 win over the Tigers in Cleveland. We flew to Boston that night. It rained like cats and dogs that Monday, so the game was postponed. Rather than wait another day, I had already made my flight plans out of Boston for Tuesday and I wasn't changing them.

So I didn't get that one final at-bat at Fenway.

I finished my career, parts of nine seasons in the big leagues, with 2,941 at-bats, 703 hits, 374 runs scored, 94 doubles, 14 triples, and 131 home runs. I averaged .239 for my career. I also struck out 577 times and walked 382 times.

I know by leaving the game at the age of 29 that I left some numbers out there on the field, since I finally had figured out how to hit big-league pitching. I would never claim that I could have finished with 400 home runs, but I had many more left in me if I had wanted to continue.

And surely, if I had been making today's type of money, or playing for a pennant contender, I wouldn't have walked away from the game.

But neither was the case.

After what was supposed to be my final game was officially post-poned, I stood in the hallway outside the visitors' clubhouse at Fenway and said good-bye to my teammates and anybody else who stopped to see me.

I headed back to the hotel, packed my bags, and awaited my flight from Logan Airport the next morning.

I was leaving the Indians.

I was leaving baseball.

I guess it was ironic that I was physically leaving Boston as I figuratively walked away from the game after 12 years of playing it professionally.

And to this day, I still have no idea what I was being paid that season.

13 WALKING 18 WASN'T ALWAYS REWARDING

MY TWO PREVIOUS TEAMS, THE INDIANS AND RED SOX, WERE about to play a doubleheader at Fenway Park to make up for the previous day's rainout, but I was nowhere near my favorite ballpark.

I was aboard a flight from Boston to Denver by the time the first game started, on my way to Saratoga, Wyoming, to begin my education under the great golf instructor, Bob Toski.

Playing baseball for a living was my yesterday.

Playing golf was my tomorrow.

And on this day, June 22, 1971, for the first time since the day I busted my ankle so badly in Mesa 15 months earlier, I was happy.

First, I had to kick the rust off my golf game after having spent the past four months in baseball. Toski, who had offered to sponsor me three years earlier, was the perfect man to help me do that.

Bob's home course was Old Baldy Golf Club in Saratoga, a beautiful spot surrounded by mountains, lakes, and streams full of fish. It was one of the most majestic courses in this country and still is.

On the night before one of our rounds, the pilot who was supposed to fly the airplane and spray the course for mosquitoes got drunk and couldn't fly that day. The Old Baldy course was located at an elevation of more than 7,000 feet. I tell you, these mosquitoes looked like small birds. After about the third hole, Bob and I placed towels over our heads and made a mad dash for the clubhouse, swinging at mosquitoes as we went.

I met a lot of good golf instructors over the years, such as Jim McLean, Carl Rabito, Brian Moog, and David Leadbetter, but Bob was the best I ever had been around. His motto was, "If it ain't broke, don't fix it," but he really knew how to fix a golf swing.

He fixed a few small issues with my alignment, but most of his time he worked on my head more than my swing. Within my first few days in Wyoming, Bob had me hitting the golf ball so well it was crazy. In that high elevation, I was hitting my driver around 400 yards consistently.

Ten days later, I was tournament-ready, he told me.

It wasn't as if I was entering my new career on my own, either.

I had met a businessman by the name of Said Haddad a year earlier at a golf tournament. Said, who was from the Washington, D.C., area, was a real estate developer better known for owning one of the largest demolition businesses in America. If somebody needed a large building, such as a hotel, knocked down or demolished, they called Said.

Said was also a golf nut.

When he first saw me play, he was sponsoring a young golfer by the name of David Oakley. I played real well that day and he approached me soon after my round with an offer.

Before I ever finalized my plans to leave the Indians, I had called Said to see if his offer was still valid. He said he would pay me $60,000 per year, plus all expenses and a membership at Miami's La Gorce Country Club, one of the most prestigious clubs in the world.

Now that I planned to play golf for a living, I couldn't live in Boston or Cleveland if I wanted to work on my golf game 12 months a year. So I moved into one of the penthouses at the Golden Strand Hotel on Collins Avenue in Miami Beach. It was a beautiful place and the perfect location. I could throw a baseball into the Atlantic Ocean from my balcony.

When I left Wyoming, I headed back to Miami, where I loved living.

One night, I went to a club to see Frank Sinatra Jr. sing, out of respect for how well his father had treated us in Palm Springs. I grabbed a table in the corner of the place when I noticed that Frank Sr. and his entourage had walked in.

I didn't want to approach him, thinking there was no way he would remember me from our brief meeting two years earlier. An hour or so passed and I headed to the bathroom. Just as I walked back to my table, he reached out and grabbed my arm.

"Hey, you don't say hello to your buddies?" he asked.

I apologized immediately, but I learned just how big a sports fan Frank was—he had read about me retiring from baseball to play golf.

The next accidental meeting I had changed my life forever.

When I was 12 years old, I had won the Junior Putt-Putt championship in Savannah, and Sam Snead presented me with a new bicycle. Fast forward 19 years: a man named Don Clayton, who owned the World Putt-Putt championships, called me. The tournament was being held in Winston-Salem and Don wanted me to handle the color commentary for the TV telecast.

During the tournament, I bumped into an old buddy who had played baseball at Savannah High. His name was Jimmy Harritos, and he also happened to be a former Putt-Putt champion.

Jimmy and I caught up on old times and I mentioned I was on my way to Washington in a few days. He suggested I call his sister while I was in town.

Jimmy was the nicest guy in the world, but he was no Warren Beatty. I could only imagine what his sister looked like.

I had regularly dated two flight attendants in D.C., but by the time I arrived, both were out of town on flights. So I called the number Jimmy had handed me.

His sister's name was Aristea Constantine Harritos, but people called her Aris.

When she answered the phone, I couldn't help but notice her deep voice. It was a Saturday afternoon, so I asked her if she wanted to go have a drink later that night. I also mentioned that I may have to leave early for another appointment, laying the groundwork in case I needed an early escape. She invited me to pick her up at her apartment, which happened to be in the same building as one of the flight attendants.

When she opened the door, I was shocked to see she looked nothing like Jimmy. She was beautiful, just as he had promised. We sat down on her couch and started talking.

It was as if lightning had struck me. She wasn't just beautiful. She was gorgeous. She had a fantastic personality. She was very smart, working as an executive secretary for a D.C. lobbyist at the time. Aris and Jimmy's parents were born in Greece, but they grew up in Savannah. She spoke fluent Greek. She had attended Savannah High but was three years younger than me, and that is why I had never bumped into her before.

I still couldn't believe she had never heard of me, since she was from my hometown, but I soon discovered she wasn't a big sports fan. I actually liked that. It was a big plus in my book.

"The only athlete I really follow is Joe Namath," she told me.

That sort of ticked me off, but I let it slide.

We went out and had a few drinks. I started to fall in love with her on that first date. Within 10 minutes, I knew I was going to marry this girl.

In the next few months, we became inseparable. I was living in Miami and she was in D.C., but we made it work.

In my first pro tournament at the Firestone North Course in Akron, Ohio, I finished 22nd. I also played in the Music City Open in Nashville. It resulted in one of the highlights of my life, but it had nothing to do with golf.

The tournament held a celebrity-pro event that week, and set up a huge tent in which to entertain sponsors and guests who had paid $5,000 to play with a pro and a celebrity. I played with Chet Atkins and

Bob Murphy that day. After our round, Chet was on stage in the tent with Roy Clark and Jerry Reed, playing in front of about 2,000 people.

They had taken a little break for some reason and Bobby Nichols knew I sang a little bit. He stood up and challenged me to grab the mic.

I figured, why not?

I asked Chet, "Do you know 'Boney Maronie?'"

Part of me was hoping he'd say no, but they started playing so I got on stage and started belting it out: "I got a girl named Boney Maronie, she's as skinny as a stick of macaroni…"

I would give anything to have a tape of that performance, because my memory is that the place went nuts. In fact, they wanted me to sing another song, but I didn't know anything else other than "The Star-Spangled Banner."

As far as making the tour, I couldn't just sign up and play. I had to head to qualifying school first.

When I first arrived at Q-school in Winston-Salem, I was paired with Lanny Wadkins. I shot the lights out and finished with a 68 that first day. At the turn, Lanny asked some guy at the drink station who had the best score thus far. He was told Leonard Thompson's 64 was the score to beat.

"Take it down!" Lanny said.

He went on to shoot a blistering 62, beating me by six shots.

Then we went to West Palm Beach for the second stage, to be held on the JDM Course, a beautiful but very challenging golf course. Lanny and I were supposed to play against David Graham and Steve Melnyck in a practice round, but Lanny was sick as a dog. He joined us at the turn and was coughing out a lung. He had a fever and just looked terrible.

Then he shot a 30 on the back nine!

Steve, David, and I—the healthy golfers—just looked at each other, shaking our heads.

The first qualifying round started the next day and I ended it one shot off of the lead, which was held by Chuck Thorpe, Jim's brother.

The following day, I was playing well again, reaching three under. I was only 11 holes from qualifying for the tour when we arrived at the eighth hole. It was a long hole with water on the right. The wind was in my face. I hit a beautiful 1-iron about 300 yards, and I had only a wedge into the green. This was back when I carried a 1-iron.

As I stood over my pending wedge shot, I started to blank out. Then I hit it just like I wanted to, but it landed in the middle of the creek right in front of the green.

At that moment, something snapped.

It was as if I had had a stroke, and yet I felt no pain.

I suddenly had no idea how far to hit the ball. My mind was a complete blank when it came to judging distances for the rest of the round. I ended up shooting an 80.

When I walked off the course, my faculties came back to me. My mind was fine again.

I withdrew from Q-school and headed back to Miami, thinking my issue was a one-day problem.

I attended the Q-school in Rockville, Maryland, a few months later and the problem surfaced again. I just couldn't calculate distances. Also, I couldn't hit the ball even 250 yards. I was a mental wreck. I went back home to Miami and was in the middle of a round with my buddy Sid Salomon when he noticed it.

Sid's dad owned the NHL's St. Louis Blues, so he arranged for Aris and me to fly to St. Louis. The team doctor checked me out and admitted me to a hospital. Within a day, he diagnosed me with mental exhaustion. I stayed in the hospital a few nights, and I had no choice but to take a few months away from golf to rest.

I am convinced now that I was overwhelmed by self-induced pressure. I had followed Ted Williams' advice about not reading the newspapers when I played baseball. However, I didn't follow it when it came to golf, and I know it caught up with me. I read anything written about me when it came to golf. I had paid too much attention to what fellow players were saying about me in the media, believing I would win a ton of tournaments.

I read one story in which Arnold Palmer said, "Now that he has turned pro, Hawk can't miss."

The toughest part for me was I knew I had the talent to compete. I was stronger than most other players. I was a long hitter, even among the tour's top players, and years later I never carried a 1-, 2-, 3-, or 4-iron in my bag. I could hit a 5-iron about 265 yards, so I carried three different wedges instead. I was a decent chipper, a great sand player, and a good putter.

I had all the ingredients but I was very frustrated.

After my short stint in the hospital, I never had another bout of that mental emptiness on the golf course again.

I headed to Q-school again, this time at Pinehurst Golf Club in North Carolina.

I played with Peter Oosterhaus the first day and shot a 73. I had hit it real well that day, but just didn't score well. The next day, the name of the course bit me in the butt. Obviously, there are tons of pine trees surrounding the fairways at Pinehurst. With pine trees come millions of pine needles.

During the second day, I hit a drive into the rough on the right. When I got to my ball, I noticed it was lying on a mound of pine needles.

I had about 220 yards to the hole, so I took out my 5-iron. I went after it hard, but little did I know that underneath all of those pine needles was a big tree root. My club slammed into it and my right wrist felt like somebody had stuck a knife in it. For the second time at a Q-school event, I had to withdraw.

The next day, the pain was so intense that I couldn't even brush my teeth with my right hand.

I headed back to Miami and had to take some time away from golf, again, this time to let my wrist heal.

My home course, La Gorce Country Club, was *the* club in town.

The food in the dining room was fantastic and its membership was a who's who of CEOs, company presidents, and the big wheels of American industry. J.W. Marriott's locker was right next to mine. Jack Nicklaus played there all the time. Bob Irsay, who owned the Baltimore Colts, threw a big party there every year.

I played golf there almost every day, unless I went out to Doral or up to Boca Rio, where my buddy Carl Rosen loved to play.

After my wrist healed, I joined Nicklaus and Gardner Dickinson during a round one day. I bogied the first hole. The second hole at La Gorce was a long par-4, a big-boy hole where the final 150 yards headed uphill.

I killed my drive, one of the best I had ever hit. As we walked up the hill, Gardner asked Jack, "Where's Hawk's ball?"

It was about 40 yards short of the green, which means it had traveled well over 400 yards.

One day I was having lunch in the dining room and I met actor James Garner, who was passing through Miami and had some time before he had to catch a flight to Los Angeles that night. We got to talking and I discovered he was a huge baseball fan. This was well after his *Maverick* days and at the beginning of *The Rockford Files*, which would become a big hit.

We agreed to play a round. I wanted to ride in a cart that day, because it was one of those steamy, hot summer days in South Florida, but he wanted to walk. It was the hottest round of golf I had ever played in my life. By the time we walked to the first tee box, both of our shirts were soaked.

The thing I remember about his game was that he hit only a few greens and still shot a 73. He got up and down from just about everywhere. He had a great aura about him. He had that deep voice and I just loved to hear him talk.

After the round, I told him that Aris was a big fan. Within two weeks, she received a signed color photo of him in the mail.

Even while I played baseball, I always followed golf. I knew who the PGA Tour players were, the stops on the tour, the contenders, and the up-and-comers.

Nicklaus was not only a great golfer, but while getting to know him, I learned he was one of the most cerebral athletes in any sport. He had just won the Masters and the U.S. Open in the summer of '72, and he knew I was attempting to make the transition from baseball when we met at the club one day to play a round. I happened to play great that day, and he encouraged me to try and qualify for the British Open.

I flew from Miami to Philadelphia and then caught a flight to Scotland a few days before qualifying began at Gullane.

The weather was absolutely terrible when I arrived, cold and windy, but I shot a 70 the first day and a 68 the second to easily make the field. I was the second-lowest American qualifier. Bruce Devlin had beaten me by one stroke on another golf course.

Just 13 months after playing my final baseball game, I suddenly found myself in the 101st Open, which would start that Wednesday, July 12, at Muirfield Golf Links.

That Monday, I played with Jerry Heard during a practice round and I felt great about my game. I had no plans to play a practice round the next day. After all, if it ain't broke, don't fix it.

As I stood on the practice range, Jack walked up to me. He wasn't feeling 100 percent, however, because he had a slight crick in his neck from playing tennis with his wife, Barbara, the night before.

"You and I are going to play Tom Weiskopf and Bert Yancey in a practice round," he told me. "Weiskopf is playing awesome. He shot a 30 yesterday on nine holes and a 64 on Sunday. I just want to see what he does when you knock the ball by him."

Like Jack, Weiskopf was an Ohio State guy, and I think Jack liked to needle him a bit.

We headed over to the first tee, where Weiskopf said hello and shook my hand. He then ripped his first drive down the middle. I was pretty nervous, but I blasted a long drive. We walked down the fairway where Jack and Yancey hit their next shots, while Weiskopf stood over in the rough, waiting for me to hit.

"Hey, Weis!" Jack said, looking at me with a wink. "Are you going to play today or what?"

Weiskopf thought his ball was the one sitting 35 yards further down the fairway. That ball was mine, however.

They had pressed us heading into the 18th, which we needed for the win. I hit it in the front bunker, the only time I had hit into any bunker all week. Jack had about a 30-foot putt to win it for us. I stood right next to him as he lined it up. It was a double-breaker, heading right, left, and then back right.

He got into that familiar putting crouch of his, and it had traveled no more than five feet from him when he said, "Hawk, I think that's center cut."

The ball went right, left, and right again, before dropping into the cup.

If that's what it took to become a great golfer, I suddenly feared I had no chance.

We had won the match. Yancey was a great guy to play with, but Weiskopf never said one more word to me the entire day after shaking my hand on the first tee. I began to wonder if the guy talked at all.

I played great that day, just as I had in qualifying.

I shot a 75 that first day at the Open, seven shots behind the leader, Peter Tupling, but I didn't putt well at all. During the second round, on one of the early holes, I pulled a long iron into the left rough. I walked up to where I thought it landed but I couldn't find it.

I asked the spotter, whose job it was to watch and then locate the ball for me, where it was.

"I'm sorry, Mister Harrelson," he said. "I was watching Tony Jacklin behind you."

I had to retrace my steps and hit a penalty shot. I stumbled down the stretch, three-putting one green after another. I three-putted 18 to finish with a 78.

I was furious.

I realized my biggest mistake of the week was telling Jack, "I promise you that I will not leave one putt short."

I hadn't.

I rammed everything by the hole and often missed my comebacker. I was disgusted with my putting. I was disgusted with myself. I stormed off the 18th green and decided to pack my bags. I was headed home, whether I made the cut or not.

Arnold saw me and I could tell by the look on his face that he was disappointed in my attitude. As disgusted as I was with myself, so was he.

I missed the cut by one measly stroke.

That fact probably saved my relationship with Arnold, because I was serious about leaving, no matter what. If I had actually made that cut and then withdrew, he likely never would have talked to me again. He was a gentleman and a stickler for the rules and for the etiquette of golf, and I had violated all of them. I had disrespected the game.

Lee Trevino was the steadiest over the four days, chipping in from about 30 feet on the par-5 17th hole to save par in the final round and beat Jack by a stroke. Jack, who was six shots behind entering the final round, shot a 66 on the final day.

"Such is life," Jack was quoted as saying in the newspapers the following day. "But I know the Grand Slam can be done."

Weiskopf finished tied for seventh, eight strokes behind Trevino.

As a contrast to my attitude when things went poorly, Jack didn't let a few bad holes get to him. One year, he started the Jackie Gleason Inverrary Classic with a double-bogey, bogey, and bogey. He was four over after the first three holes. I would have walked right off the golf course before the fourth hole. Jack? He came back and won the tournament.

By the end of '72, I was optimistic I could be a winner in a PGA Tour event. Everybody was telling me that, even Arnold.

I also started to play some mini-tour events. When they opened Orange Tree Golf Club in Orlando, the course hosted one of the Space Coast Tour events. I shot 10-under as one of only two players to break par. The other was Larry Mowry, who won the event at 15-under. Larry was winning just about every mini-tour tournament during that period. He won only one PGA Tour event in his career, but later he won five PGA Senior Tour tournaments.

On September 14, 1973, I married the love of my life near Savannah at the justice of the peace. Ralph Demopoulos, an insurance man in town and one of my best friends, stood up for me as a witness.

Aris and I grew closer as we traveled the country while I chased my golf dream.

I took her everywhere I played. Even when I was struggling on the course, we had a ball together. We drove from Savannah to Phoenix and rented an apartment there for about two months in the same complex as other golfers, such as Bobby Wadkins, Bruce Lietzke, Tom and Paul Purtzer, and all their wives.

All of us would barbeque together almost every night, talk golf, and have a few drinks. It was a wonderful time. I had several second-place finishes there but didn't break through with a win.

I credit her and our marriage with saving my life.

Before we met, I was going out just about every night. I still was drinking and getting into fights. I was smart enough to realize that if I did that long enough, somebody somewhere was either going to stick a knife in me or shoot me. The bullets missed me when I was younger, but I couldn't count on that good luck lasting forever. I figured the next guy who pulled a gun on me may have better aim than those in the past.

I had to stop my bad habits, or I would lose Aris.

So I had a new wife and a new nightlife to go with my new career.

Meanwhile, they had introduced a new rule to the American League, something called the "designated hitter." One day earlier that spring, Red Sox general manager Dick O'Connell called me about returning to baseball. I told him I needed to give golf one more year, and Dick signed Orlando Cepeda to be the Red Sox DH.

Things really started going downhill for me on the golf course, however. I was in complete self-destruct mode. I didn't even think of going back to try to qualify for the British Open. I was failing miserably.

I didn't know what to think or how to feel, because I had never failed at any sport before. But it brought back memories of my frustrating times in winter ball when Dick Howser was riding me.

My temper was killing me, too, even if it took only one bad hole. I would leave the clubhouse with the normal number of 14 clubs in my bag and come back with just a handful. Those other guys were too good to beat with only five or six clubs.

The final straw came during a two-day tournament in Savannah, of all places. I went out and shot a 68 on the first day to share the lead with Fuzzy Zoeller, Bobby Wadkins, and Lietzke. Then I shot myself out of it on the front nine on the second day.

After we finished the 18th hole, I walked off the green and over to a big oak tree right by the clubhouse at the Savannah Inn and Country Club. I took my clubs out of the cart and smashed them against that oak tree, breaking them one by one.

I then looked over and saw Aris, who was sobbing.

I had stopped going out and getting into fights because I loved her so much. Now this blowup made me realize that I had to control my temper, or I would lose the best person who ever came into my life.

We went back to the hotel, ordered room service, and talked about my future.

Finally, I came to a big decision.

"Honey, I am quitting golf," I said.

"Good," she replied.

I had a money game scheduled that next day with Fuzzy and two other guys that I had committed to play. Fortunately, I had a backup set of clubs with me.

After breakfast that next day, my phone rang. It was Mary Trank, a secretary with the Red Sox, calling from Fenway Park.

I had been out of baseball for more than three full seasons. Were they still interested in me as a designated hitter? Perhaps they wanted me as a hitting instructor.

Whatever it was that the Red Sox wanted, I realized that my professional golf career was about to be a thing of the past.

14 FINDING A HOME IN THE BOOTH

THAT TELEPHONE CALL FROM BOSTON INDEED CHANGED MY life forever.

Dick O'Connell, the team's president and general manager, was on the other end of the line.

"Hawk, we have an opening for the color guy on our TV network since Johnny Pesky is leaving the booth," Dick told me. "We want you to come up and audition for it."

The timing couldn't have been better.

It turned out they had hundreds of applicants for the job. It was the Red Sox after all, but I figured that since Dick himself called me, he wanted to give me the first crack at the job. All I had to do was show some potential behind the microphone.

I flew to Boston, spent about five minutes at the Channel 38 studio calling a replay of some game clips, and that was that.

They must have liked what they heard, because I got the job.

To say I felt natural behind a microphone or in front of a camera would be a gross understatement. I had spent my baseball career talking to the media. Before most of my games as a player, the broadcast guys from other teams, such as Ernie Harwell or Harry Caray, would interview me. They each told me I was a good interview who gave them colorful quotes and insights—and that is why they usually came to me in the first place.

At times while I played, I even pulled double duty.

As I stood at first base or in right field, I called the game as it happened just as if I was sitting upstairs in the booth. An opposing batter would strike out and I would pipe up, "He gone!" Or, "There's a long drive down the left-field line... it's fading foul."

In the back of my mind, I always thought that when my playing time was up, I would want to try broadcasting.

And now that time had arrived.

I read plenty of self-help books in those days and I found one, *Golf in the Kingdom*, written by Michael Murphy, that hit home with me. It was all about handling the negative things in your life. I liked it so much, I read it twice.

When I arrived in Winter Haven, Florida, for Red Sox spring training, I felt like a new man with a new outlook. It was as if I didn't have a care in the world, and all the pressure on me from my three years in golf had evaporated.

Before I knew it, my thoughts were drifting back toward the golf course.

I headed out to Lake Regions Golf Club, where Bobby Wilber was the pro. I bogied only the fourth hole, and then I missed an eight-footer for eagle on the 18th. I shot a 62, breaking Ben Hogan's course record by three shots.

I got back to the Holiday Inn where we were staying and I told Aris, "I might give golf one more chance."

She couldn't believe what she was hearing.

I told her that I had just broken the course record by three shots. I always knew I had the talent on the golf course to compete and win on the PGA Tour, but I didn't have the proper mental approach. Now, thanks to this book, I believed I had it.

For example, I was able to stand behind the ball before I even addressed it and visualize where I wanted to hit it. You know how you seem more relaxed before hitting your mulligan, with your terrible shot already out of the way? Well, it was as if all my first shots were mulligans.

I hadn't even called a game yet with the Red Sox and I was already thinking about leaving to try to make a living at golf again.

That night, Aris and I talked some more and she eventually talked me out of it. I knew that her final memory of me playing was my breaking all of my clubs by that oak tree in Savannah. I couldn't stand the prospect of seeing her cry again, so I backed off the idea.

I had to immediately focus on my new career.

I was paired with play-by-play man Dick Stockton, also entering his first season with the Red Sox. Dick was a veteran who knew the ins and outs of broadcasting. He taught me about the importance of pacing and timing. He also taught me to appreciate the crew and the production end of every broadcast. As I would soon learn, the directors, producers, and camera guys were the real stars of broadcasting baseball games. Those guys worked their butts off, showing up at the ballpark at 8:00 AM for a 2:00 PM game.

In turn, I like to think Dick learned some baseball from me.

All in all, I grew to like Dick very much and ours was a good match. From all indications and reviews I read, Red Sox fans loved us together, as we called 53 games on TV that season. I know this: the TV ratings were huge. Our games had something like a 90 share, which is unheard of. Remember, this was back in the day when there weren't many channels to choose from, and let's face it, the Red Sox were the Red Sox. Everybody in New England cared about how they fared and whether this particular year would be *the* year.

As I already realized from my playing days in Boston, no fan base was as loyal or as rabid, especially for a team searching for its first championship since 1918.

Things in the booth didn't get off to a great start for me, however.

In my first game during spring training, the Red Sox faced the Montreal Expos in Winter Haven. A few innings into the game, things were going well when Dick asked me, "Hawk, what do you think about the Expos' shortstop, Tim Foli?"

"Well, Dick," I said, "he's a feisty little guy who has got big balls!"

Dick reared back in his seat and made a face as if he had bit into a lemon. He then held one hand over his mouth and gasped. There was some awkward silence before he figured out his next words. I guess I forgot for a moment that I wasn't on the field anymore, where I could say anything to an audience of none and get away with it.

Nowadays, that would be nothing. But in 1975, broadcasters couldn't mention any part of the private anatomy.

I figured that I was about to get fired after just one game. As soon as I got back to the hotel, the telephone rang. It was Bill Flynn, the station manager.

"Well, you lit up the switchboard!" he declared.

"I figured I did," I admitted.

Bill didn't fire me, however. In fact, after we laughed about it some, I think he realized I was the type of guy who could add plenty of color to the broadcast, even if it was a bit off-color, so to speak.

The next game, a buddy of mine from North Andover had stopped by to say hello before the game. He told me he would be in town for a few days and he wanted to play some golf. He also told me where he would be sitting at the ballpark.

Between innings, I asked Bobby Whitehall, our producer, to get a shot of my friend on camera. I figured it'd be a thrill for him.

We returned from commercial and Bobby punched up a shot of my friend on the monitor. There he was, smiling, enjoying the game—with his arm around a beautiful blonde. That wouldn't have been such a terrible thing, if not for the fact that his wife had to be watching the game from North Andover. And I knew this guy's wife, too.

"Get it off! Get it off of him!" I shouted into my headset.

It was too late. Thousands of people in the New England area saw him with his arm around a pretty lady who was not his wife.

So, that was the start of my broadcasting career: an off-color comment one night and a ruined marriage the next. Good job, Hawk.

Things got better, however.

Gene Kirby, the team's director of broadcasting, was a great teacher, a no-nonsense guy who knew all facets of broadcasting. He had worked with such former players as Dizzy Dean and Pee Wee Reese. Gene was tough on me, and I mean that in the best possible way. He oversaw every aspect of the broadcasts and he helped me tremendously.

I wore big cowboy hats back then during the openings, and the media sometimes paid as much attention to the hat I wore as to what I said on air.

Curt Gowdy, a legend in the business and the former voice of the Red Sox, called me a few months into the season and wanted to meet with me. I knew Curt would have some great insights and advice for me.

"I've been watching you and this is the best advice I can give you," he said. "Don't try to please everybody. You just can't do it."

Curt told me that after one Rose Bowl he had called for NBC, he received hundreds of letters from USC fans blistering him for being partial to Ohio State—and he also received hundreds of letters from Ohio State fans blistering him for being partial to USC.

"That's when I knew it must have been a great telecast," Curt said. "You can't please everybody, and the sooner you realize that, the better."

A couple of weeks following that conversation, Howard Cosell called me. Howard had always been good to me when I was a player and I marveled at his memory and talent. I saw it up close once during a road trip to New York when we played the Yankees. I was in Toots Shor's with some teammates when he walked in one Sunday night in September. He was doing sports at 6:00 and 11:00 every night at the time, and invited me to come on for the earlier telecast.

As I sat off-camera waiting for my segment, Howard did something live on the air that night that simply amazed me: he handled the NFL highlights without a teleprompter or notes, reciting the statistics and scores from every game off the top of his head. I sat there watching him in awe, just wondering how his brilliant mind worked.

So whatever advice he could give me now in my new career, I was more than willing to listen.

"Hawk, I've been watching you and you're doing a good job," Howard said. "You've got to remember one thing—you can't please everybody. Don't even try to do it."

Two legends gave me the exact same advice, so it must have been true.

I knew baseball and I was immediately comfortable as an analyst. Plus, I had played with the Red Sox. I knew the town. I knew the fans. And I knew a special player named Yaz, who was still going strong. Heck, I batted behind him for a few seasons, so I knew exactly what he was thinking at the plate.

For example, in one game, I told viewers what pitch he was looking for. He didn't get it. "Now on 1-0, he has narrowed the plate down even more," I said. "He's looking for a certain pitch on the inside." He didn't get it. Another ball later, the count was 3-0.

"Is he taking?" Dick asked me.

"No, he's in control now. Yaz has narrowed what he wants to an even smaller part of the plate," I said. "If he gets the pitch at that exact spot, he will drive it into the right-field seats."

The pitch was right where he wanted it and Yaz drove it into the right-field seats, almost on cue.

Doing play-by-play, however, was a whole different animal at that point. One night in Minnesota, something happened to Dick and he couldn't make the game. I was about to fly solo and I had no idea what to do. I had to handle the opening, the promos, and the drop-ins, and also call the play-by-play and the color at the same time.

I saw that red light go on above the camera and I froze like a Popsicle. Three or four seconds passed. It seemed like a minute.

Finally, I found the words: "Hi, everybody, welcome to Red Sox baseball…"

And what a year it was for Red Sox baseball.

On one of the first days of spring training, Ted Williams walked up to me in Winter Haven and said he wanted me to see something on one of the back fields. As I said, nobody could talk hitting like Ted. He could pick apart a guy's swing and pinpoint his weaknesses and strengths within a few minutes.

Ted and I walked back to find this big, young kid in the cage. I stood there and watched in amazement as he put on an exhibition. He just hit bomb after bomb after bomb.

"Did you hear anything?" Ted asked me.

"Yeah, I heard his bat," I said.

"That's right," he said. "Bat speed is power and it makes a special noise."

That was the first time I ever laid eyes on Jim Rice. I learned he had grown up in South Carolina about 30 miles from Woodruff, where I spent my early childhood.

It was also hard not to notice that the new kid in center field was about to be something special. Fred Lynn's talent just jumped out at me. He roamed into the gaps and snagged everything within reach. He had a sweet swing and he hit with power.

At the end of that spring training, I think Dick picked the Yankees to win the American League. The Orioles, led by Jim Palmer, had won the AL East the year before, and the Yankees had Thurman Munson and Catfish Hunter. The Red Sox were coming off an 84–78 season and had finished third in the division.

But what I saw from Rice and Lynn in spring training was enough for me to go out on a limb.

"Dick, I am picking the Red Sox," I said on the air. "If these two rookies, Rice and Lynn, do what I think they can do, they have a good chance of winning this thing."

Dick had a funny look on his face, much like when I said Foli had big balls. When we headed back to Boston to start the regular season, all I read in the newspapers was, "The new color guy, Hawk Harrelson, is a shill for the Red Sox. He's a real homer."

This went on for about a month and a half as the Red Sox stumbled to a mediocre start. The media just wore me out for being a homer, something I would have to get used to over my broadcasting career.

Then Rice and Lynn started to get comfortable and show their talents.

We were in Detroit one day and Jimmy checked his swing. The bat snapped in half and Don Zimmer, who was coaching third, had to dive out of the way so he didn't get impaled. The ball never hit the bat. He had just stopped his swing and it snapped in half!

I played golf with Rice plenty of times over the next few years and saw his strength up close. One day, on about the 14th hole, he asked to borrow my driver to see how it felt. He swung it and as he brought it back down, there was nothing but the grip in his hand. He had torqued the thing in half, just like he did with that baseball bat that was headed for Zimmer.

Rice is the only man I ever saw hit a golf ball more than 500 yards more than once. We would play at Green Leaf in Winter Haven during spring training and one day he crushed one on the first hole, which was a 477-yard par-4, and it landed in the front bunker or it would have been well past the green. It was a neat thing for me to watch Jim develop into a pretty good golfer.

His development on the field and at the plate, however, was obvious to baseball fans from coast to coast.

By June 20, the club had a 36–24 record and was just feeling its way. Then the Red Sox ripped off a 10-game winning streak in early July that boosted their record to 53–37, taking over first place. They finished 95–65 and went on to sweep the Oakland A's for the AL pennant.

Rice had 22 home runs and drove in 102 RBIs that year.

I really believe he was the strongest guy I ever saw with a bat in his hand, aside from Frank Howard, of course. Nobody was as strong as Hondo. Jim Thome and Willie Stargell would be in that next tier along with Rice.

As good as Rice was in his rookie season, Lynn was even better. He hit .331 with 21 home runs and 105 RBIs to become the first player ever to win Rookie of the Year and MVP in the same season.

I knew then, after only one season, I was watching two future Hall of Famers.

Rick Burleson was steady at short. To this day, Dwight Evans was the best I ever saw in right field as far as saving runs. He also was the best at keeping runners from going from first to third. He had to fight the sun that sets over that short roof down the third-base line, something I knew plenty about. As good as they were offensively, the Red Sox won the pennant that season mainly with defense. Nothing hit the ground in that outfield. Plus, they had great leadership from Yaz.

Dick and I didn't broadcast the postseason, since the national networks always handled the playoffs and the World Series. With time on my hands, I joined a few other former players in a corporate golf tournament hosted by Allied Chemical in the Dominican Republic.

Fortunately for me, Mickey Mantle was there, too.

Billy Martin had once told me that the Mick had one of the best baseball brains he ever came across. He could slice and dice a game with the best of them. He also said, "Nobody is funnier than Mickey Mantle."

Over those four days in the DR, I found out both were true.

We attended a cocktail party one night, schmoozing the corporate leaders, when Mick suggested we duck out and find a bar to watch the game. We found a place with a TV and settled in at the bar, watching Game 6 of the World Series in Spanish. I didn't need to hear the English telecast, anyway, because Mick was there next to me. He brought up some things I had never thought of, and I liked to think I knew the game pretty well.

Alan Greenspan, an economic adviser to President Ford at the time, was the guest speaker at the conference, which hosted some of the leading textile people from all over the world. Our job was to play golf with them during the day and have a few cocktails with them at night. On the final day, everybody delivered a quick speech about their experiences during the event and Mickey stole the show, just like he used to do on the field.

Mickey performed a parody of Greenspan's speech in his Oklahoma drawl. By the time he finished, people were falling into the aisles and onto their knees, doubled over in laughter. To this day, I don't remember seeing a larger group of people laugh as hard as they did that night.

I wasn't laughing after Game 7 of the series, because I wanted the Red Sox to pull it off. The Reds won 4–3 to extend Boston's long streak of misery to another season.

Nevertheless, it was one of the most remarkable seasons in Red Sox history, just like 1967 had been for me.

What people tend to forget in what was surely one of the most exciting World Series in baseball history is that Bernie Carbo made Carlton Fisk's 12th-inning, foul-pole-clanging, Game 6–winning bomb possible. Carbo's pinch-hit, two-out, three-run homer in the eighth had tied the game, setting the stage for that blast. On the pitch before that swing, Bernie took one of the worst swings in the history of baseball.

Seeing Carbo always reminded me of the day he arrived in Boston. Mister Yawkey usually wore something like a brown sweater, brown slacks, and hush puppies. He didn't wear a suit and tie or try to impress people. He would visit players in the clubhouse before every game, and when Bernie first walked in, arriving from St. Louis, he introduced himself to a couple of players and then turned to Mister Yawkey.

"Hey clubbie," he said. "I'm hungry. Can you go get me a hamburger?"

"Uh, Bernie," someone said. "That's Mister Yawkey. He *owns* the club."

I read that Carbo admitted publicly that he had a severe cocaine and booze addiction during his career, especially during the '75 Series, but I had no idea. I had never heard anything about it back then.

I have to admit that watching that young team develop, win the pennant, and then reach the seventh game of the World Series was one of the highlights of my broadcasting career, and it happened in my first season in the booth.

The next season, however, the Red Sox started terribly. They had lost 10 straight at one point in early May and were 8½ games out of first place. I really loved Darrell Johnson, the manager, as a person, but we had a few disagreements along the way. In Cleveland one night, Yaz came up late in the game with a couple of guys on base with no outs and the Red Sox down by a run. He was facing left-hander Steve Mingori.

"He's got to be bunting here," I said on the air.

D.J. let Yaz hit away, but he struck out and the Indians won the game by one run. Word must have got back to D.J. about what I had said on the air, because he invited me to go have a drink with him and Yaz.

"Hawk, I can't have him bunting," he told me right in front of Yaz.

"Why not?" Yaz asked. "I don't hit that guy very well anyway. I thought about bunting on my own, but I didn't want to show you up in front of the guys."

The club had a 40–40 record at the All-Star break. The start to the second half of the '76 season would be crucial, but the Red Sox lost five of their first six. We headed to Kansas City, where we checked into the Adam's Mark Hotel right next to Royals Stadium. After the Red Sox lost the opener, I went down to the hotel bar and happened to walk in just as a big fight broke out. Next thing I know, I got hit two or three times in the back of the head. I had walked in there to grab a beer and was minding my own business when some guy hit me from behind.

I woke up with a headache the next morning, July 18, when Dick O'Connell called me. He said he had decided to fire D.J. and wanted me to take over as manager.

I had no intention of doing that, so I suggested Yogi Berra, who had managed the Mets a season earlier before being fired. He had returned to the Yankees as a coach. Dick didn't like that idea, so I reminded him the Red Sox had a third-base coach who all the players already loved: Don Zimmer.

The Red Sox fired D.J. and hired Popeye that day in Kansas City, and the club responded immediately. Under Zim, they won 21 of their next 31 games, but it wasn't enough to win the AL East. The Yankees won the pennant, but then were swept by the Reds in the World Series.

I had gone from a golfer with a bad temper to a first-year broadcaster to being asked to manage the Red Sox in a span of two years. I didn't give the job strong consideration, as you'd think I would. I just knew Aris wouldn't understand it all. It wouldn't be fair to her that I would suddenly be a manager on a high-profile club in that market.

This was my first of three offers to manage. Following the 1977 season, Cleveland owner Ted Bonda called me to play golf one day. We hit it off during the round, and on about the 17th hole, he asked, "How do you feel about managing?"

The Indians weren't very good then, not even close to being a contender. It was a losing proposition, I believed, but I wanted to see how badly he wanted me.

"I would do it for $400,000 a year," I said.

"I can't afford that," he said.

So I turned him down. I was relieved he didn't meet my asking price, because I had several reasons not to manage and didn't really want to do it.

After Buddy LeRoux purchased the Red Sox in 1978, he made overtures to me about managing, but nothing ever came of it.

I knew that a club couldn't have a manager who was willing to fight his players if they didn't run hard to first base. Of course, there was Billy Martin, but there's an exception to every rule. And players didn't mind fighting their managers, either. We would have had brawls in the dugout every other day, like Billy's famous fight with Reggie Jackson in the dugout at Fenway in 1977.

I had an indirect hand in that episode, without ever intending to.

The night before it happened, O'Connell and I were having a drink after the Red Sox–Yankees game in the press club at Fenway. Billy and Dick Howser, one of his coaches and the same man who nicknamed me Hawk about 17 years earlier, came upstairs and sat down with us. Billy told us Reggie was driving everybody on his ballclub crazy.

I'll never forget seeing Reggie for the first time. He walked into our Athletics clubhouse as a rookie in 1965, took off his shirt, and was as ripped as any football player I ever saw. He then took batting practice and hit several bombs. We veterans stood there with our mouths agape. He was quiet and respectful, too. Nobody had a problem with him then.

"Billy, when Reggie came up from the minors at Kansas City, he was a great kid and we all loved him," I told him. "He was humble, he always hustled and he was respectful to every one of the veterans. But he has changed, there's no question about it. Maybe being in New York has changed him, I don't know. I think the only way to handle Reggie now is to embarrass him and bring him back to earth."

Thurman Munson was the leader of the Yankees at the time, and he absolutely hated Reggie. And most of his teammates had similar feelings toward him.

The next day, with Reggie playing right field, Rice hit a rocket to right-center for a double. The next time Rice came up, Reggie had moved more into deep right-center, where the double had landed. This time Yankees' pitcher Mike Torrez hit Rice on the fist with a fastball and forced him to pop up over second baseman Willie Randolph's head.

Reggie had no chance to reach it and it dropped for a hit. Billy promptly went to the mound and started to point at Reggie.

That resulted in their huge fight in the dugout a few moments later. The cameras caught the fight and Billy had embarrassed him on national television.

After the game, he and Howser came up to the press club again.

"Hawk, you will never guess what happened after the game," he told me. "The first guy in my office was Thurman and he said, 'Skip, you did the right thing.' Then Lou Piniella came in and said, 'You did the right thing.'"

Apparently, after that episode, they all got along much better with Reggie.

Thurman was just the type of guy not to take crap off anybody.

And he didn't like Fisk at all.

Before a series against the Yankees in New York, I had been invited to Mantle's restaurant to appear on a radio show. I had been asked about the two catchers and I said, "Fisk is better."

I said it because I was a Red Sox guy at the time, not because I believed it fully. Truth is, they were both great in their own way.

I got to the ballpark and walked down to the batting cage, where the Yankees were taking batting practice. Thurman told me he didn't appreciate what I'd said.

"Screw you, Thurman," I said. "You couldn't carry Carlton's jock."

He dropped his bat and started to walk outside the cage toward me. Bobby Murcer and another Yankee jumped in between us. After the game, I told Billy if he started anything with me the next day, the Yankees might lose their catcher.

The next day, I watched batting practice and Thurman didn't say a word to me.

On August 2, 1979, I was playing golf at the South Bend Country Club on an off day when I heard the news over the little radio I always had in my golf cart: Thurman's airplane had crashed in Canton, Ohio. I sat there in the golf cart and cried. I found out later that Lou was supposed to be with him, but fortunately, he didn't make the trip.

After my third season in the booth, a little guy by the name of Jack Satter had asked me and Rice if we wanted to do some commercials for his company, the Colonial Provision Company, which owned the contracts to sell hot dogs at Fenway Park (called Fenway Franks) and at Yankee Stadium (Yankee Franks). Most people may not realize it, but hot dogs are made differently depending on the region of the country. For example, the dogs made for New York were a little spicier than the ones made for New England.

Jack's offer sounded good. The next thing I knew, I had gotten myself into the sales business during the off-season, selling deli meats, hams, turkeys, and hot dogs throughout New England.

I quickly noticed another difference between the cities in relation to my new job. We were allowed to offer buyers a few perks in exchange for their business, such as tickets to an event or a game. If I offered most buyers in the Boston area something, they would politely decline, stating it was against company policy. On the other hand, if I didn't offer any perks to the buyers in New York, they gave me the cold shoulder.

Anyway, I always loved hot dogs and the sales job was a natural for me. I jumped into the sales business with both feet during the winter months. I realized I had an advantage with my name recognition, which often helped me get my foot in the door with most buyers. It didn't take long for me to sell a lot of products for Jack's company and he soon made me a vice-president.

I always figured the winters were easier to take if I had places to go, people to see, and things to do. I knew it sure beat sitting around watching TV.

My neighbors, however, weren't so thrilled about my new off-season gig.

Jack had bought me a new Cadillac that operated on diesel and sounded like a semi-truck. The grocery sales business was an early morning business, so when I cranked up that Cadillac at about 4:30 every morning, our neighbors woke up instantly.

One winter, Aris and I took a trip with some of Jack's other employees and his preferred customers to Aruba. There was a group of about 30 people in all, and on our return trip to Boston we had to stop at Kennedy Airport in New York to catch our connecting flight. As the plane approached New York that night, a flight attendant pulled me and another guy aside.

She whispered, "Now, when we crash…"

I am not sure I really digested much of what she said after those first four frightening words, but it was something about asking us to help passengers get out those emergency doors. Apparently, the captain had discovered the landing gear on that DC-10 was inoperable. He then announced to the passengers that we had to circle Kennedy and dump all of our excess fuel.

A few of the women passengers heard that announcement and started screaming.

Well, this one guy, who just happened to be one of my customers, believed his last moments on earth would be the perfect time to confess all of his sins. So he told his wife that he had been having an affair with her best friend.

A few minutes later, I heard banging underneath the airplane as the landing gear fell into place. As we approached Kennedy, I saw the fire trucks aligned along the side of the runway, but our pilot's landing was smooth as expensive bourbon. Most of the people on our trip headed to the Hertz and Avis counters to rent cars to drive to Boston, but Aris and I continued with our connecting flight as planned.

A week later, I learned that customer and his wife were getting a divorce.

The moral of that story: be sure to find out if the landing gear is stuck for good before confessing your sins.

Jack owned about 5 percent of the Yankees. He had a type-A personality and was a pretty good motivator, but he didn't hold his booze very well. One time we were up in owner George Steinbrenner's suite at Yankee Stadium and Jack was feeling a bit tipsy. He made some snide comment about one of the Yankees' recent trades.

"Jack," George said, "do you know what the most useless thing on the planet is?"

"What?" Jack asked.

"A limited partner in the New York Yankees when I am the majority owner!" George declared.

Jack didn't say a word for the rest of the night. George could be a great host when he wanted to be, but I always regarded him as a bully, a real tyrant most of the time, as I would see for myself in the following years.

Eventually I grew tired of selling meats for Jack, who became more and more demanding. I made him a lot of money but it was never enough. He just became too bossy, wanting more and more from me, so I gave up my side job and focused solely on calling the Red Sox games.

The sports talk shows were drawing some huge audiences in Boston in those days, and sometimes they picked up on what I said in the booth.

Zimmer got into a pattern where he allowed guys to hit away on 3-0 counts. I mean, it wasn't just something he did for the three-four-five hitters, or Yaz—he let *everybody* in the lineup swing away. I called it out several times on the air.

Well, Zim and I had been very close. After all, it was my suggestion that got him the job in the first place, although he may never have known that. But my so-called criticism and the fact that sports talk shows were talking about it soon drove a wedge between us. It got to the point where we would get on the team bus and Zim wouldn't even look at me.

After a game one night near the end of the '76 season, O'Connell and I were in the press room at Fenway when he asked me what he should do about Zimmer. I said he should either fire him or give him an extension, and if it were up to me, I'd give him an extension.

The press room at Fenway was one of the best in all of baseball. Sometimes, they even served lobster or filet mignon or shrimp. Dick made sure of that for a reason: he figured it would be another tool toward getting the media on his side. Dick was a brilliant guy. He was a former Navy intelligence guy and he had a way of appearing tipsy when he was not, just to get information out of people.

They also employed a bartender who was as liberal as Ted Kennedy when it came to pouring drinks. He poured about three shots in every cocktail. His name was Walter, but Milwaukee Brewers broadcasting legend Bob Uecker had labeled him "The Assassin."

"He fixes you two drinks and then you're dead!" Ueck would say.

There were a bunch of reporters in there the night Dick and I talked about Zimmer's future. I sat in the corner of the room, having a stiff drink that Walter had poured me, waiting for the traffic to clear out when Dick told me he'd decided to give Zim the extension.

"Well, why don't you announce it right now in front of all these media guys?" I asked.

Dick grabbed a napkin, took a pen out of his coat pocket, and started writing: "The Boston Red Sox are offering Don Zimmer a one-year contract extension…" He walked over and handed it to Popeye, who read it and started to cry. I guess he thought he was about to be fired. So Dick made the announcement right there and that cut down the public bashing of Zim.

Zim's undoing was the team's collapse of 1978, as the club led the division by 14 games in August only to see the Yankees surge down the stretch. Rick Burleson was lost to injury and the club brought in Frank Duffy to play short. Their defense was not very good down the stretch.

It ended with a four-game series still known as "The Boston Massacre" before Bucky (bleeping) Dent's game-winning home run off of Mike Torrez edged over the Green Monster to make it official.

That was a big moment in Red Sox history. It was the collapse of all collapses.

Despite the outcome, I had a blast being around the Red Sox away from the ballpark.

By the late 1970s, disco was sweeping the country.

I loved disco and *Saturday Night Fever*, and I happened to be a pretty good dancer. Problem was, a few Red Sox players knew it. We were on a road trip in Texas one night after a game against the Rangers, and we happened to be in a nightclub holding a dance contest. I was sipping a drink when I heard several of the players yelling at me to enter.

I ignored them, having no interest in dancing or entering a contest. Somebody pushed me from behind a moment later and I found myself on the floor with some girl I didn't know. We just started dancing and won the contest.

I was never averse to having wholesome fun like that, but despite my flamboyant reputation as a player, I drew the line at topless bars and X-rated movies. The club was in downtown Milwaukee in the summer of 1978 when *Debbie Does Dallas* hit the theaters. It was playing a block or two from our hotel and I overheard a few of the players talking about heading over to watch it.

Curiosity got the better of me.

I wanted to see which players had paid to see the movie, so I wandered over there and snuck inside the theater. The whole club was in that place. It was the only time I had seen a pornographic movie, but I stayed for only a few minutes. Not to sound like a prude, but I have never been to a topless bar in my life, not even for a buddy's bachelor party.

I had come to know many of the Red Sox players and regarded them as my team, just as I would with any team for which I called games as my career progressed.

Stockton was hired by CBS after our fifth season together and he was replaced by Ned Martin, who was a broadcasting icon in New England. Just like Dick, Ned was also a consummate professional. He never hogged the microphone and gave me plenty of space. It was an easy transition for me.

I also started doing some play-by-play after Dick left, but turned it over to Ned for huge moments, like when Yaz got his 3,000th hit, against the Yankees of all teams. (Willie Randolph didn't give much effort on that one, but that's the way it was then with the legends of the game. Other players took care of them when it came to milestones.)

As for Popeye, he finally was let go with a few games remaining in the 1980 season, in which the Red Sox stumbled to an 83–77 finish.

All in all, I really loved broadcasting Red Sox games throughout New England. I learned some valuable lessons during those first few seasons that have carried me through my broadcasting career. If in doubt, I always went back to the ball, so to speak. I talked about the pitcher and the catcher.

It seemed as if my popularity in New England had picked up right where it left off before I was traded in 1969, and it continued to grow with each broadcast. My mug appeared on billboards for Busch beer and the Yellow Pages around the city, wearing a cowboy hat.

I owned two sub shops before two businessmen, Jordan Friedman and Paul Klapper, came to me with an offer. They wanted to give me a 20 percent stake in a new restaurant if I agreed to put my name on it. That sounded good to me, so I agreed to it on a handshake deal. They called it "Ken Harrelson's Boston 1800." It was a really nice place with great food. The place was bigger than the popular Pier 4 around the corner, and it didn't take long for our restaurant to become pretty popular, too.

I was upstairs in my office one day during the off-season, handling some paperwork, when a waiter came up and told me a couple people downstairs wanted to meet me. I walked down to see Liz Taylor and Richard Burton sitting in a booth. I introduced myself and joined them. They were headed to Europe that day and were killing time before their flight from Logan International, which was only about eight minutes away from my restaurant.

I sat there staring at them as she ate lobster and he had a steak. I was mesmerized by how she doted on him throughout their meal. She ran her fingers through his hair constantly. Burton was just a little bitty thing but he sure had a presence about him. His voice was captivating, like Yul Brynner's or Barry White's voice.

Bill Veeck, the owner of the White Sox, came in there almost every day and sat in the same booth, as if it were his office.

One night, the Red Sox were in Chicago, where it had rained before the game. Bill fretted over a possible rainout, so I realized he had to be running the club on his day-to-day gate receipts. When the game was called off, he sat there depressed and angry. I figured he needed those gate receipts to pay his bills.

He also was drinking a lot, buying a lot of drinks, and at times being too loud. Finally, one day, I approached him and asked him about his drinking.

That was the final day I saw him in there, so obviously, I had offended him.

Sadly, that restaurant was gutted by a fire while I was in Miami. I don't know if it was a suspicious fire or not, because I had nothing to do with how the insurance was settled. I had not even signed a contract with those guys for my ownership stake.

Other than that drawback, things couldn't have been better. I was back home in Boston. I was making a living again in baseball, loving my time in the broadcast booth and happily married to the love of my life.

Our family also had expanded in Boston.

Our daughter, Krista, was born January 9, 1976, and I was right there in the delivery room. Watching her birth was the highlight of my life. Two years later, on February 8, 1978, we had a son, Casey. Now I had a beautiful loving wife, two beautiful children, and I was not out running around anymore.

The world seemed right to me.

One day soon after Casey's birth, I read an article about the side effects of birth control pills. I was talking to one of my best friends, Bob Witt, on the telephone, when he asked what I planned to do that particular day.

"I'm getting a vasectomy," I told him.

"I ought to get one, too," he said.

So we made a double appointment. When we arrived at the doctor's office, I flipped a coin to determine whether Bob or I went first. I lost. My fears were overblown, because all I felt was a little pinch.

As I stood up to put my clothes on, I told the doctor I wanted to have a little fun with my friend, so I started screaming.

The doctor and I then walked into the waiting room and I tried my best to look like I'd just had open-heart surgery. Bob sat there dabbing his forehead just like Gabe Paul had done during my contract negotiations a few years earlier. I had to calm him down and convince him I had been joking before I could get him to walk into the doctor's office.

I was also playing some of the best golf of my life. I broke three more course records that summer, including the record at Winchester Country Club northwest of Boston.

Life was good.

15 WELCOME TO THE WINDY CITY

TOM FREEMAN, A DOCTOR AND A GOOD GOLFING BUDDY OF mine from Savannah, called me one day in August of 1978. He hit me between the eyes with some terrible news.

"Hawk, your mom has pancreatic cancer," he said.

"What does that mean?" I asked.

"It means she's going to die. She has about six months left."

She's going to die.

My mother was only 63 years old, and I had not yet prepared myself for the idea of her dying. I was born a mama's boy, I grew up a mama's boy, and I was still a mama's boy now in my late thirties.

I had no idea what pancreatic cancer meant, but I soon learned it was 100 percent fatal in those days. There was no cure.

I talked to Mama over the telephone often over the next few months, and she always sounded upbeat. She had her good days and bad days, but she battled on. My mother was a fighter.

About 11 months after Tom's first call, he called me again to say I'd better get home to say good-bye.

I flew down to Savannah and walked into her bedroom. There she was—this once-big and beautiful woman now weighed no more than 95 pounds. Her eyes appeared sunken into her face. We made some small talk and I tried my best to smile and to act upbeat, but I was still shocked at seeing her in this state.

She told me she had to go to the bathroom, so I picked her up and carried her to the toilet.

She seemed so light, so frail. I noticed her stool was white as ash. I cleaned her up and carried her back to her bed.

"Mama, you are not going to make it," I told her.

Tears ran down my cheeks as I said those words.

"Son, I am ready," she said, smiling back at me. "I am ready."

I kissed her, told her I loved her, and walked out of the room. I knew she realized just how much I loved her. I also knew it would be the final time I would ever see the woman that meant everything to me. God, I loved her so much.

A week or so later, I was in the press box at the old Cleveland Municipal Stadium when Jack Rogers, Boston's traveling secretary, whispered into my ear that I had a phone call. It was my hometown friend Ralph Demopoulos, who at times was like the father I never had.

"Ken, she's gone," he told me. "I am sorry."

"Good," I said. "I have prayed almost every day for the last six months, asking God to take her."

Finally, He had answered my prayers.

She had no quality of life over those last few months. She had been a strong and very proud woman. It just broke my heart to see her in that condition. I flew back to Savannah to plan the funeral.

Because of the mental state I was in, I really don't remember much about her funeral all these years later. I know one thing: it was the last funeral I ever attended.

She is buried in a cemetery right across from the third hole of the Savannah Golf Club.

After Mama died, Iris revealed to me what Mama had told her years earlier. When the man she married had left us when I was 12, she had no intention of ever marrying again, at least until I was grown. She had been afraid that I wouldn't get along with whoever she would marry, and she never wanted to put me second.

That sounded just like her, putting my needs and wants before her own.

She did meet a man later in her life named Bill Robertson and she must have felt the time was right. I was happy for her. They married and he was at Mama's bedside with her when she died. I know Bill had treated her well and took great care of her when she was sick.

Mama had left me a couple of small houses in Savannah, which she had purchased years earlier as rental properties. Since Bill had been so good to her, I gave him one of them after she died. He thanked me profusely the day I told him. Mama and Iris had a falling out years earlier, and she left Iris nothing in her will.

Then after I gave a house to Bill, Iris stopped speaking to me for about the next seven or eight years following Mama's death.

Bill re-married within months of her passing, and I took that as a slap in the face to her memory. I was angry with him, which I regret all these years later.

Mama had kept all my trophies throughout the years and some baseball memorabilia that was special to me, such as autographed bats Mickey and Kaline had given me. When I went back to Savannah to claim them, Bill told me that his new wife accidentally had thrown everything into the garbage.

I was never good at accumulating baseball memorabilia, or taking care of it once I did receive it.

While broadcasting Red Sox games, I received a box in the mail at Fenway one day. I opened it to see a baseball with two signatures on it—Babe Ruth's and Ty Cobb's. The box contained a return address and I tracked down the sender and called her. She was an 87-year-old Red Sox fan.

She told me that her husband was gone and that she had no children. She wanted me to have the ball because she'd enjoyed my broadcasting of the Red Sox games. I thanked her but told her it was too valuable for me to keep, but she insisted.

I thanked her and I hung up the phone with tears in my eyes.

Do you think I know where that baseball is today? I have no idea. Just like the glove Satchel Paige wore in his final game, it's gone with the wind.

On one of Boston's trips to Comiskey Park that following season, I walked into that old rickety elevator to head to the press box. A well-dressed man and his young son entered at the same time. I recognized him from his picture in the newspaper.

It was new White Sox owner Jerry Reinsdorf.

The Red Sox blew a tough one that night, a game they should have won. I was really ticked off and my mood was probably all over my face as I got onto the elevator to leave the stadium. Jerry and his son Michael happened to get in the elevator with me for the ride down.

"Tough one tonight, huh?" Jerry asked me.

"If your son wasn't here," I said, "I would tell you just how tough it was."

I think that first meeting may have meant something to Jerry. I know it did for me. He knew right away how much I hated to lose, even though I wasn't a player anymore.

A few months later, I had been invited to speak at a University of Massachusetts event in Boston, where the audience was made up mostly of college students. A kid asked about the contract statuses of Carlton Fisk and Fred Lynn. I said I thought Haywood Sullivan, who was now a part-owner of the Red Sox, had been messing around with those two superstars when he should have locked them up long-term with fair contracts. I didn't think he wanted to pay either of them what they deserved.

Well, a sportswriter for the *Boston Globe* quoted me word for word.

His story prompted Sullivan to call Channel 38 station manager Joe Dominio, demanding I be fired. Fortunately, the station controlled my contract. Today, I may not have been as fortunate, since most clubs control their TV contracts.

Following that season, in which the strike erased 50 games from the schedule, one of Chicago's minority owners, Eddie Einhorn, called me. He said he wanted me to join Don Drysdale and become the new broadcasting team for the White Sox.

I had been making $65,000 each season with the Red Sox, but the White Sox were offering $200,000 per season, plus a $200,000 bonus. I called Joe to set up a meeting at Pier 4, and when he heard the financial details, he understood I had to take the deal.

So I did.

We had family in South Bend, Indiana, east of Chicago, and I knew Aris would be happy with me working there and us living closer to them.

Later, Joe and I were having a beer and he asked me if I had any suggestions for my replacement. I suddenly remembered seeing Tony Conigliaro doing the nightly sports in San Francisco that previous season.

"Joe, Tony C. does a great job on sports out there," I said. "The camera loves him. Give him a shout and see what he says."

They flew Tony in and hired him on the spot. His brother, Billy, was driving him to Logan Airport after the meeting that day. Tony was ecstatic. He was coming home to call games for his beloved Red Sox. As Billy drove, Tony mentioned he had met a girl the previous night. Before he could give his brother the details, fluid shot out of both of Tony's eyes. Terrified, Billy stepped on the gas, reaching about 100 miles per hour on Revere Parkway on his way to Massachusetts General Hospital.

It was January 9, 1982. Tony C. had suffered a massive heart attack and soon lapsed into a coma. Sadly, he would never get to spend one day in a Red Sox broadcast booth. He never came out of that coma and died eight years later.

It was strange how our careers had intertwined. He had hit 32 home runs in 1965 at the age of 20 to lead the league, and I had hit 23 that season in Kansas City. Ted Williams later told me he was the greatest young home run hitter he had ever seen. One day when I was playing first base in Washington early in the '67 season against the Red Sox, Tony hit a routine grounder to short. When the throw went toward the line, I reached for it and he spiked me, resulting in a lot of stitches in my leg. I knew it wasn't on purpose.

Then I had a big series on our return to Fenway in August as we beat them two out of three games. A few days later, Tony C. got hit in the face by Jack Hamilton. I will never forget seeing his picture on the cover of *Sports Illustrated* sporting that big black eye. That was a bad, bad injury.

Anyway, the Red Sox suddenly had a gigantic need for a right-handed bat in their lineup. That would lead to my free-agent signing later, after I had popped off about Charlie O. (In Hamilton's defense, Tony had a big, wide stance and he didn't move well in the box. It seemed if a pitcher threw it there, the ball chased him down.)

So I replaced Tony in the Red Sox lineup during the '67 season.

Now that I had left the booth in Boston for Chicago, it opened a spot for him to replace me. He accepted it and before he could enjoy it, he suffered a heart attack and a stroke. Tony will go down as one of the most tragic figures in Boston sports history.

Aris and I flew out to Chicago and found a home we loved at White Eagle Country Club. Before the sale went through, we discovered the taxes were more than $15,000 annually and we quickly changed our minds. We eventually found a home in the suburb of Lisle, where the schools were rated the best in Illinois.

She and the kids flew out to begin their new lives in the Midwest. I stayed behind back east and prepared to drive a car full of our possessions to Chicago. One of those possessions was the kids' parrot. I stuck the bird and its cage in the backseat and drove from Boston to Chicago in the middle of the winter, on icy roads and in the snow. When I stopped at a hotel, I had to take the parrot inside with me. Within days of my arrival at our new home, the parrot died. The kids replaced that parrot with a frog, which would crap all over the cage.

It is funny the type of things you remember.

But we had a gorgeous new home, and a new life in a new city.

When I first started in the booth doing White Sox games, Drysdale handled the play-by-play and I did color. We would do three innings on television, three on radio, and the final three back on television.

Working for the White Sox, I learned something real quick: Reinsdorf was my type of guy. Not only would I learn how smart he was—only the most intelligent man I would ever know—he was fair.

Veeck basically had bankrupted the club when Jerry bought it. The White Sox were in shambles and there was nothing in the minor league system, but Jerry improved everything. Chicago really was a White Sox town at the time. I think the Cubs were drawing a few thousand fans per game.

Unlike Veeck, Jerry was willing to spend money to sign top free agents, such as Carlton Fisk following the 1980 season.

After a month or so in Chicago, Jerry asked me when I was going to bring my family to a game.

"When you make this ballpark safe," I told him, "I'll bring them."

At the time, Comiskey was probably the most dangerous ballpark in the major leagues—inside and outside of the park. So Jerry went to work. Sure enough, he turned it into one of the safest parks around just by forming a plan and spending money to execute it. I knew within a month that I loved my situation with the organization.

When I broke into the major leagues, the Dodgers' Sandy Koufax was the best pitcher in the game, but he was not the epitome of pitching the way I envisioned it. Drysdale was. He hit 154 batters in his career. One time when Dodgers manager Walter Alston walked out to the mound to tell Don to walk a guy, Don plunked the batter instead.

"Why waste four pitches when one will do?" he asked.

That was Don.

In today's game, it's a rarity when a pitcher lasts nine innings. It's even rarer for one to last nine innings and pitch a shutout. In 1968, Don threw six straight shutouts, the last on the night Bobby Kennedy had been shot. He didn't give up a run in 58⅔ innings, which remained a record until the Dodgers Orel Hershiser broke it 20 years later. He finished his career with a remarkable 167 complete games.

Don won the Cy Young in 1962 with a 25–9 record, and by the time he retired after the '69 season, he had three World Series rings with the Dodgers and had appeared in nine All-Star Games. He finished with a 209–166 career record, with 2,486 strikeouts and a 2.95 ERA.

He and I hit it off right away.

I had played golf with him some in the past at those celebrity events, but never got to know him well before we were paired together. He played his entire 14-year career in the National League and had been broadcasting for the Angels, but we had crossed paths plenty of times over the years.

Over the ensuing five years, it was as if I had a 6-foot-6, 240-pound big brother.

We traveled together. We ate and drank together. We fought together. We cussed each other out often.

I will never forget that one thing Don often told me: "I hope that when I die, it's not in a hotel room."

In all modesty, I believe we were one of the first combos on the air with our credentials. He was a Hall of Fame pitcher. I had been a decent power hitter. So together, we could get inside the minds of both the pitcher and hitter in any circumstances of any game we called.

Not to mention we told hundreds of baseball stories over the air. Don was the best at it. He had a great voice, a great memory, and an awesome knowledge of the game. When I didn't like what he said, I told him—on the air—and he did the same to me. White Sox fans loved that give-and-take and our bickering. A lot of people told us that they thought we were the best broadcasting combination in baseball, and I know it was because we argued often. That doesn't happen as much on the air today.

Howard Cosell, who initially helped me so much when I got into broadcasting, had also worked with Don, and he once told me he loved our chemistry and how we related to each other. Howard lived in the Hamptons and often called me at home in Lisle, which was an hour behind his time, at 6:00 in the morning.

I politely asked Howard if he could call a little later in the morning. Maybe that ticked him off, because Howard never called me again.

I didn't mean to do that, because I liked Howard.

Another opportunity came along that year involving us moving back to Boston. I talked to NBC Channel 5 about possibly delivering their 6:00 PM and 11:00 PM sports segments. I had a five-year offer on the table, starting at $400,000 per year.

Aris was adamant against leaving our new home. By this time, I had gotten to know, respect, and love Reinsdorf, too, so I turned it down.

Plus, I had a great partner to work with in Don.

When I started working with him three years earlier, he had been divorced from his first wife and loved the nightlife. He was a handful for anybody who got in his way, especially if he had a few drinks in him. He wasn't exactly a mellow drinker. He could be downright angry and mean at times.

One night in Cleveland during the 1982 season, at the old Cleveland Hotel downtown, Don and I went to the bar after a game. After two or three drinks, I was ready to call it a night but Don wanted to stay. It grew later. At 1:00 AM, nobody else was there and the bartender wanted to close the bar. Don flipped him a $50 bill to stay open, so then I couldn't leave. Finally, after about another hour, Don was still firing them down when I told him I was going to bed.

So I left him at the bar by himself. The Cleveland Hotel must have had the longest hallways of any hotel known to mankind. It seemed I had to walk 90 yards in one direction, then turn a corner and walk another 40 yards to get to my room. I always carried a roll of quarters in my right pocket, and they weren't for parking meters or laundry machines. I had broken my hand three times and nothing made a more powerful fist than one wrapped around a roll of quarters.

As I got off the elevator on my floor, I saw two guys walking straight at me in the long hallway, and they stood shoulder-to-shoulder, blocking my path. I stuck my hand in my pocket and grabbed that roll of quarters just in case. Just as I reached them, they parted at the last second.

I went to bed, thinking nothing of it until the next morning.

Apparently, Don left the bar soon after I did. He got into the elevator with two other guys already in there. One hit him over the head with a blackjack and they ripped off all of his gold chains, and took his Rolex and cash. Don always carried a roll of big bills in one pocket and a roll of ones and fives in the other.

I knew he had to be pretty drunk or there was no way they would have been able to get that big guy down with just a blackjack.

I also figured it had to be the same two guys I'd seen in the hallway, although the Cleveland police never caught them. In fact, they blamed Don publicly for carrying so much money and for wearing too much jewelry, as if it had been his fault he got robbed.

The next morning happened to be a getaway day, so we checked out of the hotel. Don looked like crap. He had a big red mark on his head, bruises on his face, and was still partially drunk.

"Don, you can't work today," I told him.

"I'm alright," he said.

We did the opening to the broadcast and it was pretty good. The big guy took a few big blows, got ripped off, still feels his booze, and can still do live TV like nothing happened.

Then the game started and Don started to nod off.

"Don," I whispered, "go to sleep."

So he did. He took his headset off, put his head down, and went to sleep. I handled the play-by-play and the color for the rest of the game.

I once suffered my own injuries broadcasting in Cleveland, of a much different sort.

One night at the old Cleveland Stadium, Don and I arrived and started to get ready for the game when it began raining. Just as I had put the headset over my ears, a bolt of lightning struck the stadium and zapped the power. It was as if a shotgun had gone off inside my ear. Since that moment, I have been unable to hear very well out of my left ear. Then I waited too long to talk to a lawyer, who told me I had a good case, but the statute of limitations had expired.

Let me tell you, Don was not a guy you wanted to pick a fight with. He and I, as close as we became, almost came to blows one night. We were eating dinner at Verne Fuller's restaurant in Cleveland and Don started getting a little tipsy. When he got tipsy, he became very critical of the current players.

He started knocking a couple of the young pitchers on the White Sox roster. He just hated any pitchers who were scared to pitch inside, and he didn't care how vocal he became about it. Anyway, I drove us home since he had been drinking heavily and he continued on and on about the pitchers.

I told him to stop. He refused. So I said, "Let's go."

I hopped out of the car, ran over to the passenger's side, and opened the door. He got out and stood up. "Take your best shot, big boy!" I told him.

I was all cocked and ready, sizing up that 6-foot-6 body, planning to hit him right in the gut.

Just when I was expecting a big right-hand punch from him, he smiled.

I was relieved. I really didn't want to fight him. First of all, he was one of my best friends. Secondly, both of us would have been banged up from that fight.

When I thought about it, Don wasn't any different than I was when I was younger and drinking gin. When Ken Harrelson drank gin, Hawk would get ticked off and wanted to fight without needing a good reason. Norm Cash of the Tigers once told me the same thing. He couldn't drink gin without wanting to fight, and I heard it from several other guys through the years.

When I switched to Smirnoff vodka later, I became a different guy. I just wanted to have fun and mellow out, so I have stuck with it all these years.

But Don just never seemed to find that level, where he could drink without getting too angry. How many guys do you know whose favorite breakfast was liver and onions and two Heinekens?

Then, finally, he met Ann Meyers, the former star basketball player for UCLA, and his whole life changed. They married in 1986, had three kids, and he settled down. No more smoking. No more drinking.

He was a different man, other than his penchant for driving fast.

One time I stayed at their house in Rancho Mirage, California, during a series against the Angels. We always visited with "The Cowboy," Angels owner Gene Autry, and one night after a game we talked until 1:00 in the morning. Then we drove from Anaheim to Palm Springs, about 80 miles or so, to get to Don's house.

Well, Don was the fastest driver I had ever been around, this side of Mario Andretti. I trailed him in my rental car, trying to keep up with his Rolls Royce. I couldn't. We got past Riverside and he had to be going

100 miles per hour or more, so I just let him go. It got to the point I would never ride with him behind the wheel.

Anyway, while staying at his house those few days, I got to see the new Don. He wore an apron and cooked. I still smoked back then, and Don would walk around emptying every ashtray just as soon as a butt landed in one. I couldn't believe the change.

Annie was so good for him.

One thing I loved about Don: nobody, and I mean nobody, knew as much about pitching as he did. Not in my lifetime anyway. He was the best "flaw-picker" I ever saw. He could watch a guy throw and tell you right away what his weaknesses were. Don had a wealth of knowledge inside that brain of his.

And he was a natural at broadcasting, interviewing players and describing the action on the field.

Harold Baines was a great player with the White Sox, a terrific clutch hitter during the late innings. He also was a heck of an outfielder. The only things he didn't do well were run and talk. Harold was one of the quietest people in baseball. He just didn't say squat.

One night, we called a game that lasted only a little more than two hours and we had some airtime to fill. Harold had been the hero of the game, so the directors asked Don to head down to the field to interview him for five or six minutes. Don looked at me, rolled his eyes, and headed downstairs.

Don asked Harold question after question that night, rambling on as much as he could. The interview lasted five minutes, but Harold said about 15 words the entire time. Don did a wonderful job filling the time, and when he returned to the booth, I stood up and applauded.

They ended up with 99 victories and won the division by 20 games. Of course, great pitching also helped. Three starters—LaMarr Hoyt, Richard Dotson, and Floyd Bannister—went 42–6 over the second half of the season, and that was almost unheard of in the history of baseball.

That club had the greatest chemistry of any team I had ever seen, but it ended up losing in the American League Championship Series to Baltimore, which went on to beat the Phillies in the World Series. Guys like Baines, Jerry Koosman, and Greg "The Bull" Luzinski were natural-born leaders on that team.

Luzinski was one tough guy.

One night in Toronto, he hit a home run. The next time up, he took a fastball in the helmet. It sounded like a shotgun had gone off, but Bull never moved. He just dropped his bat and stared at the pitcher. Herm Schneider, the White Sox trainer, ran out to check on him.

"Get back in the dugout," the Bull told him.

He then jogged down to first base like nothing happened.

During spring training the following year in Sarasota, the Bull approached me one day and asked if I'd be interested in buying his boat. He owned a 23-footer he wanted to sell so he could upgrade to a larger one. The boat had a galley, slept four or five people, and came with a beautiful trailer.

"Just take over the payments and it's yours," he told me.

The payments were about $500 per month, so I told him we had a deal. I planned to ship the boat to Chicago and dock it at the marina off Lake Shore Drive, until I discovered what dockage fees in Chicago cost.

Before we headed north for the regular season, I took Casey and Krista out on it one day in Sarasota Bay and we had a great time. A buddy of mine by the name of Demetri owned a popular restaurant in Sarasota which served great pizza and Greek food. I needed somebody to look after the boat during the baseball season and I trusted Demetri.

Demetri called me about two weeks later.

"Hawk, I took about 12 or 15 friends out into the gulf and we hit something," he told me. "Your boat is sinking."

The Coast Guard rescued Demetri and his friends and then had the boat towed back into the marina. They tied it to a dock and a terrible storm happened to hit Sarasota that night.

Demetri called me again a few days later.

"Hawk, your boat is in three pieces," he said.

The insurance company took care of it, paying me what it was worth, and I broke even. I gave Demetri the trailer. So we got one great boat ride out of it, but that marked the end of my boating days.

As the '85 season ended, the White Sox had finished third in the division with an 85–77 record, and I was about to begin a much more complicated ride in my career.

16 SOMETIMES, THE TRUTH HURTS

AS YOU NOW KNOW FROM THE END TO MY PROFESSIONAL golf career, I have battled my temper over the years.

I realized my temperament wasn't cut out for managing a ballclub. It just wouldn't have worked out. I had turned down those three offers to manage, not wanting to put Aris through all the things a manager's spouse must deal with.

You also just can't have your manager getting into the face of one of his players, wanting to fight him every time he failed to run out a ground ball or missed the cutoff man. That worked for Billy Martin, but that would not have worked for me. Players don't mind fighting their managers, either, if they are challenged, so what kind of manager would I have been?

Plus, those one-run losses would have torn me apart.

In addition, I was an old-school guy when it came to fighting on the field. My teams would have broken major league records for fights. If the opposing pitcher hit one of our guys, I would have had our pitcher hit two of theirs.

On the other hand, I figured that being a front-office executive or a general manager was a different animal. That was something that was attractive to me.

The man in that position does not come face to face with a player who may have been dogging it. The GM does not run out onto the field to scream at an umpire, who may have blown a call at home plate. The man in that position tries to put the pieces of the puzzle together for the organization to be successful on the field.

After buying the White Sox from Bill Veeck, Jerry Reinsdorf had spent quite a bit of money trying to build a winner for Chicago. The club had come very close to winning it all, losing to Baltimore in the 1983 ALCS. If they had only gotten by the Orioles that year, most baseball experts, including me, think they would have had little trouble beating the Phillies in the World Series.

Now, only two years later, however, something had to be done. The club appeared headed in the wrong direction.

Jerry wanted a championship, or at least a contender. As he would prove in the years to come with the Chicago Bulls, he was a professional sports owner who did what he had to do to get one.

But he was a baseball man first and foremost. He knew baseball much better than he knew basketball, because it was his first love while growing up in Brooklyn. He also knew the game better than any other baseball owner I ever met and he could slice and dice what happened over nine innings better than even most players I knew.

More than that, I liked him very much. I loved working with him. He deserved success in the game of baseball. He deserved a world championship. There was nothing I wanted more than to see the commissioner hand Jerry the World Series trophy.

One day late in the '85 season when the team was struggling, Jerry and White Sox co-owner Eddie Einhorn and I were talking, shooting the bull when Jerry suddenly turned serious. He asked me what I thought about the state of the organization.

"I think there are a lot of holes," I told him.

"Like what?" he asked.

"Well, do you want me to write down what I think is the state of this organization?" I answered.

That was exactly what he wanted.

So I went home, sat down at the kitchen table, and pulled out a legal pad. I started writing. I wrote and wrote and wrote. I covered every subject and key position with the White Sox. I went from Eddie to Roland Hemond, the general manager, to the minor league system, to the bench coaches.

I ended up with pages and pages of notes.

I handed them all to Jerry, who read them and then asked me to fill in the names of people I thought would be good candidates for each position. I think he wanted to see the contrast between who he already employed and who I might suggest. So I wrote a name here and a name there and I handed it back to him.

"Why did you leave the GM job vacant?" Jerry asked.

"Well, you have to make that decision," I said.

"No," he said. "I want a name for that position."

My first thought was Chuck Tanner. I always loved Chuck. He had managed the White Sox previously and I think he would have been a fantastic director of baseball operations.

Then I started thinking about the job myself.

As I had in the past, I thought about Aris and how I never wanted her to be exposed to all the attention that came with me taking a high-pressure, high-profile job in a major media market.

I was talking to her about the team's problems and Jerry's request when she asked me bluntly, "Honey, do you think you could turn this around for them?"

"Darn right I could!" I told her.

"Then do it!" she said.

It had taken me a long while to reach this point. I always wanted her blessing in anything I did. I needed her blessing. I had passed on three managing opportunities earlier. I had passed on other jobs in baseball over the years, for various reasons. But this time was different and I could sense it. Most importantly, I knew the woman I loved so much was accepting of the whole thing and supported me.

So I wrote my name down next to GM and handed the paper to Jerry. He read it and simply said, "Okay, you got the job."

It was October 2, 1985.

My official title was executive vice-president of baseball operations, and I intended to hire a general manager to work for me. I essentially replaced Roland Hemond, whom everybody loved including me. Roland had held the job for 15 years and was bumped upstairs to become a special assistant to Jerry.

I wasn't naive. I realized the new job came with plenty of downsides. I had been a big-league player, a pro golfer, a part-time deli-meat salesman, and then a broadcaster for 11 seasons. I had been earning a good living between my broadcast salary and my endorsements, which included the "Beat the Hawk" bit I hosted on the local NBC affiliate, where I also sometimes delivered the sports news on weekends.

The GM job didn't pay quite as much, so I had to face a significant pay cut for a much more demanding, more pressure-filled job. All my endorsements would go away. I would also have much less free time. There would be little time for golf and all the other things I enjoyed away from the broadcasting booth.

I think I took the job because of Jerry and Eddie, both of whom I respected very, very much. And I always loved a challenge.

Jerry had all of the club's financial books sent to me within the first month. There were large volumes of material. I read them page by page, and what struck me immediately was that the club had been spending more money on the maintenance of Comiskey Park than on the entire minor league system. That shocked me.

The ballpark literally was falling down. Even though Jerry had made it safer, it was obvious to me the south side of Chicago needed a new stadium for the White Sox. Jerry knew it as well as anyone. He had already made up his mind the club had to have a new stadium and he also knew we needed leverage to get one.

So one day, he was quoted in the newspapers saying the White Sox might move to St. Petersburg, Florida.

You can imagine the response. All the writers lit into him. I don't think Jerry had any serious thoughts about moving the ballclub. He just knew the team needed a new stadium and that was his leverage to get one.

When I held my first press conference, I told the media, "I know you have a job to do and I understand it—and I promise I won't lie to you."

As I said, I always interacted well with the media. There was a reason writers swarmed around me after games throughout my playing career. I dealt with them fairly and honestly. I gave them colorful quotes and always made time for them.

With this new position, that would turn out to be a huge mistake.

Doubling down on that honesty mantra, one of my first acts was to tell a few key people in the organization one simple rule: "Don't ever lie to me."

A few guys I had in mind to hire for the GM role, however, didn't want it, so I basically served in that capacity, too.

I hired my former manager Alvin Dark as the director of player development in the minor leagues. I hired my former teammate Duke Sims to manage in the minors. All the minor league managers got bumps in salary in excess of $30,000 each.

Right from the start, my philosophy was, this is not a small-market team; we were the Chicago White Sox. If you are going to manage them, or coach them, or be a pitching coordinator for them, then you should be paid accordingly.

For example, Jim Leyland had been Tony La Russa's third-base coach, making $35,000 the previous season. He came to me one day in the off-season and said, "Hawk, I know we didn't have a good year, but I really felt I did a good job. I wonder if I could get a raise. I…"

"Jimmy, you can talk to me all you want, but I already know what you are going to make next season," I said.

By his expression, I could tell that he was worried.

"I think you are the best third-base coach in the American League," I told him. "You are going to make $50,000 next season."

He looked at me, smiled, shook my hand, and walked out. He surely wasn't expecting that.

While I am on the subject, I will tell you that Leyland and Don Zimmer were the best third-base coaches I ever saw. You have to have guts and great instincts over there. But I always believed something that goes against common baseball wisdom: I always believed managers should put their best coaches at first base. A team will lose more games with a bad first-base coach than it will with a bad third-base coach.

Let me give you an example. That '83 White Sox team that lost to the Orioles in the ALCS beat more throws into second base by pure hustle and good baserunning instincts than any team I ever saw. Those are the plays that extend innings and get a team extra outs. If the runner on first gets a good jump on that play in the hole, he can make it to second safely.

That runner on first has to be told constantly—and I mean constantly—"Check your outfielders. Don't get doubled-up on a line drive. That guy in right field has a great arm…"

The runner at first should constantly be prepared for what is about to happen. There is just more action at first than at third base. In a lot of games during a 162-game season, the third-base coach gets little or no action. But there is never a game in which the first-base coach gets no action, unless the pitcher throws a perfect game.

Today, how many managers put their best coach at third base?

Every single one of them.

Within days of telling Leyland about his raise, Pittsburgh general manager Syd Thrift called me and inquired about hiring Jimmy to be the Pirates' manager. I gave him a glowing recommendation, and that was enough for Syd, who hired Jim to be his manager. What happened? Jim became the NL's Manager of the Year twice in his 10-year stay with the Pirates and he won a World Series in his first season with the Florida Marlins before leaving to build the Tigers into a powerhouse. He finished his career with 1,769 career wins.

I knew Drysdale would be perfect as our pitching coordinator. He would oversee the pitching coach and the entire staff during spring training and act as a consultant as the season progressed. Nobody I ever met knew more about pitching than Double-D.

Even though Don and I were like brothers and he was interested in the role, he told me up front that he wasn't going to do it for free.

After I talked to Jerry, I went to Don and said, "Twenty-five thousand."

"That's not near enough," Don replied.

Now remember, he would keep his primary job on the TV broadcast, which obviously paid him much, much more. He also had some endorsements. This additional role would supplement his income, but it also would take up a lot of his time. So I talked to Jerry some more about it and then I doubled the offer. Don accepted.

Jerry didn't particularly like that number, thinking it was too high. Remember, this was in the mid-1980s, before salaries of managers and coaches exploded along with the players' salaries.

I had other good ideas in addition to adding Drysdale. I hired my old teammate Moe Drabowsky to help coach the relief pitchers. I knew Moe could teach them toughness and how to pitch inside. He always had a terrific mind for the science of pitching.

Having two pitching coaches, one for starters and one for relievers, always made sense to me and I don't know why other teams weren't doing it. Now, every team in baseball does it.

I had the same philosophy about hitting coaches. I hired Willie Horton as a "power" hitting instructor. I always thought it made sense to have one guy coach the guys who hit for power and another to coach the guys who hit for average. After all, there are two different approaches. Now, every team does that, too.

I also wanted to infuse some toughness into the organization.

Drysdale was tough. So was Willie. I hired my former Red Sox teammate Rico Petrocelli, one of the toughest guys I ever played with, and Duke Sims to manage in the minors. I wanted the minor league teams in the organization to adopt the same attitude so those players would be ready to play White Sox baseball when they were promoted.

I thought if we won all the fights on the field, we would win more games, too. Those things galvanize clubs into pulling together and winning together.

But I also knew the roster needed improvement. Baseball's winter meetings were held in San Diego and I was warned by a few friends in the business to be careful—a few other clubs' general managers thought they could pick my pocket on players.

I knew better.

The first guy I tried to trade for was Buddy Bell, Texas' third baseman. He was a terrific player and we needed a guy with some pop in his bat, but the Rangers just wanted too much for him. Not many people realize that Buddy finished his career with more than 2,500 hits.

We did get Dave Schmidt from the Rangers to bolster the bullpen and we got pitcher Joe Cowley, who ended up winning 11 games that season, and catcher Ron Hassey from the Yankees for pitcher Britt Burns, who never pitched again because of a hip condition. I had told George Steinbrenner about Burns' hip but the Yankees wanted him anyway.

Among other moves, I selected Bobby Bonilla off the Pirates' AAA roster in the annual Rule 5 draft, which allows major league teams to draft other clubs' minor league players.

Syd Thrift loved Bobby, but for some reason he was left unprotected, and I thought he had the potential to be a superstar. Once the season started, however, Bonilla didn't get a lot of playing time. Rather than stick to my decision, I called Syd back and gave him the chance to get Bonilla back. The Pirates sent us right-hander Jose DeLeon in return. DeLeon was off to a 1–3 start in Pittsburgh, but I thought he had potential to be a solid starter.

Another trade I made soon after I got the job, because of Don's superior knowledge of pitching, involved getting infielder Wayne Tolleson from Texas. A right-hander we had at the time, Ed Correa, was only 19 years old and to outsiders he had a promising future. But Don had picked up on something.

"He is an accident waiting to happen," Don explained. "He will blow up."

By that he meant he would encounter an arm injury because of his throwing motion and mechanics. So what happened? Correa went to Texas and won 12 games in 1986, finishing with 189 strikeouts on the season. I was getting crucified by the Chicago media for getting rid of him.

The following season he blew up his right shoulder just as Don had predicted he would, and he never pitched again.

Not one Chicago writer wrote about that, of course, but they wouldn't have known the reasons I traded him in the first place. I couldn't very well come out and say that my pitching coordinator knew he would get hurt one day, could I?

The season didn't start as well as any of us had hoped. We were 7–18 and riding a six-game losing streak. I really believed it was the right time to make a managerial change and bring in Jim Fregosi, who always had impressed me when he managed the Angels from 1978 to 1981. Jim also was a master at handling a pitching staff.

Eddie Einhorn suggested I make a call to Billy Martin.

It was no secret in baseball circles that I always admired Billy and we got along very well through the years.

Strategy-wise, I thought nobody could top Billy as a manager when he was at the height of his career. He also was one tough competitor, and I considered myself cut from the same cloth. We both loved to win, hated to lose, and got ticked off when things didn't go our way.

And obviously, we both had terrible tempers.

Billy somehow made his work for him as a manager, even though it was largely the reason he managed for five different clubs in his career, including five famously separate stints with George Steinbrenner and the Yankees. When he wasn't fighting a player like Reggie Jackson or feuding with a general manager or club owner, he was kicking dirt on an umpire's shoes or berating the media or whatever bar patron crossed him at the time.

Billy was never afraid of anybody, and truthfully, neither was I.

Billy was calling Yankees games on television at the time. I wanted Fregosi, but I honored Eddie's request and called Billy to set up a meeting in my hotel suite in downtown Chicago.

Billy had told me that he tried to trade for me a few times during our careers, but it never worked out. In turn, I told him I would have loved to have played for him. He was my type of guy. I knew he certainly was a better manager than a broadcaster, and he knew that, too. He needed to be managing somewhere.

We shot a few games of pool in my hotel suite on Michigan Avenue that night and talked baseball.

Then I cut to the chase. I could tell that Billy wanted the job badly.

"Hawk, I will come here in a minute if you ask me," he said. "I love this town and would love to work for you. I want this ballclub."

The moment we finished talking, I opened the door to my suite to see a cameraman from the local NBC affiliate standing there, pointing his camera at us. Somebody had tipped him off.

Within hours, our meeting was all over the news in Chicago.

It didn't look good. I ate it with the media and never threw Eddie under the bus, because that was my job. The job of a GM is to take the heat. I also never told Jerry what Eddie had told me to do.

The media was killing me over the next few days, so I called Dallas Green, the general manager of the Cubs.

"Dallas, you owe me a dozen golf balls," I told him.

"Why's that?" he asked.

"Because your club is in last place, and I have taken all the media attention off of you," I told him. "I am the one catching all of the crap."

I held a press conference to try and quiet things down.

"I really believe if we wanted to make a change, Billy would be our manager," I said. "But we had two options when I met with Jerry and Eddie last night: do we keep Tony or not? I suggested we keep him. Billy will manage again. He's like a fish out of water when he's not managing."

The team's inconsistent play continued. The club got hot and won 10 of 12 games, so I thought maybe we were going in the right direction. Then we lost 18 of the next 27 games. At that point, we were 26–38, way back in the AL West standings, and there were no signs things would improve.

I finally told Jerry we had to make a change. He told me to do what I had to do.

After I let La Russa go, I didn't call Billy Martin, as the media had speculated I would. I named Doug Rader the interim manager and told him, "If I can't get Fregosi, you're the guy for the remainder of the season."

I then flew to Louisville to talk to Fregosi. I was very honest with Jim, telling him that if he took the job he'd be stepping into a very tough situation. He still wanted it, so I hired him on the spot.

Before the season had even begun, I had Plans A, B, and C in my head. Plan A was for Tony to succeed and take us to the postseason. Plan B, if the team got off to a slow start, was to hire Fregosi. Plan C was to turn to Billy if the first two didn't work out.

I also had to deal with Tom Seaver, who had come to my office several times requesting a trade to any team back east. He wanted to be closer to his home in Connecticut.

I had tried to trade him earlier in the season and quickly found out that nobody wanted Tom; at 41, he was way past his prime and still making a lot of money. Finally, I called Lou Gorman, the GM of the Red Sox, who I knew needed starting pitching. All Lou would give me for Seaver was jack-of-all-trades Steve Lyons, so I accepted the deal June 29 simply to make Tom happy. As a future Hall of Famer, I felt he deserved to be taken care of. When I told him about the trade to Boston, he was like a kid on Christmas morning.

I always believed I did some good things for the organization that went unnoticed, too, or were at least overshadowed by our struggles in the standings.

For instance, I moved the Appleton, Wisconsin, farm team to South Bend, Indiana, which is about 95 miles east of Chicago. That helped make South Bend a White Sox town. Years later, the guy who owned the club sold it to the Cubs and now it is strictly a Cubs town these days. You can't find a White Sox T-shirt or hat in any stores there.

Over the years, every time the subject of the 1986 season surfaced, I have been crucified in Chicago. It's as if I am the guy who traded Babe Ruth, or caused the Black Sox scandal, or lit the first match to ignite the Chicago Fire of 1871.

I used to joke that the title of my autobiography would be "You Gotta Lie," because everybody in baseball, and professional sports for that matter, lies. They lie to the media, to the players, to the owners, to the fans, and to each other. I never liked it, but I guess I did it, too.

I realize that I have been lampooned in Chicago, a city I have grown to love, for all of these years over what happened during the 1986 season.

I have lived with that fact because I had no other choice.

My tenure as director of operations/general manager ended on September 26, with the club 20 games below .500 and 22½ games out of first place.

I had come down to breakfast one morning earlier to see Krista sitting at the table with tears in her eyes.

"What's wrong, honey?" I asked her.

She didn't say anything. She just got up from the table and slowly walked upstairs to her room. I looked at the newspaper on the table in front of her chair. On the front of the sports page was a column which called me every name in the book for single-handedly wrecking the White Sox in only one season.

That was the final straw for me.

The job did what I feared it would do: it had affected my family.

I had no choice but to try and protect them again.

So, I resigned.

I believe I did a good job. I made some good trades, getting rid of some dead wood. I will go to my grave with my head held high.

No matter what has been said and written for all these years.

17 GEORGE, LOU, AND THE BIG APPLE

THERE'S A SAYING ABOUT NEW YORK THAT YOU EITHER LOVE it or hate it.

Being a product of the Deep South, a guy who came up to the big leagues in a Midwestern city like Kansas City, a former Red Sox player, and a guy who loved the nightlife, I always believed that New York wasn't meant for the Hawk.

To be honest, I believe one of the reasons I must have felt that way was that I just didn't understand New York. I didn't understand the traffic, how people could live in such congestion and what it took to be happy in such a large, complex city that never sleeps.

I never was one to get much sleep as a player there, because of the noise, the sirens, and the traffic all night long. And I also admit that I may have stayed out into the wee hours a time or two and then tried to play a baseball game the following day. If you don't have some self-discipline off the field as a big-league baseball player, that city could eat you alive.

Let's face it, there was and is only one New York.

But on top of that, I absolutely hated Yankee Stadium.

Don't get me wrong. I loved the tradition, the sacred monuments beyond center field, and the rich history of the place. I cried the first time I walked in there as a player on July 29, 1963.

My childhood idol, Mickey Mantle, was out of the lineup that day with a broken foot, but when I walked up to the plate for the first time, I wanted to call a timeout and call Mama to tell her about it. I singled to center field off Al Downing (you may remember him for giving up Hank Aaron's record-breaking 715th home run as a Dodger 11 years later) in the second inning of our 5–0 win that day. Yogi Berra wasn't behind the plate that day, but he pinch-hit later in the game. (It was my first season and his final season in the big leagues.)

Once I got over that awe factor, however, I realized the ballpark didn't suit me or my strengths as a hitter. It was way too big for a right-handed power hitter. I compared it to trying to hit a home run over the Grand Canyon. It was more than 430 feet to left-center and 461 to center.

Every time I stood at home plate, I felt like I needed binoculars to see the outfielders. I gained so much respect for Joe DiMaggio. How in the world did Mister Coffee ever hit 46 home runs in one season while playing half of his games there? He must have been something special. I know many right-handed hitters in my era agreed with me when I considered his 1937 season to be the *real* single-season home run record, rather than Roger Maris' 61 or Babe Ruth's 60.

Red Sox legend Bobby Doerr once told me that every time they played a series at Yankee Stadium, Joe hit three or four long flies that were caught in front of the fence. They would have been home runs in any other ballpark.

There had been so much speculation all those years earlier of the Yankees and Red Sox trading their superstars, so Ted Williams could take advantage of Yankee Stadium's short right-field porch, while Joe could take advantage of the Green Monster.

I once wanted to separate the myth from the legend myself.

When we played golf together years later, I once asked Joe how many home runs he could've hit if he'd played in Boston.

His answer? About 70.

I believed him.

During my career, I hit about five or six just short of the fence at Yankee Stadium that would have been home runs anywhere else. One time, I hit a bomb when Mickey was playing center field. He went back, turned around in front of the 461 sign, pounded his glove a few times, and stood there waiting on it. I had gotten all of it and yet it was nothing but a long out.

Fast forward about 20 years.

Things in New York had changed after I retired from baseball. The monuments were still there. The tradition was richer than ever. The pinstripes still meant something special. They had added two more World Series flags, from the 1977 and 1978 seasons. The fences now were much shorter.

And there was a new boss in town.

I always said there should be a bust of George Steinbrenner in Cooperstown, simply because he turned the Yankees into the monster they became after he bought them in 1973. A season earlier, they didn't even draw 1 million fans, but George made it an event to go to Yankee Stadium again. He made you a celebrity if you visited his suite at the ballpark. He paid millions for the biggest-name free agents.

He deserved credit for making the Yankees not only relevant and competitive again, but turning them into the top sports franchise in the entire world.

One day soon after I resigned from the White Sox, Steinbrenner called me at my home in Lisle and said he wanted me to work for him.

Steinbrenner wanted me to work *for* him? I was somewhat flabbergasted, because just a little more than a year earlier I had told him off in no uncertain terms.

Just weeks after I was named the White Sox general manager, I was with Jerry Reinsdorf in St. Louis for the 1985 World Series between the Cardinals and Royals. Most teams' baseball executives attend the World Series each year for meetings where trade ideas are bounced around.

We sat with George one night and talked baseball. He and Jerry had been very close through the years. In fact, George called the White Sox offices almost daily to talk to Jerry about one thing or another. Jerry was the only other baseball owner I knew who could reason with him and keep him in line if needed. If I wanted to know where Steinbrenner was or what kind of mood he was in, I didn't call the Yankees—I called Sheri Berto, Jerry's executive assistant.

But as the general manager, I wasn't going to let him push me around and I let him know it in no uncertain terms. Maybe he respected me because of that, perhaps because he knew he couldn't bully me like he bullied everybody else. My mother always told me to stand up to a bully and I always regarded George as baseball's No. 1 bully. I realized that everybody who worked for him over the years had been forced to kowtow to him, for fear of losing their jobs. And if you lived in New York and wanted a job in baseball, who wouldn't want to work for the Yankees?

Now here we were, not a year after I'd yelled at him, and George was offering me a job.

George explained to me that there would be an opening calling Yankees games on SportsChannel TV in New York for the 1987 season. The job was mine if I wanted it. I would be paired with Spencer Ross and Mickey Mantle in a three-man booth.

I was excited by the thought of working with Mickey, since he knew the game as well as anybody and was so much fun to be around. I had long forgiven him for stiffing me on that autograph request when I was a kid.

"Well, George," I said, "I certainly won't come to New York to work *for* you, but I will come and work *with* you."

He laughed and then said, "Okay, Hawk, come work *with* me and the Yankees."

Once the season began, it didn't take too long to learn to love the city I once detested. After a few months, I finally understood it. And once you understand New York, you learn to love it. I suddenly appreciated the beauty of it all. The place can be electric and alive, unlike any city on earth.

Aris and the kids stayed at our house in Lisle, so I commuted back and forth and stayed in a hotel in Fort Lee, New Jersey, where some Yankees players stayed, just across the George Washington Bridge.

Lou Piniella was entering his second season as Yankees manager when I arrived and I absolutely loved him. Anybody who knows Lou loves the guy. Woody Woodward was the general manager. He was a nice guy, but I could tell within a week or two that he couldn't control George a lick.

George had always loved Piniella the player, but he never loved anyone when they managed for him. Not Yogi, not Billy Martin on five separate occasions, and not even Lou. There was something about that position that made George unreasonable. He defended most of his players and usually treated most of his general managers decently, but whoever managed the Yankees at the time usually had a bulls-eye on his back.

I got to see firsthand that George was a genuine bully and could be a real tyrant. Other times, when he entertained guests in his suite at the stadium, he could be the most generous and charming host you ever saw.

That spring, Lou had briefed me on the frequent late-night phone calls from George, who seemed to lecture Lou constantly, all the while saying, "I am trying to make you a good manager, I am trying to make you a good manager."

Lou and I frequently hung out together off the field. He was one of the funniest and nicest guys I have ever known from all my years in baseball. I loved talking to him.

During one of the early games, I noticed that Lou looked up at George's suite at the stadium when he reached the mound to consider a pitching change. I also noticed George staring back at him while making a "thumbs-up" or "thumbs-down" motion.

Lou and I happened to be having dinner that night at Christine Lee's Restaurant in Fort Lauderdale.

"I was watching Steinbrenner today during the game," I said. "What was he doing?"

"Well, George was just trying to make me a good manager again," he said, laughing.

"What do you mean?" I asked.

"Well, when I go out to the mound, if he wants me to leave the pitcher in, he gives me the 'thumbs-up,'" he explained. "And if he wants me to take him out, he gives me the 'thumbs-down.' So if you watch George when I head out there, you will be able to see what he wants me to do."

I just couldn't believe that a club owner would get that involved in the decisions a manager made every day on the field. Lou seemed to take it all in stride, knowing it was just how Steinbrenner operated. Lou loved New York and loved managing the Yankees, so he put up with George's meddling most of the time. And at other times, he played George like a fiddle.

The season started and Lou didn't have much of a pitching staff to work with. One day, he walked out to the mound at Yankee Stadium and I saw him position himself so he could easily look up at George's box without the fans noticing. I looked over at George and he had a thumb up and then he put it back down. He did it again, back and forth.

I couldn't wait to get down to Lou's office after the game to see what that signal meant.

"I had to ask him that myself," Lou said. "You know what he told me? He said, 'Well, when I do that, you have to make the decision on your own, but you had better be sure to get it right!'"

I almost fell down laughing. Only Steinbrenner would say something so ridiculous.

It seemed Lou and I spent half of our time together swapping stories about George. We were like two old housewives gossiping about the crazy neighbor, except this crazy neighbor was the boss.

One night after a tough loss in Baltimore, I went to Lou's hotel suite to play cards. We were playing Stan Williams, the pitching coach, and Gene "Stick" Michael, the third-base coach, in a few games of gin. When the phone rang in the middle of a hand, Lou picked it up and immediately I could hear Steinbrenner ranting and raving on the other end. This went on for a minute or two, so Lou gently laid the phone down on the table and made a motion for Stan to deal the next hand. We quietly shuffled the cards and dealt them by gently laying them on the table, so George couldn't hear what we were doing. We must have played three or four hands in silence as Steinbrenner continued ranting over the phone.

Finally, there was a pause, so Lou grabbed the phone off the table and said, "Alright, Mister Steinbrenner, I appreciate it, I will talk to you tomorrow."

He hung up and the four of us almost fell off our chairs laughing.

Lou didn't have a great ballclub to work with that season, other than Don Mattingly's everyday stardom. He put on a show that season, hitting .327 with 30 home runs and 115 RBIs. He broke Ernie Banks' and Jim Gentile's single-season record by hitting six grand slams. He set another record with a homer in eight consecutive games in July. But what made him great in my eyes was how he flashed the leather every day at first base. He was a magician with the glove.

The Yankees also had Rickey Henderson, who was the greatest offensive player I ever saw. I played with Yaz and against Mickey, Maris, Musial, and Kaline. The reason I make that claim about Ricky is how he impacted a game. He drove pitchers—especially young pitchers—crazy once he got on first, and he hit for average and for power in the leadoff position.

But those two guys and Dave Winfield weren't enough to overcome spotty pitching. The Yankees finished 89–73, nine games behind the first-place Tigers. That was enough for George to want a change, so he made Lou the general manager and rehired my buddy Billy Martin—for the fifth time.

I loved both Lou and Billy, so I had mixed feelings about George's latest move.

This was less than two years after Billy and I had met in downtown Chicago to discuss the White Sox job. I always considered him a friend and we had played golf together often over the years.

Let's just say Billy didn't always take the game of golf as seriously as I did.

We were preparing to tee off one day at Ocean Reef Golf Club in an event sponsored by Allied Chemical, which paid us to play with their best customers, when someone asked, "Billy, what do you think you will shoot today?"

"Seventy-seven!" he said. "I got the scorecard already filled out!"

That was typical Billy.

Billy's group went off first that day and I teed off in the following group. I had never played the course before and I didn't have a clue about the greens or the pin locations. As I stood in the first fairway, eyeing my second shot, I told my playing partners, "Man, that pin is way, way back there."

I hit a great shot and the ball headed directly at the pin. All of a sudden, I saw sand spray everywhere. We drove our cart up to the green and I saw the problem: some jokester had stuck the pin in the bunker behind the green. It didn't take a genius to figure out who the culprit was.

Later, we approached a dogleg-left that had a high, elevated green. The pin looked like it was touching the sky. I hit a perfect shot again, headed right at the pin. Then I heard the clunk of my golf ball hitting an oak tree. This time, Billy had stuck the pin on the branch of the tree.

He was such a character, and now he was the Yankees skipper for the fifth time in his career. The changes were not limited to the field, either. Bobby Murcer replaced Spencer Ross in the booth, joining Mickey and me.

The Yankees started 9–1 that next April and it appeared George's managerial move was a stroke of genius. But I had noticed a real change in Billy by this time. He was doing some crazy things off the field, crazy even for him, and his bad habits finally caught up with him one night in Texas.

It was about 2:00 AM on May 7 when everyone at the Arlington Hilton was awakened by the fire alarm. I had no idea if it was a real fire or not, so I trudged out into the parking lot, half asleep, where about 100 people stood around in their pajamas. I saw Bobby and we started talking to a few other people when a limo pulled up. Mickey got out first. Then I saw Billy get out. I could tell immediately that Billy's face was messed up. I was about 50 feet away and it was dark, but Billy's mug was a bloody mess.

About a minute later, a second limo pulled up and Steinbrenner got out of it. George had been on the road trip with the Yankees.

It turned out that Billy had been in another bar brawl and obviously had received the worst of it. He told the police and Steinbrenner that two guys jumped him in the bathroom and beat him up for no apparent reason. Billy had been thrown out of the game, a 7–6 loss to the Rangers, earlier that night for kicking dirt on an umpire.

I walked into Billy's office the following night before the game, after he had met with the media wearing a big pair of sunglasses. I closed the door behind me. Billy saw me and took off his sunglasses. I couldn't believe how bad his face looked. The left side was a purple mass and there were stitches behind his ear. I wouldn't have known it was him if it weren't for Billy's distinctive nose.

"Those guys almost killed me, Hawk," he said. "I guess I can't go anywhere anymore."

Later, Mickey told me the truth: Billy had started the whole thing at a club and a bartender kicked his butt out in the parking lot. He kicked Billy in the side of the head with one of those pointed cowboy boots commonly worn in Texas. If that boot had landed about two inches higher on his temple, the blow might have killed him. There were no "guys" and it didn't happen in the bathroom, as he had claimed to the police.

I don't know why Mickey didn't jump in to help Billy and I never asked. Maybe he was inside the club when it happened and had no idea where Billy was.

I saw Mickey get into only one fight the entire time I knew him. We were at Jack Haley's Apartment Lounge in Kansas City one night after the Yankees had beaten the Athletics pretty good when I was a player. I saw Mickey talking to some big guy who played basketball at Kansas, then they walked outside. I heard a bunch of yelling back and forth, so I got up from my bar stool and headed out after them.

The guy, who was still holding his beer can, said something Mickey didn't like and Mickey hauled off and landed a huge punch. The big guy went down as his beer can flew clear across the street. That guy came into the Apartment Lounge the next night, sporting an eye as black as coal, but I never asked either of them what their fight was about.

Anyway, despite Billy's shenanigans, the Yankees held first place through June 19 and then things started to go bad. They were swept at Detroit and lost seven of eight games. They still were 12 games above .500 at 40–28 but were clearly headed in the wrong direction.

That day, George decided to fire Billy—for the fifth time overall and for the second time in three seasons—and bring Lou back down from the front office to replace him. It was the typical musical chairs that George orchestrated, replacing a familiar face with another familiar face. It still had to be one of the rare times in baseball history a manager was fired when his team was 12 games above .500.

Nothing surprised me with George. All a manager had to do was lose three in a row or six out of seven and it would get him fired. He had owned the club for 15 years and had changed managers 15 times—he was batting 1.000.

The Yankee players were stunned.

"I have pretty much learned to expect the unexpected here," Mattingly was quoted as saying. "But I do feel bad for Billy."

By late August, the Yankees had lost 10 of 15 games as we headed to Seattle. George had been criticizing Lou in the newspapers. On the final night of a three-game series at the Kingdome, I just ripped Steinbrenner a new one. I really let him have it on the broadcast, stating he was the culprit for the Yankees' tailspin, not Lou.

The more I talked the hotter I got, and before I knew it I had rambled on and on, ripping into the boss.

"The best thing Steinbrenner can do is back up a truck to Yankee Stadium and get some of these big-priced free-agents he had signed out of here!" I said. "Lou can only manage what he's been given."

The next day was an off day as the Yankees headed back to New York. I called Aris and told her I'd probably be coming home. I was sure I was going to be fired. He had fired dozens of people for lesser offenses, but he was at his home in Ocala, Florida, so I felt safe heading to the Yankees' office to get my mail that day.

As I got into the elevator, Mickey walked in. He was there to get his mail, too.

Just as the elevator doors were about to close, a hand reached in to keep them open.

It was George. He had just flown up from Ocala.

He got onto the elevator, turned his back to me, folded his arms across his chest, and faced Mickey.

"Hawk, I heard what you said about me," George said, even though he was looking at Mickey. "Well, you might be *right*."

The elevator doors opened and George headed to his office. That's all he said and he never once looked at me.

Nothing ever bothered Mickey much. He couldn't have cared less if Steinbrenner ever got mad at him. After all, he was *Mickey Mantle*. What could George do to him?

I could go on all day about my admiration for Mickey. For starters, as Billy once told me years earlier, he was one of the smartest men to ever play the game. Secondly, he could tell a story like nobody else in the game, and I could have listened to him talk about the old days forever. He had a naturally comedic way about him. He probably could recite the Declaration of Independence and have me laughing.

One time he confided in me.

"Hawk, you know what the biggest mistake I ever made was?" he asked. "I named my son Mickey Mantle Jr. But how in the heck did I know I would grow up to be 'Mickey Mantle'?"

Baseball researchers would have to go a long way to find three more colorful broadcasters in one booth at any time in the game's history. In between innings, Mickey and Bobby would do or say something to get all three of us laughing so hard that we had trouble composing ourselves before we came back on the air.

Mickey told so many funny stories I couldn't possibly remember them all, but one of the better ones involved Joe Pepitone.

As I have said, players often did favors for the superstars of the sport, when it came to a milestone or a record. When Mickey's next home run would be his 535th, passing Jimmie Fox on the all-time list, the Yankees happened to be in Detroit facing Denny McLain during McLain's 31-win season in late September of 1968.

The Tigers were ahead 6–1 that day and had already clinched the AL pennant, so McLain looked in at Mickey and asked, "Where do you want it?"

Mickey held out his hand across the plate to give McLain a spot to hit. He threw it right there, and Mickey fouled it back. He threw it there a second time, and Mickey fouled it back again. He threw it there a third time and Mickey connected. The ball rocketed out to right field, tearing a seat out of the upper deck at Tiger Stadium. He passed Fox with that shot. He tipped his hat to McLain as he rounded first and McLain stood on the mound applauding.

It reminded me of the one time I tanked at the plate on purpose. I was in winter ball in Venezuela and Daryl Knowles, who was in the Orioles system at the time, was on the mound. He had good stuff and a real funky motion and I always had trouble with him. In Venezuela, players earned bonuses for records and milestones.

The catcher looked up at me and said, "Hawk, Daryl needs one more strikeout to break the league record."

So, I took three straight strikes and Daryl got his bonus. That's just the way the game was played back then. We looked out for each other, at least the guys we liked, when nothing was on the line.

Back to Mickey's story: Pepitone followed him to the plate that day in Detroit. Peppy was a great guy, whom everybody loved, but he wore this really bad hairpiece that looked like a divot left over from your best swing with a 9-iron.

Peppy looked out at McLain and demanded, "I want one right here, too."

McLain threw one right at Peppy's ear, and as he fell to the ground, his hairpiece just hovered in the air above him. Mickey claimed McLain's pitch split the distance between Peppy's head and his rug.

Mickey's many stories kept me laughing that entire season and helped me deal with what a zoo George had created. Sparky Lyle coined the term with his book, *The Bronx Zoo*, and it couldn't have been better titled.

The offices had such a different atmosphere when George was in town. It was tense, extremely quiet, and everybody walked on eggshells. When he was in Florida or somewhere else, the Yankee employees smiled a lot and there were plenty of pleasant conversations.

George enforced plenty of stupid rules, too. For example, if he walked by an employee's office and the lights were on, and that employee was not in that office, he or she would be fired immediately. Working there was really something you had to see to believe. There is no way to accurately describe his craziness.

George never admitted this, but he was aware of everything that was ever written or said about him publicly. When you work for guys like him, you either take it or you don't. Most people took it because they wanted to work for the Yankees.

Still, he usually treated me with respect. He loved Bobby and he loved Mickey, too. It always ticked us off the way he treated other people, but there was nobody he would not berate once in a while, even those two guys. If you stood up to George and he respected you, sometimes he backed down, but he always had a caveat.

For example, he wanted to trade Bernie Williams early in his career in the 1990s, but Gene "Stick" Michael, the general manager, told George, "You can trade him, but you have to fire me first."

"Okay, Stick, but you had better be right on this one, or you will be gone," George told him.

Stick was right as rain. Bernie became a five-time All-Star, collecting over 2,300 hits, in 16 years with the Yankees. Stick was one of the few general managers who ever stood up to George regularly, other than Brian Cashman, who came along much later.

The play on the field during the 1988 season was marred by the league presidents' directive to the umpires to strictly enforce the balk rule that was on the books but rarely enforced. It seemed they were calling two or three balks every night, stopping the flow of the game. The pitchers had no idea what was a balk and what wasn't. I reached a boiling point one night on the air and I ripped AL president Bobby Brown and NL president Bart Giamatti to shreds.

Afterward, I felt bad and wanted to apologize. I called Giamatti and we had a great conversation.

The Yankees concluded the season with an 85–76 record, finishing only 3½ games behind Boston—even though they finished fifth. In one of the American League's greatest pennant races, the Red Sox, Yankees, Tigers, Brewers, and Toronto Blue Jays all finished within 3½ games of each other.

George naturally fired Lou again, for the second time in less than one calendar year, and replaced him with Dallas Green, who had been fired by the Cubs.

On October 2, the final day of the season, after a 4–3 loss at Detroit, I did the best thing I ever did in New York: I puffed on my final cigarette.

I had smoked anywhere from three to five packs a day for the previous 30 years, since Lew Krausse Jr. taught me how to smoke underneath those grandstands at Elmira. In fact, sometimes during that turbulent 1986 season, I had two or three cigarettes going at once, each resting in separate ashtrays. I was down to a pack a game working for the Yankees, but I knew I needed to quit altogether.

I had just turned 47 years old and I finally realized it was a terrible habit, dangerous to my health and to my future.

My sister was a heavy smoker who had died of lung cancer when she was only 40. I was so proud of what Iris had done with her life after such a tough start, having to get married at the age of 14. She wrote a few books and became a gourmet cook. She also learned to speak fluent German, Russian, and Spanish. She lectured at Duke University and at the University of Toronto. She became an accomplished pianist. She also dabbled in acting and landed a few roles on stage in New York. And she was an interior designer, having turned my penthouse pad in Cleveland into a beautiful home.

But we had a falling out several years before she died when I turned down her request to borrow $250,000. She had wanted to open a nightclub in downtown Savannah and I didn't have that much cash at the time. Plus, I didn't think her business idea was a good one. When I refused her request, she walked out the door and I never saw her again.

Apparently, she never stopped smoking.

I had promised my kids I would quit once the 1988 season had ended. I knew I could do it, because throughout my life, I always could give up something if I put my mind to it. Being in military school for three years taught me that. I had given up gin because it made me angry. Now, I had to give up smoking or I was a sure bet to someday have lung cancer.

I got through breakfast that Monday without a cigarette, and it was very painful. Then I got through lunch. The pain grew worse. I got through Tuesday and the pain lessened a bit. On Wednesday, I had made it three days without one and I was home free. It was all a mind-set.

And I haven't smoked since.

It was soon announced that the Madison Square Garden Network bought the rights to broadcast Yankees games, replacing SportsChannel for the 1989 season and beyond. Naturally, their executives wanted to hire their own announcers. They hired Bobby, Tommy Hutton, and Lou for the booth.

I was suddenly unemployed for the second time in three years.

I took a few calls from teams looking to fill GM jobs, but I didn't really listen—I had already determined that had to be the worst position in baseball.

Then I formed a new plan.

I had been in professional baseball every year since 1959, not counting those three seasons trying to make it in golf. I just wanted to go to our winter home in Orlando and do nothing but play golf and relax for at least a year. I never really had spent a year not working before, but I wanted to try it.

There would be no pressure on the golf course, not like when I had to make a living at it. There would be no maniacal club owner critiquing my every word from the broadcast booth. There would be no umpires turning games into four-hour marathons. I wouldn't be traveling around the country with a ballclub, checking in and out of hotels and eating room service every night.

I couldn't wait.

Anyway, I left New York with a different feeling than when I had arrived two years earlier.

I certainly didn't understand George Steinbrenner any better than before, but I finally had fallen in love with his city.

18 BACK HOME AGAIN

I WAS DRIVING FROM MIAMI TO MY ORLANDO HOME ONE DAY after playing in Dan Marino's celebrity golf tournament in January of 1990, when my car phone rang.

It was Jim Corno, the president of SportsChannel Chicago.

"Jerry and Eddie want you back in Chicago. Would you want to come back and call White Sox games again?" he asked.

It caught me by surprise. I had fielded some broadcasting offers, but none with teams I wanted to work for, and I had been enjoying my time relaxing and playing golf.

But I did miss baseball.

So we started talking numbers within a minute or two. Jim said he might be able to offer as much as $180,000 a year, and more down the road. Five years earlier, I had been making more than $400,000 with the same job, including my endorsements. Then I had taken a pay cut to become the general manager. Then I had spent two years calling Yankees games.

Now, if I accepted this job to return to Chicago, I would have to take a further pay cut.

But it wasn't a pay cut from being unemployed, so I took Jim's offer.

Gary Thorne had called play-by-play the previous season, with Tom Paciorek doing color. Thorne had moved on to ESPN, opening a spot, so I would be paired with Paciorek in the booth. My buddy Don Drysdale had left Chicago two years earlier to work with the great Vin Scully in the Dodgers' broadcast booth.

I am sure some fans in Chicago figured it was strange that I was coming back after having called White Sox games for four seasons and then spending only one year as the club's general manager.

But I had no reservations about it because of my relationship with Jerry Reinsdorf. We had parted on great terms and remained very good friends. I also loved Corno and I trusted the people I would be working for.

Once I returned, I admit it was tough for a while. Because of the way I had left, and because of the Tony La Russa firing, the media constantly peppered me with questions about the past.

I just handled it all by lying to them, telling them there were no hard feelings and all that hogwash. I did my best to be diplomatic and graceful.

Broadcasting White Sox games again wasn't the only thing I had keeping me busy.

I may have originally planned to spend a year playing golf and relaxing at our new Orlando home, but a conversation I had with Jerry the previous year kept creeping back into my head.

Jerry was the head of Major League Baseball's expansion committee at the time, and he knew the game would be expanding into new markets soon. He suggested I think about getting a group together to try and bring a team to Orlando.

The more I thought of it, the more I liked the idea.

In terms of population, Florida was the largest state without a baseball team. With its growth expectancy, I believed Florida could host more than just the spring training sites. It had been one of the fastest-growing states throughout the 1970s and '80s and it was showing no signs of slowing down.

A few years earlier, we had purchased a new home in the Bay Hill Country Club development, where we had visited friends over the years during the winters. Arnold Palmer had redesigned Bay Hill and lived there himself.

Orlando, the state's second-largest city behind Miami, already had the NBA's Magic and would be the perfect place for an expansion franchise, I figured.

I went to work and it didn't take long before I had a good group of guys involved. The money man behind the effort was Abe Gosman of Boston. Abe had made millions in the health care business. I also met with Buell Duncan, the CEO of Sun Bank, and he also loved the idea.

I called Drysdale to see if he would become our general manager if we got the club. Don loved the idea. The man I hired to work on the project for me, Thom Rumberger, was a prominent attorney who lived in Winter Park.

We were competing against Bill duPont, the owner of the Magic, for the rights to the Orlando franchise. Bill had already put together a group, but his group didn't include anyone connected to the game.

One day, Thom and I went to meet duPont, to see if we could combine our efforts. Pat Williams, the general manager of the Magic and a man who couldn't have been nicer during the entire process, was very much involved. I really liked Pat. He was a great guy, a very unusual guy, and I say that in the most respectful and complimentary way.

As for duPont, I thought the guy was an absolute jerk.

Finally, after going back and forth on our plans, he said, "We will let you buy into our organization for 5 percent."

I looked at Thom and shook my head. duPont was going out of his way to insult me.

"Bill, you are going to mess this whole thing up for the city of Orlando," I said. "You will not get this team without baseball people involved. You will not get this ballclub unless I am involved."

By the summer of 1990, there were 16 cities in the running. Six months later, by December, that list was cut to six cities: Orlando, Denver, Washington, D.C., Miami, Buffalo, and St. Petersburg. The price tag for a new team would be around $95 million.

Drysdale was our point person, meeting with the expansion committee in New York.

One thing was working against us, however. Carl Barger, the president of the Pittsburgh Pirates, also was on the expansion committee. He wanted a franchise in Miami, because he was close friends with H. Wayne Huizenga, who had made a fortune with his Blockbuster Entertainment and already owned part of the NFL's Dolphins. He had promised the members of the baseball expansion committee that he would build a dome and would not share a stadium with the Dolphins if he got the rights to the Miami club.

In early June of 1991, baseball owners voted for Miami and Denver to be awarded franchises, both of which would be placed in the National League.

It was a huge disappointment, but I hadn't given up yet.

Even with a new team in Miami, I figured we still had a shot for a second Florida franchise since baseball had not finished expanding. We had targeted an area of land near Lake Nona, away from the Interstate-4 corridor that was very congested even then, to build a domed stadium.

Gosman dropped out of our group so we brought in Tom Hammons, a businessman from Sarasota who owned a ton of Burger Kings across the South.

We also had met with Dick Nunis, an executive vice-president at Disney, hoping for his support. However, he wanted no part of it. He figured having Major League Baseball nearby would take business away from his Disney properties. I thought baseball would have enhanced it, as the two would have complemented each other.

At this point, I had spent a ton of my own money, somewhere near $700,000, most of it for attorney's fees to try and pull this off for the city of Orlando. But when I learned Orlando would not receive one of the expansion teams, we shifted our focus to the St. Petersburg area.

A dome in St. Petersburg had already been built. We were one of three groups trying to place a team there. The team eventually went to a group headed by Vince Naimoli. They named them the Devil Rays.

Orlando still does not have a Major League Baseball team, and I blame duPont for that. He is the sole reason baseball did not come to Orlando when the opportunity was there. Huizenga's Marlins won the 1997 World Series and then he dismantled the club with that disgusting fire sale of talent. And he never built a dome as he had promised. The latest owners of the Marlins used taxpayer dollars to get one built in downtown Miami on the old Orange Bowl site in 2012.

Nevertheless, it was one of the most disappointing failures of my life. It really set me back. I had put a lot of time and effort into it. It ranked right up there with my failure to make it in pro golf.

"We had a real good group," I told the media when baseball announced its expansion plans that day. "We met all the criteria that they had laid down. We just didn't get it. But I will be back with the White Sox next year. That's a better alternative than maybe some of the other guys have."

I had no choice but to put the whole expansion franchise effort behind me and focus on my broadcasting career.

In addition to working with Paciorek, USA Network hired me for its Monday night national broadcasts. My first two color guys were Bert Blyleven and Bucky Dent. Some people never realized how great a pitcher Bert, or "The Dutchman" as most people called him, really was. He won 287 games, pitched a remarkable 242 complete games, and deservedly entered the Hall of Fame in 2011.

Bert called Minnesota's games regularly, and one story illustrates how many young players never bother to check baseball history.

One night, Twins starter Johan Santana asked manager Tom Kelly to take him out in the ninth inning even though he had a shutout going.

Bert walked up to Santana after the game and asked him why he didn't go for the shutout.

"Man, shutouts are hard to come by," Santana said. "Did you ever pitch a shutout in your career?"

"Only 60!" Bert shot back.

The first time Bert ever stepped into the booth with me after retiring from pitching will forever be etched in my mind. Before the game at Anaheim, he just wouldn't shut up. He was a chatterbox, bouncing from one subject to another. He always was a funny guy with a great personality.

I was handling play-by-play and I heard the director's countdown in my headset. When we went live, I said, "Coming to you from the Big A in Anaheim, I am Ken Harrelson along with my broadcast partner, Bert Blyleven. Bert, this is a really good pitching matchup tonight. How do you see it?"

Bert didn't say a word. He just continued looking at me. He just couldn't get one word out. Finally, eight or nine seconds later, an eternity on a live broadcast, he uttered something.

It was funny, only because he wouldn't shut up before we went on the air.

By my second stint broadcasting White Sox games, I had my own style. It was no secret to anyone listening that I openly hoped the team was successful, just as I had with the Red Sox from 1975 to 1981 and for the Yankees for those two seasons I worked there.

I make no apologies for it. If I worked for a club, got to know the players, owner, managers, and coaches, then it was natural for me to pull for them, everything else being equal.

Who doesn't want to watch, write about, play for, or broadcast for a winner rather than a loser?

That was the competitor in me, I guess. And being a former player, I could relate to the current players. White Sox stars such as Paul Konerko and Frank Thomas came to me at times, wanting to know what I noticed, if they happened to be in a funk at the time.

One time I went to Konerko's locker to cheer him up when he was struggling.

"It's obvious to me that you are thinking behind the ball," I told him. "It's your mechanics. Your thought process needs to be out front, in front of the plate, in front of the baseball. You know what I mean?"

The next night, he hit a home run and had a couple of RBIs and was quoted in the newspaper saying, "Hawk Harrelson really helped me with my approach."

Well, Ron Schueler, the White Sox general manager, read it and had a hissy fit. He told all of the coaches, "I don't want anybody on this team talking to Hawk Harrelson about hitting. It's your job, not his."

I always thought that was pure stupidity. If a hitter can benefit from some advice, who cares where it comes from? Schueler and I never got along after that. We almost got into a fight at a bar one night in Toronto when he shot off his mouth to me, but thankfully, Drysdale pulled me away before I could get to him.

I liked helping guys if I could and I didn't see anything wrong with it. One time during my two years in New York, relief pitcher Dave Righetti was really struggling. I wasn't an expert on pitching mechanics by any means, but I knew a guy who was.

So I called Drysdale.

"I am sending you some video of 'Rags,'" I told him. "Let me know what you see."

Sure enough, Don picked out a flaw in his motion and relayed it to me. I told Rags what Don had said, and he promptly reeled off 14 consecutive saves.

My advice was not limited just to baseball, either.

Frank Thomas was always very reserved in front of the media, but among his teammates in the clubhouse, he opened up and displayed a great personality.

"Frank, just be yourself when they put those microphones in front of you," I told him. "You change when the media comes around, but people need to see your personality because you've got a great one."

One year when the AL All-Star rosters were announced, reporters gathered around Frank to get his feelings about being on the team. I was nearby and heard the entire exchange.

"Frank, how's it feel to be an All-Star?" someone asked.

"It feels great. It's a big honor," he said. He went on to detail what it meant to him and how he looked forward to the All-Star Game. He added, "We are neck and neck with the Indians for first place. There's also a part of me that wouldn't mind the three days of rest to get ready for the second half of the season."

The story in the *Chicago Tribune* the next day said Frank didn't want to play in the All-Star Game. I couldn't believe it. I had stood there and heard the entire exchange and that is not at all what Frank had said.

I already had described George Steinbrenner's moods and how, before I ever worked for the Yankees, I got a read on him when I was a general manager of the White Sox, thanks to Jerry's assistant, Sheri Berto, who started to work for him around 1971.

Jerry thought the world of her, as did anybody who ever worked in the Bulls or White Sox organizations. I loved her. She had such a great personality and always was on top of things.

In November of 1991, she required surgery to have a benign tumor removed from her uterus. It was supposed to be a simple procedure, but the doctors accidently cut a vein and she bled to death overnight. She left behind a husband and a three-year-old daughter.

All of us were heartbroken, but none more than Jerry. He was absolutely crushed. Sheri was not just an employee, she was like a family member to him.

Sheri's husband filed a malpractice lawsuit, in which I and many White Sox and Bulls employees had to testify. The defense claimed that she "was only a secretary," a strategy to limit the damages. Believe me, she was so much more than a secretary. Jerry had confided in me before her surgery that he was about to make her a partner.

When my day came, I walked up to the witness stand, the only time I ever had to do something like that. I think it was the most nervous I had been in my entire life.

The lawyer, a big, good-looking guy wearing an expensive suit, grilled me for about 20 minutes. He threw question after question at me, while I continued to state the many reasons why Sheri was more than just a secretary. I explained how she had to deal with Steinbrenner on a daily basis, among other things. She handled duties more suitable to a vice-president of a large company.

After I answered his last question, he walked by me and said, "And you can put that on the board!"

He had brought my home run call to the courtroom!

Fortunately, Sheri's husband won the case and her family was awarded more than $17 million, one of the largest malpractice awards in Illinois history. When the Bulls' new practice facility was completed, Jerry named it the Sheri Berto Center to honor her memory.

Heartbreak hit me again two years later.

On July 3, 1993, I was calling the White Sox–Orioles game in Chicago when Jack Gould, one of the team's minority owners, walked into the booth and whispered those horrible words: "They found Don in his hotel room tonight in Montreal. He's dead."

I was stunned. I couldn't get a word out and I started to cry. I thought about Annie and the kids, who would never grow up to know their father as I knew him. I immediately thought back to something he always told me when he had been drinking: "When I die, I hope it's not in a hotel room."

If he said it once, he had said it dozens of times. That was his greatest fear, and tragically, it came true.

Don had never shown up at the stadium that night in Montreal for the Dodgers-Expos game. They sent somebody to the hotel and found him lying on the floor. He died of a heart attack. I later learned he had struggled with angina for years, but he never once told me of his condition.

I waited a few moments to compose myself and then I told our audience.

"In 19 years of broadcasting…this is the toughest thing I ever had to say. ESPN Radio is reporting that Don Drysdale is dead…at the age of 56," I stammered.

About the same time, some 850 miles away in Montreal, his partner, Vin Scully, said, "I have had to make a lot of announcements. Never have I been asked to make an announcement that hurts me as much as this one. And I say it to you as best I can with a broken heart. Don Drysdale, who had a history of heart trouble, was found dead in his hotel room tonight."

When the Dodgers went through Don's possessions at the hotel, they came across a tape of Robert Kennedy's final words from June 4, 1968, immediately before he was assassinated; he had wished Don good luck as he attempted to pitch his sixth consecutive shutout that night against the Pirates.

Annie called me a day or two later, requesting I give the eulogy.

"Annie, I just can't," I told her. "I would never get through it."

I swore since Mama's funeral that I wouldn't attend another one and I haven't. I didn't even go to Don's. I can't explain it, but I just don't do funerals.

And I would never be able to compose myself long enough to give someone's eulogy, especially someone so close to me.

Another thing I felt bad about around that time was the players' strike. Team owners wanted a salary cap. Among other things, they claimed the small-market teams had little chance to compete with the larger-market clubs. A work stoppage loomed and everybody knew it.

My sister, Iris, and me in the early years. I was proud of the way she accomplished so much later in life.

Aris and me at the Savannah Inn and Country Club on the day we were married in September 1973.

At spring training with the Kansas City Athletics in March 1966. *(AP Images)*

Here I am after winning the Baseball Players' Golf Tournament for the second year in a row in 1966. Those tournaments made me wonder about making a living playing golf instead of baseball. *(AP Images)*

After several seasons putting up with Charlie Finley's madness and a couple years in Washington, I joined the Boston Red Sox in 1967. *(AP Images)*

Making the cover of *Sports Illustrated* near the end of the 1968 season. Considering I was traded to Cleveland within the next seven months and later broke my leg, maybe the *SI* jinx was real.

Red Sox fans protesting my trade to the Indians outside of Fenway Park in 1969. I considered retiring from baseball and becoming a professional golfer rather than going to Cleveland. *(AP Images)*

At spring training with the Cleveland Indians in 1971. *(AP Images)*

After retiring from baseball, legendary golf instructor Bob Toski helped get me ready for the world of professional golf. *(AP Images)*

I returned to the game of baseball in 1975, only this time as a broadcaster for the Red Sox. *(AP Images)*

In 1982, I became a part of the Chicago White Sox's broadcast team: seated from left to right are me, Jimmy Piersall, Joe McConnell, and the great Don Drysdale. Standing against the wall are Jerry Reinsdorf and Eddie Einhorn. *(AP Images)*

As head of baseball operations for the White Sox, I didn't always see eye to eye with manager Tony La Russa. *(AP Images)*

Casey, Aris, Krista, and me in my office—the booth—before a game in St. Petersburg against the Tampa Bay Rays.

The King and I—with the great Arnold Palmer watching someone putt. Those days on the golf course with Arnie are some of my greatest memories.

The Red Sox brought back members of the 1967 "Impossible Dream" team in 2017. From left to right are me, Rico Petrocelli, Jim Lonborg, and Carl Yastrzemski. *(AP Images)*

As the years have flown by, I can still do one thing very well: make the love of my life laugh.

On Wednesday, August 10, 1994, the White Sox team charter from Oakland to Chicago was somewhere over the Rocky Mountains when a few of the players invited me to come to the back of the airplane.

I walked into an impromptu team meeting with key members of the team discussing the issue. They were looking for a little perspective.

I looked around at all of the players and pointed my finger at them. Bear in mind, everyone I addressed at the time was a millionaire.

"Let me tell you something," I said. "If you guys follow through on this, if you go on strike, it will be the biggest mistake of your lives. Baseball may never recover from it."

I didn't like or trust Donald Fehr, the director of the Major League Baseball Players Association. I was convinced, and still am, that he didn't have the players' best interests at heart. He sure didn't care one bit about the game of baseball or its future. He even was quoted as saying he was not a baseball fan. I believed he just wanted to declare war on the owners, to have the players go out on strike and boost his own career.

To put it bluntly, Fehr was similar to Jim Jones to me. Remember Jim? His followers drank the poisoned Kool-Aid in Guyana and almost 1,000 of them died.

Well, the players were gulping down Fehr's Kool-Aid like a cold beer on a hot summer day, even though no one would die from it. I figured baseball's future surely would be severely wounded by a players' strike.

Sure enough, soon after that team charter landed in Chicago, players across baseball walked out—August 11 would go down as the final day of the 1994 season.

I was crushed for many reasons, but most of all, I wanted to see if the White Sox, who were 21 games over .500 and leading the AL Central, could reach the World Series to face the Montreal Expos, who had a 74–40 record at the time. Instead, the Fall Classic was canceled for the first time in 90 years. (As a side note, the strike also hastened Michael Jordan's return to basketball from his attempt to make it in baseball.)

At the time, Frank Thomas was hitting .353 with 38 home runs and 101 RBIs—unbelievable numbers through only 113 games. Tony Gwynn of the San Diego Padres was hitting .394 and every fan wanted to see if he could become the first player since Ted Williams to finish at .400 or better.

"I've had a career year," Frank said, "and I am not going to get to finish it."

A new agreement was reached the following spring before replacement players took the field, but for the next three seasons, baseball was in trouble as far as many fans were concerned.

It would take an unusual season, and an unlikely reason, to bring them back again.

19 THE WORST DAY

TOM PACIOREK, MY PARTNER IN THE BOOTH DURING MY second stint broadcasting White Sox games, was one of the greatest all-around athletes to ever play in the big leagues. He came from a family of great athletes; in fact, his older brother John still holds the major league record for having the most career at-bats with a perfect 1.000 batting average. John had been called up to play the final game of the 1963 season with the old Houston Colt .45s and he had three hits to go with two walks in five plate appearances that day.

The next spring, John didn't make the big-league team coming out of spring training and he never got called up again after a back injury had taken its toll.

Tom had been a great defensive back at the University of Houston, good enough to be drafted by the Miami Dolphins, but he chose base-ball and hit .282 over almost 1,400 games and more than 16 seasons in the big leagues before retiring in 1987.

Before coming up, he had played on what was probably the great-est minor league team ever, the 1972 Albuquerque Dukes, managed by Tommy Lasorda.

And just as Dick Howser had tagged me Hawk, Lasorda stuck a nickname on Tom: "Wimpy."

Obviously, it wasn't a macho or masculine nickname, but it was all his. It seemed nobody in baseball called him Tom.

The story goes that Lasorda had taken his players to this great steak-house for dinner one night and while everyone on the team ordered steaks, Tom ordered a hamburger. That prompted Lasorda to mention the character from the Popeye cartoon who ate only hamburgers.

"Come on, 'Wimpy,' order a steak!" Lasorda said.

Wimpy stuck like glue to Tom, just as Hawk had to me.

It didn't take long for me to bond with Wimpy, on the air and off, when I returned to Chicago. On the air, we told stories and argued just like Don and I had years earlier. Our audience loved our repartee and Wimpy was extremely popular with White Sox fans. He had played for the team from 1982 to 1985 when I called their games with Don. In addition, Wimpy had one of the best senses of humor and he was very good at his job as a color analyst.

Off the air, he was fun to be around and he could hit the golf ball a mile.

What was not to love about him?

One of his favorite storytelling subjects was Lasorda, known by baseball insiders as "AG1"—America's Guest No. 1. By that, I mean Lasorda never paid for anything no matter where he went. When the Dodgers handed out meal money in envelopes on the airplane, Lasorda would stash his away. Wimpy claimed that Lasorda once went an entire season without opening an envelope. Tommy had perfected the art of taking many of his players to a real nice restaurant and then would get everything they ordered comped.

I have always believed Lasorda was one of baseball's greatest ambassadors.

Anyway, in 11 seasons in the booth together, Wimpy and I had plenty of arguments on the air, mostly to entertain our viewers, but we had only one serious fight off the air.

It involved Michael Jordan.

I had played plenty of golf with Michael over the years. After all, we both worked for one of Jerry's teams. Most importantly, I liked Michael.

When he worked out with the White Sox farm team in Sarasota in the spring of 1994 in his attempt to make it in baseball, he called me one day and invited me to drive over and watch him hit. That day, he was swinging the bat pretty decently. I saw a couple of minor things he could improve, but I thought that over time, with hundreds of at-bats, he could work those things out and be successful.

That day, Michael hit for 10 minutes, took a break, hit for another 10 minutes, took a break, and then hit for another 10. That amounts to a lot of work in the batting cage. That much work at once is tough on the arms and shoulders and very tough on the hands.

When he finally finished, Michael asked me, "You wanna play some golf today?"

I was never one to pass up a good golf game, especially with a guy like Michael.

I arrived at the Gator Creek course before Michael. When he arrived, he had both hands wrapped in tape and I noticed blood soaking through the tape on his right hand. I realized that day what the NBA already knew: he was absolutely relentless in his pursuit of excellence.

He and I teamed up against Donnie Robinson and Mike LaValliere that day and we lost only because of me. Michael played really well and I played like crap. I drove back to Orlando and learned the next day that Michael had stuck around after our golf game to play gin for a couple of hours. That day summed up his competitive nature: baseball, golf, and gin. He wanted to compete and to succeed at everything and I really admired that part of him.

During that spring training, I couldn't wait to see Michael's first live at-bat in a game. It came in an intrasquad game against James Baldwin, a pretty good right-hander for the White Sox. Michael hit a rocket to left-center as Warren "The Deacon" Newson raced after it. Newson dove and made the greatest catch he ever made in his career, robbing Michael of a double.

I watched Michael's swing get better and better and smoother and smoother as he worked as hard as any White Sox player.

But once the players went on strike that summer, Michael refused to cross the picket line and that was a big factor in him returning to the Bulls for good. And as everyone on the planet knows, he was the best at that game.

I played golf with Bob Cousy, the former Celtics great, often when I lived in Boston. One day, I asked him, "Who's the best player you've ever seen?"

"Bill Russell," he said.

Years later, after the Bulls had won three titles, I saw Cousy again at a sports banquet. After we caught up on our lives, I asked him, "Bob, can I ask you the same question that I asked you years ago? Who's the best you ever saw?"

"Michael Jordan," he said.

Since I became so close with Jerry Reinsdorf over the years, I witnessed up close how valuable Michael was to not only the Bulls but to the entire city of Chicago. Jerry and I had been discussing sports trades one day when I happened to say, "Well, nobody is untradeable."

I mean, if you think about it, Babe Ruth was traded once. So was Wayne Gretzky. Kareem Abdul-Jabbar was, too. I always figured if the return was enough, anybody could be dealt.

"Except one player," Jerry interrupted. "I can think of *one*."

He didn't have to say his name. I knew who he meant. And he was right.

Remember when Michael single-handedly beat Utah in Game 5 of the 1997 NBA Finals despite playing with a severe case of the flu? When the Bulls returned home the following day, he went to see Herm Schneider, the long-time trainer for the White Sox who always was one of the best in the business at getting injured or sick players healthy. Michael looked gaunt and obviously was still very sick.

Jim Karvellas, the Celebrity Golf Association commissioner, had asked me earlier to ask Michael to call him. The CGA event was coming up at White Eagle Golf Club outside of Chicago and the event desperately needed Michael's appearance to sell more tickets.

"Hawk, I haven't picked up a golf club in two months," he said. "I can't play."

"I'll tell you what," I told him. "We'll get Mario Lemieux and the three of us will play together and just have some fun. Just think about it, and I'll check with you later."

Mario was a regular on the CGA tour and a great guy. About 10 minutes later, I walked back into Herm's training room and Michael still was there.

"Tell Jim I'll play," he said.

I called Karvellas right away and he made sure news of Michael's entry made the newspapers the next morning. By noon, the event was sold out. The Bulls went on to win their fifth NBA title the next night by finishing off Utah, and of course, Michael was named the Finals MVP again.

It seemed the entire city of Chicago turned out to watch Michael play that CGA event at White Eagle. He had a dozen security people walking with us, but that didn't stop him from signing hundreds of autographs that day. We had a great time, too. Mario hit great shots all day and continued smiling. I hit bad shots and somehow continued smiling. And Michael hit bad shots and still continued signing and smiling over 18 holes. He never complained one bit.

Mario shot 70, I played awful and shot 80, and Michael, as he had warned me, didn't break 90. What mattered most is how he had helped Jim and the tournament, knowing he wouldn't be at his best. He could have easily begged off and nobody would have thought anything of it, since he had been sick and just brought the city another NBA title.

That's the Michael Jordan I know.

He is a once-in-a-lifetime athlete.

When he was at his best, Michael had this big, long, looping swing and he could hit the golf ball a long way. Then he hooked up with a new swing coach and suddenly he was taking a shorter, choppier swing and really struggling.

"Michael, you've got to get away from this guy," I told him. "He has messed up your swing."

Later, when his son played basketball at the University of Central Florida, I called Michael to see if he wanted to play Southern Dunes in Haines City with me. He had obviously left that swing coach behind, because he was back to hitting it a long way again. I didn't tell a soul about our golf game that day because of Michael's immense popularity. Well, by the 13th hole, word somehow leaked out and it seemed that half the people in town were following us, hoping to get an autograph from him.

What I loved about Michael was his competitive desire to succeed in whatever he did. He never lost his child-like qualities when it came to playing a game, whether it was basketball, baseball, golf, or gin.

Anyway, back to my one-and-only fight with Wimpy.

Before a White Sox game one night, he overheard me telling somebody the story about Michael's golf swing and how this new swing coach had messed him up.

"Why are you sucking up to Michael so much?" Wimpy asked.

"Screw you, Wimpy," I said. "Michael is a better golfer than you are and can hit the ball a lot further than you do!"

I said it to tick him off and I got hotter than I should have, probably because I knew a side of Michael others may not have known, like his helping Jim and the CGA when he didn't have to. He performed a lot of charitable work.

But that comment was all it took to escalate things. We argued back and forth and I could tell Wimpy was getting extremely agitated. And he is a big, strong guy. He is all of 6-foot-4, so fortunately, we never came to blows.

As the first pitch grew near, we grabbed our headsets. By the time the final out was made that night, we had forgotten the whole thing.

That was the only time he and I ever shared a cross word off the air.

It was appropriate that Wimpy's car was exactly how I pictured the cartoon character's car. He would drive all over the Midwest in that car and practically live in it, sleeping in it instead of grabbing a hotel room when he drove long distances. It was full of clothes, fast-food wrappers, and just plain junk. I think he had to move garbage out of the way just to fit into the driver's seat. There really is no way for me to accurately describe just how messy it was.

Wimpy had a type-A personality and it was hard for him to sit still at times. He had been diagnosed with attention-deficit disorder, which required medicine to help him focus. One time we attempted to tape an opening and it just wasn't working. He screwed up take after take, until he blurted out, "Dammit, Wimpy! Take your medicine!"

If you think it's strange he referred to himself in the third person, it wasn't strange to me at all.

There were times I walked into the booth before a game and Wimpy would be curled up on the floor, sound asleep. He had just come from the golf course—he loved to play just about every day—and had decided to rest up before our broadcast began.

In my mind, Wimpy will be forever linked with another one of my favorite people.

Following the 1999 baseball season, I was about to hit my tee shot on the third hole at Southern Dunes one day when my cell phone rang. I noticed it was my daughter's number, so I answered.

"Dad, have you heard about Payne Stewart?" Krista asked.

Her tone struck a chord in fear with me, but I had no idea how devastatingly the day would play out before I went to bed that night.

I had known Payne for years because we both lived in Orlando and played golf together. I started calling Payne "OB," for "out of bounds." When he wore those Bermudas, it made his legs look as thin as out-of-bounds stakes. He always laughed when I called him that.

Payne was married with two beautiful children and I never saw him in a bad mood. He was outgoing and loved to have fun, and I think that's why we bonded. Some guys on the PGA Tour didn't like him because he was so gregarious. I loved him because of it. When we played together, Payne didn't give a crap if he shot 80, because he was determined to have a few laughs and enjoy the day. And that's how he lived his life.

I could beat Payne often, but sometimes, he and I played with Scott Hoch. I could never beat Scott, who always seemed to play me like it was the U.S. Open. A lot of people on the tour didn't like Scott at all, but I did, because I understood him. I always felt bad for him missing that two-footer that would have won the 1989 Masters, which Nick Faldo won in a playoff.

One day, back when Payne had a house on the 12th tee at Bay Hill, I teed off and hit a flare to the right. Before I could pick up my tee, I heard this loud voice yell, "What are you doing?"

I looked over to see Payne standing outside of his house, watching my group.

"Widen your stance!" he said. "You're standing there like a big sissy!"

I widened my stance and ripped another one about 330 yards down the middle of the fairway.

One day in May of 1999, I was about to tee off at Isleworth Country Club in Orlando when I saw Payne practicing on the putting green. He was preparing for the upcoming U.S. Open and waved me over to show me the new SeeMore putter, which had just been released.

"This is the greatest thing I have ever seen," he said. "I just started using it and I can't miss a putt with it."

As I admired his new putter, Payne told me he would have a new SeeMore placed in my locker at Bay Hill. I started using it and liked it, too. It seemed easier to keep my putts on my intended line.

A month after he gave me that putter, on Father's Day at Pinehurst, Payne holed an 18-footer with his new putter to beat Phil Mickelson by a stroke to win the U.S. Open. I watched it on TV, feeling elated for him. I could see in his eyes how much that championship meant to him. I knew many of the players on the PGA Tour and it couldn't have happened to a nicer guy.

Anyway, that day on Southern Dunes in October, when I picked up Krista's call, her next words stunned me.

"Dad, Payne's in trouble. Something's wrong with his airplane," she said.

I immediately rushed to the clubhouse, where all the TVs were tuned to the horrible news: Payne's private airplane that had just left Orlando for Dallas had apparently lost cabin pressure.

Somebody in the clubhouse mentioned Payne was traveling with two of his agents. Then someone else said they thought Scott Hoch was on the plane, too.

My heart just sank. I rushed home and turned on the TV again, watching the tragedy unfold. Fortunately, it turned out that Scott was not on the flight, which eventually ran out of fuel and crashed in a field in South Dakota. Payne was only 42.

I sat there in my living room that day, tears running down my face. I couldn't believe he was gone. I thought of his wife, Tracey, and their kids and how they had to be absolutely crushed.

Then the telephone rang. It was Wimpy.

"Tough day, Wimpy," I said. "How are you doing?"

"Hawk, I just want to let you know that I am quitting," he went on. "I want to see my children more and watch my grandchildren grow up."

I had trouble processing what he was telling me. Wimpy and I were popular as a broadcast team and I simply loved being around the guy. Why would he want to quit now? The news was like a shot to my gut, on top of the shock of Payne's death.

Wimpy went on to tell me that the producers had wanted him to change some things about his work, but I never did discover what he meant specifically. Nobody had mentioned any problems about his work to me. But more than that, he said he just wanted to spend more time with his family.

That morning, I had lost a golfing buddy in the prime of his life.

That afternoon, I learned I would lose my broadcast partner.

I cried most of the day and most of the night.

Getting to know Wimpy still is one of the greatest joys of my baseball career. Just as Don was like the brother I never had, Wimpy was like the little brother I never had.

To know Tom Paciorek was to love him. And I loved the guy.

To this day, I receive tons of letters from people who miss hearing us together. We teamed up again for one series at Seattle in 2017 when Steve Stone took a series off and it was just like old times: Wimpy and I bantering back and forth in the booth about the good ol' days.

I still have that putter Payne gave me. It is one of my most cherished possessions. I would give anything to use it during just one more round with him, or to see him come racing across the fairway one more time to bum a cigarette.

Like anyone who lives long enough, I've experienced plenty of bad days in my life, such as when I was told Mama had cancer, or when someone whispered into my ear that Don was dead, but October 25, 1999, had to be one of the worst.

Payne and Wimpy will be intertwined in a strange way forever for me because of that day.

20 A CHAMPIONSHIP FOR THE SOUTH SIDE

THE WHITE SOX HAD CONTENDED FOR THE POSTSEASON almost every season for the first 15 years since my return to Chicago, from 1990 to 2004, but they just couldn't get over the hump and get to a World Series.

Let alone win one.

They had lost to Toronto in the 1993 American League Championship Series. In their only other playoff appearance during that period, they had been swept by the Seattle Mariners in the 2000 AL Division Series.

Sprinkled in between had been *nine* second-place division finishes.

Gene Lamont had taken over for Jeff Torborg before the 1992 season, but I never considered Lamont to have the "it" factor when it came to leading a club to a championship. He knew the game of baseball as well as anybody, but knowing the game is not even half of what makes a great manager. All managers know the game pretty well—a great manager has to be able to motivate his players on a daily basis, to get the most out of them every day over 162 games.

Still, Gene was named AL Manager of the Year in 1993. After the strike-shortened season the following year, he was fired after the White Sox were swept in four games by the Indians, which left them with an 11–20 start in 1995.

He was replaced by his third-base coach, Terry "Boomer" Bevington.

I really liked Terry, and he certainly was an excitable guy. A couple of times he walked out to the mound to make a pitching change, but forgot to have any relievers up in the bullpen. He was fired after his third season.

The club then turned to Jerry Manuel, who had been a bench coach for Jim Leyland's World Series champion Florida Marlins the previous season. I thought Manuel had a chance to be a heck of a manager, but his first two White Sox teams finished 2 and then 11 games under .500.

The 2000 team had a real chance to do something, taking over first place only 15 games into the season and running away with the AL Central, finishing 95–67, as Manuel was named AL Manager of the Year.

That award didn't stop my old buddy, Lou Piniella, from outfoxing him in the playoffs, however.

In the first game of the series in Chicago, I was watching on TV from Orlando, as I usually did for all playoff games since the networks picked up the broadcasts. (People have asked me why I handled it that way, but if I was not working, I never liked fighting the crowds at the ballpark. I wanted to be in my living room right in front of my television, where I could focus on the game and often picked up more things than I would sitting in somebody's suite with all the commotion.) The game was tied 4–4 heading into the top of the 10th with Keith Foulke on the mound for Chicago.

Mike Cameron singled to start the inning for the Mariners. After Alex Rodriguez flew out, everybody expected Cameron to try to steal second to get into scoring position. The first pitch to Edgar Martinez was a ball. Lou walked out of the dugout and right past his first-base coach Johnny Moses. He put his hands in his back pockets as he normally did, faced the outfield, and started to talk to Cameron. Lou was trying to give the impression that Cameron had missed the steal sign.

After Lou walked back to the dugout, Manuel ordered a pitchout on the next pitch. Now Martinez had an advantage with a 2-0 count.

Cameron then stole second on the next pitch before Martinez hit a two-run homer that led to the winning runs.

After the game, I got a hold of Lou and asked him what he'd said to Cameron.

"Well this is the playoffs, Hawk, and you have to pull out all of the stops," he said. "I told him, 'The Dow is down and the NASDAQ is up,' among a few other things that had nothing to do with baseball."

Lou had played Manuel like a fiddle, just hoping for a pitchout to give Martinez an advantageous count, which led to his home run. Then the Mariners went on to sweep the White Sox.

A few writers had called me after the series to ask my opinion.

I said, "We just got outmanaged."

It was that simple.

When I headed to spring training in Arizona the following February and walked into the clubhouse for the first time, I saw Manuel heading straight toward me. At that point, we didn't like each other much anyway, and I had no idea what he possibly would say to me.

He just said, "Your boy sure got me, didn't he, Hawk?"

I replied, "Yes, he did."

And he continued walking.

Three years later, the White Sox went to New York to face the Yankees in a crucial three-game series in late August. They were leading the division over the Twins by only one game at the time. We beat Roger Clemens 13–2 in the first game and David Wells 11–2 in the second game to get to 71–62.

Mark Buerhle was set to start the third game, his first time on the mound at Yankee Stadium. A sweep would have given the club great momentum headed down the stretch.

When I walked into the clubhouse before that Sunday game, Buerhle stormed past me.

"Can you believe this crap?" he said. "He's not pitching me today."

Instead of Buerhle, Manuel had decided to start a rookie, Neal Cotts.

Sandy Alomar, one of Manuel's bench coaches, was livid. He told me, "This is one of the worst decisions I can ever remember."

I tried to get into the tiny visiting manager's office at Yankee Stadium before the game to discover Manuel's rationale, but I couldn't because of the swarm of media. I went on the air in the lead-in to the game and said flatly, "This is a lose-lose situation. Mark Buehrle should be starting this game as scheduled. I don't know what Manuel is thinking."

Sure enough, Cotts faced eight batters and got only one out. He left the game in the first inning with the Yankees up 4–2. The game, and the sweep, was lost by the end of the first inning. After the game, one of the writers walked out of Manuel's office and told me he said he wanted to give Buehrle an extra day of rest.

That made no sense, since Buehrle already had his normal four days of rest and had been looking forward to his first start at Yankee Stadium. The next night in Detroit, Buehrle, still shaken by the switch, gave up five runs to the Tigers in the first two innings and the club lost again, 8–4.

That was the beginning of the end of that White Sox team, which went 15–13 from the moment Manuel made that awful decision, finishing in second place, four games behind the Twins.

The club had entered the season as the heavy favorites to win the division, so that terrible finish left general manager Kenny Williams with no choice. He fired Manuel.

I was talking to Kenny one day when he had asked me about possible replacements, and I had written down two names—Ozzie Guillen and Sandy Alomar.

Guillen had been like a coach on the field when he played shortstop for the White Sox. I remember repeating on the air often that he would become a great manager once he retired from playing, if he wanted to go that route.

I love players with great baseball acumen, and Ozzie had it. He always knew what the other eight players were supposed to be doing at any given time, in any situation.

Ironically, the Marlins again had won a World Series the previous year, and again, the White Sox plucked one of their coaches. The first time it was Manuel, seven years prior.

This time it was Ozzie, who basically had managed that team in Miami as a bench coach for Jack McKeon, who was getting up there in age.

Right from the start in 2004, Ozzie had the White Sox playing their behinds off. Then Frank Thomas got hurt. Then Magglio Ordonez got hurt. I swear that if the club didn't lose those two guys, they would have won the World Series that season.

They still held first place in the division through mid-July, then stumbled with a terrible August because he injuries had taken their toll. They finished 83–79, but it was obvious to me that Ozzie knew what he was doing from the dugout.

There are some guys who you just know will do a great job and get results. Ozzie was not afraid of anything. He was not afraid of the media or his players. There is no doubt that some managers are afraid of one or the other, or even both, and it prevents them from making the right decisions.

The next season, he had his team playing lights-out again, jumping to a 15-game lead over Cleveland. Then the Indians got red hot and the White Sox cooled off. They were struggling in August when I walked into his office and told Ozzie, "These players need you now more than ever."

He didn't say a word to me and I walked out. Within minutes, he went on a rant in front of the media and that was all any writer in Chicago wrote about or anything the TV guys talked about for at least a week.

The team then got hot on the field, holding off the Indians and sweeping them in Cleveland during the final weekend of the season. A.J. Pierzynski later told me, "We had been choking like rats and he took all the pressure off of us."

After Ozzie's rant, he became the story—not the struggles of Jermaine Dye or Paul Konerko, or Frank's elbow injury. The media stopped asking about all those things, and started to focus on Ozzie's mood and whether he would explode again.

Down the stretch, Ozzie made out some lineups that had me shaking my head, but they all seemed to work. They won the division by six games and most of it was Ozzie's doing. Piniella later told me that Ozzie's rant was one of the greatest pre-calculated moves he ever saw from a manager. It removed all the pressure from a team that was choking.

That team cruised through the playoffs, sweeping Boston in three games before beating the Angels in five to win the pennant and reach the World Series.

If there was any downside to that run, it was that Frank didn't get to enjoy that playoff run as an active player. Everybody on the team hurt for him. For his first seven years, there was not a better hitter in baseball. In my opinion, he, Manny Ramirez, Miguel Cabrera, and Albert Pujols are the four best right-handed hitters in the last 50 years of this game.

The National League champions were the Houston Astros. Years earlier, when Astros manager Phil Garner was in Milwaukee, he and I got into a verbal battle through the media after I felt he had his Brewers pitchers throwing at our guys a bit too much during one series. I guess Wimpy must have said something, too, because Garner ripped us to the media.

"If Hawk Harrelson and Wimpy think we're hitting their guys on purpose, I am available," he told the media one day after a game. "Those two guys should know better. They played ball. But obviously, they are two idiots. My challenge is for them to come down here and I will fight them right now."

That's all I needed to hear. I had had enough of it and called him while the Brewers were in Oakland. I wanted to take him up on his offer. I had looked at the map and figured out a spot that was exactly halfway between Chicago and Milwaukee.

"Phil, check your schedule," I told him. "When you got an off day, let's meet at the Six Flags amusement park. I want to settle this thing."

Garner backed down like a big baby. He didn't say much or even answer my challenge. I could tell he wanted no part in meeting me. I was hot enough about it at the time that I really wanted to kick his butt.

Now that Garner was managing the Astros, I couldn't have hoped for a more fitting matchup.

Fortunately, Ozzie's club dominated Garner's bunch from the start, recording only the 19th sweep in World Series history.

Two days after the final game in Houston, I flew from Orlando to Chicago to prepare for the championship celebration on Michigan Avenue, which I had been asked to MC. The city was electric. As we rode the bus from the ballpark toward downtown on that chilly day, one of the security guys said the crowd was larger than when the Bears had won the Super Bowl in 1985.

I had been given a list of who to introduce that day and it included Mayor Richard M. Daley, a few other local politicians, all of the players, and, of course, Jerry. I happened to notice a certain U.S. senator from Chicago not-so-subtly trying to get my attention before the ceremony started. He walked by me and then stood next to me and smiled, but he never said a word. I could just tell by his body language that he wanted to be included in the ceremony, so I double-checked the list.

The name Barack Obama wasn't on it, and I wasn't going to veer away from the script I had been given.

To that point, I had known Jerry for 24 years. To say it was the most emotional I had ever seen him would be a gross understatement.

After I introduced all the players, it was Paul Konerko's turn to speak.

"Everybody wonders what happened to that last out," he said, reaching into his pocket and pulling out a baseball. "Mister Reinsdorf, this is for you. You earned it!"

He dropped the ball into Jerry's hands. Within two seconds, Jerry had tears running down his cheeks.

Jerry will tell you it was the greatest day of his career. His Bulls had won six NBA titles, but I knew this meant more to him. As much as

Jerry loved his Bulls, it was an entirely different feeling when it came to the White Sox. Baseball was his first love.

I was happy for a lot of reasons. For Pauley. For Buerhle. For A.J. For Frank, even though he didn't get to play in the Series. For Ozzie. For the city of Chicago.

But mainly, I was happy for Jerry. He became the third owner in sports history to bring at least seven championships to one city.

That's an amazing accomplishment.

I had never seen one man do so much for a city and yet be so maligned so often by the media all those years. I never saw him complain once about it, either.

For reasons I'll never understand, from the time he bought the club in 1981 until that championship, Jerry had many detractors in the Chicago media.

There was none bigger than a guy by the name of Jay Mariotti, a columnist for one of the Chicago newspapers in the 1990s. For years, Mariotti tried to make a name by ripping Reinsdorf.

Mariotti and his cohorts, such as Bill Gleason of the *Chicago Sun-Times,* ripped Jerry for just about anything he did, but especially for wanting a new stadium to replace the crumbling Comiskey Park. The fact is, Jerry had pumped millions of dollars into the old ballpark, as I discovered when I was an executive in 1986. I mean, how many facelifts can a stadium get until it is time for a new one?

For the White Sox to succeed and stay in Chicago, they needed a new stadium and it had been obvious to everyone, except a few sportswriters.

I always believed Gleason, an old-time writer, was anti-Semitic in his criticism of Jerry. He hated Jerry with a white-hot passion. Finally, the *Sun-Times* fired him and he ended up at the *South Bend Tribune,* where he continued to rip Jerry from farther down the road.

But Mariotti was the biggest weenie of them all. One night in Minnesota, where the press box was somewhat tight, he leaned back in his chair as I happened to be walking down the aisle behind him. I accidentally bumped into his chair. He jumped up as if he wanted to fight me.

"Why don't you move your chair out of the way?" I asked.

He then got into my face and started cussing me.

"Jay, I know what you are trying to do," I told him. "All you got to do is put one hand on me and I will kick your butt!"

There was no doubt he wanted me to punch him first just so he could sue me. That's just the type of guy he was. Even though I was much older, I could tell by looking at him that the fight wouldn't have lasted very long.

I received a letter from his lawyer soon after that, threatening to sue me. For what, I have no idea. I showed the letter to Jerry and he just laughed about it.

Not long after that episode, I was driving home to South Bend from Chicago when I heard Mariotti ripping me on the air during his radio show. I called into the station and told his producer I wanted to speak with him. Not surprisingly, Mariotti wanted no part of that.

I was more than ready to turn that car around, drive to his studio and settle this thing with this little weenie once and for all.

On the air one night, the subject of Mariotti came up and I called him a "hineybird."

My partner, Darrin Jackson, looked at me and asked, "What's a hineybird?"

"Well, a hineybird flies in perfectly executed concentric circles for a while until it eventually flies up its own behind and disappears forever," I told him.

Viewers had to be either shocked or amused at that line. Anyway, that's exactly what happened to Mariotti. He left for ESPN and then encountered legal troubles in California. Today, he's living in oblivion.

I always felt I had to defend Jerry from the Chicago media because he refused to do it himself. He is too classy to stoop to their level or get down in the dirt or even strike back. Doing those things never bothered me.

I often said Jerry is probably the smartest man I ever met. His résumé spoke for itself. He once developed a real estate company and then sold it to American Express for more than $100 million. He also was a former prosecutor. He left that job because he said he grew tired of putting people in jail. His leadership guided the Bulls to six NBA titles. He is already in the Basketball Hall of Fame. I am sure someday he will become the first inductee to also have a space in Cooperstown.

Jerry was the baseball owner, not George Steinbrenner, who broke down the salary structure limitations for managers, coaches, and scouts. After he started to pay them better, other owners had to follow.

He also was the first to bring a comprehensive drug-testing program to baseball, implementing one with White Sox employees before Major League Baseball even had one. He was the first one to take the test, then Eddie Einhorn, and then me.

Furthermore, there was no owner in baseball who knew the game as well as he did.

There is nothing I enjoy more than talking baseball with the legends of the game. Over the years, I have had the privilege of speaking with people such as Ted Williams, Alvin Dark, Gene Mauch, Whitey Herzog, Mickey Mantle, Billy Martin, hundreds of scouts and coaches, and other household names. I could sit and talk baseball eight days a week.

So I think I have some credence when I claim that Jerry is right up there with his knowledge of the game.

Most owners are bean-counters, bill-payers, and CEOs. Jerry really *knows* baseball. He can analyze a game as well as anybody I have been around. He even can pick up on small things that the average baseball insider doesn't see.

Many in the media blamed Jerry for the players' strike in 1994, but all the blame should have been placed on Donald Fehr. It took a lot of strategic planning to get the game back to where it is today, and Jerry was right in the middle of it. He worked in tandem with Bud Selig, who became commissioner in 1998, to regain baseball's popularity among the fans.

At the time Bud took over for Fay Vincent in 1992, baseball was in bad shape. Not many owners liked Fay and he was known as "the umpires' commissioner"—the men in blue seemed to be the only people who supported him. There were 30 different owners with about 30 different agendas. None of them really cared about the other owners. They were out for themselves, aside from Jerry.

Then I saw Jerry and Bud work together to get 29 of them headed in the same direction. There was always Steinbrenner, who had his own agenda, but eventually he had no choice but to come along with the others on issues that grew the game.

More importantly, Jerry is one of the most honest people I have ever known. His word always was his bond. A handshake was a contract to him. If he said something or promised something, I could always count on it.

As I watched him operate all these years, I called his motto "STP"—stability, tradition, and pride. He was always willing to pay the price for whatever the White Sox needed at the time. He hired good people and stuck by them. The Bulls and White Sox organizations have been full of employees with 20 years or more tenure.

As far as the media was concerned, the thing that finally came with those championships was the respect Jerry deserved. The media now respects the man as it should have all those years earlier.

That is another reason why the 2005 World Series title was so satisfying for me.

After the sweep of the Astros, as I watched the players and the city celebrate, and simultaneously feel such great relief and joy, I found myself thinking back to October of 1967.

I was not sure I felt real pain for losing that World Series with the Red Sox—until I experienced what the White Sox felt by winning it.

Here I was, 38 years later, mourning that loss to the Cardinals in which somebody swiped my glove and I stunk at the plate—just as if it had happened yesterday.

Why was that?

Did it finally take experiencing the joy of a championship to realize the pain of losing one?

I really don't know the answer.

Championships last forever, but the greatness that it takes to win one is sometimes fleeting. Ozzie left after the 2011 season. He had a brief run with the Marlins but doesn't have a job managing a team today, and that troubles me. There is nothing contrived about him. He is genuine. There is innocence to him; if he is asked something, he answers it honestly. The answer may not always be politically correct, and sometimes that scares people such as owners and general managers who make the decisions.

If I owned a team, he would be the first guy I would call if I needed a manager.

Unless that team was in Miami, of course.

Ozzie was fired by the Marlins in 2012 after saying that he "respected" Cuban dictator Fidel Castro. That was something nobody should ever say in Miami. When I read those comments that day, I thought Ozzie had just screwed up a good situation. He was the perfect fit to manage a team in Miami, but I knew he wouldn't be able to survive after making that comment.

I'll never forget when we got off the airplane following the final game of the 2016 season, in which the White Sox finished 78–84. Robin Ventura resigned on the final day.

"Whatever happened this season was really not your fault," I told him. "We had some pitchers who could not pitch and some players who could not play."

We hugged that night and the truth was, Robin knew as much baseball as any manager I had been around. It just didn't work out for him. Some players didn't bust their butts for him as they should have.

The team promoted bench coach Rick Renteria, who managed the Cubs in 2014 before they fired him and hired Joe Maddon. I think Rick will become a great manager given a little time, because it didn't take long during the 2017 season to notice he had the White Sox hustling and playing the game the way it should be played.

No matter all the great things I said about Rick on the air, I never wanted it to be construed that I was putting down Robin in any way. I loved Robin like a son and he was one of my all-time favorite players, so I had been very hesitant to compliment Rick on the air early, thinking some people would take it as a slight to Robin.

As I write this, the White Sox have rebuilt their farm system, which is stocked with tons of prospects. Renteria, I think, is the perfect manager to get them to reach the top again, just like Ozzie was the perfect guy in the mid-2000s.

I may not be around to see it, but the White Sox should contend for another World Series title when their prospects start to mature sometime around 2019 or 2020.

They should become a contender again.

I won't be calling games then, but my hope is that Jerry is there to hold the trophy again.

21 "CATCH THE BALL AND DON'T MESS WITH JOE WEST"

I HAVE OFTEN JOKED ON THE AIR IN RECENT YEARS THAT THE title of this chapter describes the first two rules of Major League Baseball.

Catch it—as in, play great defense—and never, ever tick off an umpire by the name of Joe West.

The truth is, however, nobody respects umpires or the job they do more than Ken Harrelson.

You can put that on the board and etch it in stone.

Umpires are just regular people.

There are bad umpires just like there are bad lawyers, bad doctors, and some bad players. Sometimes, good umpires have bad days just like people in any other profession, including managers and broadcasters. But for the most part, they are very, very good at a job that is very, very difficult.

And before I became a broadcaster, I got along with them better than almost any player.

If I remember correctly, I believe I was thrown out of a big-league game only twice in my nine seasons—and one of them was premeditated—so what does that say about me?

I may have had a terrible temper when some guy got in my face, or when things were going badly on the golf course, but I rarely directed it toward an umpire—my punch that missed its mark down in Venezuela notwithstanding.

When I was with the Red Sox, we were playing in Washington and there was a big crowd that day for some reason. Normally, the Senators didn't set the world on fire when it came to attendance and that is one reason they moved to Texas and became the Rangers.

Anyway, I had been invited to a big party after the game.

We had jumped out to a 7–0 lead that day and I knew we were going to win easily. As I stood in right field, I realized I was coming up to the plate the next inning. I decided if the umpire called a pitch the wrong way, I was going to yell my head off and get out a little early.

Sure enough, the ump punched me out on a close pitch on the outside corner. I started cussing right away and he followed through on my plan, giving me the heave-ho. I didn't like this umpire anyway so that made it easier to blow up in the first place.

As I left the dugout to walk toward the clubhouse, I tried to hide my smile.

Just as I had planned, I arrived at that party about four innings early.

That episode was no different to me than managers who calculated when and how to get tossed. Of course, they are trying to change their team's momentum or get their players' adrenaline flowing, not get a jumpstart on a good party. When I played first base, I often heard a manager, during the middle of an argument, tell an umpire, "I am not leaving here until you throw me out!"

Billy Martin used that line all the time. The Orioles' Earl Weaver did the same thing. We used to say, "Earl's got 29 men on his roster: 25 players and four umpires!"

Of course, there were always certain umpires looking for confrontations, too. They overheard everything a player said, no matter how far away they were. We called them "big ears" for a reason. Many of them had big memories, too, like elephants.

When I played, we had scouting reports on umpires, just as teams have today, and we would go over them in a pregame meeting. Pitchers especially had to know the book on umpires, but all we ever cared about was consistency. Nothing ticked me off more as a player than an umpire who called pitches high one inning and low three innings later.

Normally, when I was called out on a strike I didn't agree with, I just shut my mouth. When I did that, I knew I gained their respect. The next time I came to the plate, it was common to hear, "Hawk, I am sorry. I missed that last one."

That type of apology always told me that guy was a good umpire.

There is little doubt that umpires and players got along much better in my day than they do now.

There were plenty of times when I was having dinner at a nice restaurant somewhere and I noticed umpires eating at another table. You know what I sometimes did? I sent them a good bottle of wine.

Can you imagine that happening today?

Today, the player-umpire relationship is adversarial, at best.

At times, so has been the broadcaster-umpire relationship, at least as far as I was concerned. I do realize I have been tough on umpires from the booth during my career and I have heard about it—from Jerry and whoever was commissioner at the time.

One night in 2012 at Tampa Bay, a couple of the White Sox players had been hit by Devil Ray pitchers. Naturally, Chicago's Jose Quintana then threw a pitch behind the Rays' Ben Zobrist an inning later.

Umpire Mark Wegner immediately tossed him. Then he threw out manager Robin Ventura, who had defended Quintana.

I went berserk on the air.

"What are you doing? What are you doing? This is absolutely brutal. This is unbelievable....Totally absurd...That just tells you that there is an umpire here in the American League who knows nothing about baseball..."

I didn't stop there. I continued to rant about Wegner for an inning or two, claiming he should be suspended, among other things.

In my mind, all Quintana did was follow up and self-police the situation, protecting his teammates. If Wegner had let it go and moved on, the issue would have been over.

Afterward, I realized I may have gone too far with my criticism, so I called Mark and left a message, apologizing for my rant.

I got a call from Bud Selig, the commissioner, and he let me have it pretty good. Then I got a call from Joe Torre, who oversaw the umpires for Major League Baseball at the time.

"Hawk, I understand what you were saying, but can I ask you one thing?" Joe said. "Just don't make it sound like that umpire can never be a good umpire. They are learning the same way a player learns. They are better in their fifth year than they are in their first year, just like a player..."

Joe had such a calm presence about him and he was absolutely right. I love Joe Torre. He has been a classy guy his entire life and he has my respect.

But it was a rough few days, because many people in baseball were talking about my explosion. I was the story when the game should have been the story, and I regretted it.

My tirade may have gone a little overboard that night, but I do know that some umpires today are so scared of confrontations and the possibility of a benches-clearing brawl that it affects how they call a game.

I believe some umpires don't want pitchers pitching inside, fearing a little chin music may lead to a major dustup. So they may give the pitcher a few inches on the outside part of the plate and subsequently call it tighter on the inside part of the plate.

Pitching inside and sending messages are a huge part of this game, however. It always has been. Umpires can't take that tool away from pitchers. Players and managers have had a way of policing the game for 100 years without needing umpires' help to do so.

Most managers felt that way, anyway.

But there have been others who let it go, without responding.

When Albert Belle was with the White Sox in 1998, he got drilled twice one day and no White Sox pitcher responded. Belle was making more than $10 million per year as the club's highest-paid player. If he had been lost to injury, the club's chances that year would have been over.

After the game, I walked into manager Jerry Manuel's office and asked, "Albert gets drilled a couple of times and your pitchers did nothing. Are you going to do anything about this?"

He said, "We'll file it."

File it?

The best managers in the game, such as Terry Francona, Joe Maddon, Mike Scioscia, Bruce Bochy, Dusty Baker, and many others, are old-school guys who don't just "file it." They do something about it that very day to protect their players.

In my day, very seldom did a manager even have to tell his pitcher what to do. Pitchers just knew. Drysdale was the best at it. Nobody ever had to tell Catfish Hunter a thing, either. Or Bob Gibson, or Jim Palmer, or Nolan Ryan. They protected their own, and they had to hit in those days, too. They were not protected by the DH rule until 1973, and even then only in the American League.

Remember back in 1993 when Ryan plunked Robin Ventura, who then charged the mound and found himself stuck in a headlock, as Nolan punched the top of his head?

Later, I asked Robin what he was thinking as he charged out there.

"Well, I was ticked off at first, because he threw it at me," he told me. "Then after I started to run out there, I thought, 'Oh man, what am I doing? This is Nolan Ryan!' Then I ducked right into a headlock."

Reinsdorf came up with the best line regarding that fight.

"Robin was the only guy ever to get five hits off Nolan Ryan in one game," he said.

There were plenty of hitters who just never had the mental makeup to charge the mound, no matter how obvious it was that they were being thrown at.

I remember one day in Oakland, Frank Thomas took a pitch in the ribs. The next time up, a pitch sailed behind his head. It was the first game of a three-game series and he did not hit very well for those three games, and that was no coincidence.

When we left Oakland, Frank sat down beside me on the charter flight.

"Hawk, I let them do it to me again, didn't I?" he said.

"Yes, you sure did, big guy," I said. "If you would go out to that mound just one time and pinch the pitcher's head off, it would stop all of this crap."

But Frank wouldn't charge the mound. It just wasn't in his DNA. He was a mild-mannered guy. I always maintained a hitter needed an edge at the plate. Guys like Yaz or Kaline would get ticked off and respond by hitting a bomb.

I can admit here that I never charged the mound once, either. I had made up my mind early in my career that if I charged the mound, I was not going to get anything done anyway, because other guys would be there fast to break it up.

I was hit only six times in my entire career in 3,364 plate appearances, mainly because I was very good at getting out of the way of a pitch and pitchers didn't throw at me very much. I think my reputation for meeting a guy outside his clubhouse after a game early in my career may have helped.

I think there was only one time that I knew I was purposely hit by a pitch. And it was by a buddy.

When I faced Oakland's Chuck Dobson, a former teammate of mine in Kansas City, one day at Fenway, I just knew he would throw his curveball down and away, so I waited and waited for it. Finally, I got one. I reached out and stroked it over the Green Monster for a three-run homer. After the game we headed over to Lucifer's bar, where most of the players drank together.

The Dobber walked right over to me.

"Hawk, you know I can't allow that to happen without responding," he told me. "I've got to do what I've got to do."

"I know that, Chuck," I said. "Do what you've got to do."

In my next at-bat against Chuck a few weeks later in Oakland, he hit me right in the ribs with his first pitch. I just dropped my bat and jogged to first. I don't think I was smiling at the time, because it hurt like heck, but that was the way the game was played then and we all accepted it.

That meeting-outside-the-clubhouse thing didn't leave me when I entered the booth, either.

During one game in 2006, the White Sox' A.J. Pierzynski was hit twice by Texas' Vincente Padilla, who had a reputation for throwing at guys. That day, I went crazy on the air, ranting and raving a little. I knew none of the White Sox would do anything about it and that also ticked me off some, so after the game, I headed down to the Rangers clubhouse. I stood outside for six or seven minutes before one of their outfielders came out.

"Hey, is Padilla in there?" I asked. "Tell him to come out here."

The guy returned a few minutes later.

"He says he is not coming out," he told me.

I walked away frustrated. I just wanted to see how he would respond. I loved A.J. like a son and I guess I felt like a father defending him. I was 64 years old at the time; Padilla was about 30. What would I have done if Padilla mouthed off or swung at me? I would have laid him out and dealt with the suspension later.

The umpiring issue is one of the few things for which Jerry has gotten on me over the years. I have received plenty of texts from him in the middle of a game along the lines of, "Lay off the umpires!"

Which brings me to my old pal Joe West.

Besides often repeating my two rules of baseball, I also once said, "Right now, Joe West doesn't know what he is doing. He is becoming a joke in the umpiring profession…"

And, "Joe West should be suspended! He is an absolute disgrace to the umpiring profession…"

It's all there on YouTube, among a few other things that popped out of my mouth. As every Chicagoan knows, I had been rather hard on Joe over the air for many years.

When he called a balk on White Sox pitcher Mark Buerhle one day in Cleveland, I snapped. But I later realized he was not calling it on Buerhle, as much as he was calling it on manager Ozzie Guillen. He and Ozzie had a lot of problems over the years, and Joe was one of those guys who, if you gave him respect, would bust his butt to call a fair game.

For all of those things I said once upon a time about Joe, I want to apologize right here and right now.

I really believe Joe is one of the greatest umpires I have ever seen. There was never an umpire more talented than Joe. I know what I am saying will shock White Sox fans, but if you go over the transcripts, I never, ever called Joe a *bad* umpire. I just ripped him for some individual calls he had made over the years.

And maybe I have had a change of heart, because I eventually got to know the guy behind the mask.

We were in Texas when my broadcast partner, Steve Stone, said to me, "Joe West is back. Isn't that great?"

"Where's he been?" I asked.

"You didn't hear? He had throat cancer," he told me.

After the game, I bolted from the booth straight to the umpires' room. Another ump opened the door and had to be shocked to see me standing there, and he was especially shocked when I asked to see Joe.

"He's in the shower," the ump said. "Come on in."

I walked in and saw Joe with soap all over his face.

"Listen," I said. "I don't mind fighting with you. I don't mind arguing with you. I don't mind ripping you on TV. But there's one thing I can't have and that is you getting sick on me!"

Joe laughed.

That was the icebreaker for us. I felt horrible not knowing Joe had cancer and I wanted to extend that olive branch.

A few years ago, my friend Dewey Tomko called me one night. Dewey was a world-class poker player who owned a sports grill in Orlando very close to my home in Bay Hill. He said Joe was there and suggested I stop by.

I hung up and told Aris, "I've got to go over to Dewey's."

"Why?" she asked.

"Because Joe West is over there."

"And tell me again, why are you going over there?" she asked.

Joe and I had a beer together at the bar that night. We talked about everything happening in our lives and that was that: I liked him almost immediately. I always respected him, but now I saw firsthand what a great guy he was. We really got along well and it surprised me a bit.

A few weeks later, Dewey called me again.

"Guess who's back?" he asked.

"Come on, Aris," I said. "I want to introduce you to Joe."

She and I drove over to Dewey's and as soon as we walked in, Joe said, "Mrs. Harrelson, you sure have my condolences…"

We all laughed and that sealed the deal for me. I suddenly was in the Joe West Fan Club. At the end of the night, Joe asked me to play golf at his home course in Claremont. I never realized he shared my passion for golf. We played a round together on his course and had a great time.

Then I invited him to play in Winter Haven one day. Joe and I spent 18 holes swapping stories about baseball and about our lives.

He has a great personality and is full of great stories. And I also discovered that Joe is a pretty good golfer.

Now I guess you could consider us friends.

If anybody is qualified to be the chief of umpires, it is Joe. Knowing him, however, still hasn't stopped me from ripping a man in blue once in a while on the air. Especially if the guy did not hustle to get into position. What bothered me the most about umpires over the years usually had something to do with whether they were in position to do their jobs correctly.

A few years ago when we were in Oakland, I noticed a veteran umpire trying to work his way from the field up a flight of stairs toward the umpires' room. He could barely manage the steps because of his weight. In my opinion, the guy shouldn't be umpiring.

As far as the new replay system, some fans may not like it because it takes calls out of the umpires' hands and it eliminates the human factor, but I love it. They just needed to get the time limit for a replay under control. The games are already long enough.

Baseball has searched for ways to limit the duration of games for years. A few new rules dropped the average length of a game to 2 hours and 56 minutes during the 2015 season, but it was up to 3 hours and 5 minutes in 2017. And that probably is too long for most people. In my era, games normally lasted from 2 hours to 2 hours and 30 minutes at the most.

I always said, "Control the umpires and you will control the length of the game."

Umpires like Joe don't want the games lingering on and on any more than the fans, players, or broadcasters do.

When it's all said and done, I was very pleased that Joe and I patched things up and became good buddies.

In fact, when he retires from active umpiring someday, I firmly believe he should become Major League Baseball's head of all umpires.

He would be the perfect guy to teach young umpires and also force the veterans to hustle.

I know what you must be thinking: whoever would have thought Ken Harrrelson would become the president of an umpire's fan club?

The fact is, I long ago retired from messing with Joe West.

22 "HOW MANY SHOTS YOU GIVING ME?"

WHEN I WAS IN HIGH SCHOOL, I WRAPPED A BELT AROUND most of my books on the first day of school and then threw them into my locker, where they stayed until I turned them in on the final day each year.

In other words, I was a dummy who didn't read much.

It would have shocked my teachers to know I became a voracious reader over the years, other than the sports pages of course, following Ted Williams' advice.

My material of choice? Self-help books.

I must have read 50 of them, always searching for the so-called golden egg of a book that would help me understand my feelings, my mind, and my approach to life.

I found only that one by Michael Murphy, which I read twice and helped my golf game the year after I stopped trying to make it on the PGA Tour.

The others? Most were full of crap, and a waste of time, in my opinion.

In my constant quest to know what made me tick, I also had one meaningful visit to a therapist.

Dick Schwartz, a prominent psychologist in the Chicago area, had written books and hundreds of magazine articles about the human mind and what triggered or controlled behavior.

Fifteen minutes into the session, Dick had me in tears. He explained I had an entire family inside my mind, a family I had never known. I had a Mister Choke, a Mister Happy, a Mister Anticipation, and a Mister Angry, as he labeled them.

"All of those elements make up who you are," he explained. "They will be with you until the day you die and you have to accept them as part of your family."

Dick also taught me that any pressure I had faced, whether it was in everyday life or in athletics, had been mostly self-induced.

Everything he said seemed so profound. It all made perfect sense.

"Embrace all elements of your mind," he said. "Each one will always be a large part of who you are."

So I tried to do just that.

One of my finest moments in golf, right behind qualifying for the British Open, happened at Dan Marino's Celebrity Golf Association event in 1999 at Weston Hills Country Club in Miami.

Former big-league pitcher Rick Rhoden dominated the celebrity tour in those days, winning a majority of the events. I am being completely honest when I say that even though I had played golf with Nicklaus, Trevino, Player, and Palmer, Rick was the best golfer I ever saw from 100 yards to the pin.

In the first round, he and I were paired with NFL quarterback Trent Dilfer. All three of us shot 69, so naturally, we were paired again for the final round. Rhoden blistered the front nine with a 31, while Dilfer shot himself out of contention. I shot a 31 on the back nine to tie Rick for the lead.

We both finished 7-under and nobody else in the field had broken par.

So we headed back to the 18th hole—a 580-yard, par-5—to begin a sudden-death playoff.

First prize paid $30,000 and it occurred to me to ask Rick if he wanted to split the first and second-place winnings, no matter what happened in the playoff.

Then I remembered Rick had a sponsorship deal with Maxfli.

"Rick, how much does Maxfli pay you when you win a tournament?" I asked.

"Ten thousand," he answered.

Screw it, I thought. I couldn't very well ask him to split the pot since he would earn another 10 big ones if he won the event.

It was very hot that weekend, so I told Aris and Krista to go shopping that day and then come out to the course when the tournament would be nearing its conclusion. With only a few holes remaining, I hadn't seen them anywhere on the course and wondered if they had made it or if they were still off spending our money.

Rick hit his first tee-shot in the playoff right down the middle, as he always did. I then hit a long drive left into the 10th fairway. Rick followed with his approach shot to the front of the green.

When I reached my ball, my caddy, Joe Hajduch, a good buddy and a former U.S. long-drive champion, told me I had 280 yards to the pin.

There was water on the right and the pin was way back on the top of the green. I knew the greens were running fast, so with my 3-wood I could land my ball on the front part of the green and hope it ran up to the hole. I hit a rocket out of there, but unfortunately, it ran through the green.

It was the last thing I wanted to do.

As I walked to the 18th green, I finally spotted Krista and Aris standing high above it on a riser.

Then I discovered just how much trouble I faced when I saw my ball had run down the hill behind the green. I noticed I had no margin for error on my next shot.

I also saw John Brodie, the former 49ers quarterback and a great golfer, standing next to the green with a drink in his hand. He just looked at me and shrugged his shoulders, as if to say I had no chance to do anything with it. I looked over and saw Bobby Murcer, whom I had worked with in the booth in New York. He made the same helpless expression to me. Then I saw Jack Marin, the former NBA player, who made a wincing expression.

By the time I sized up my possibilities, I knew I couldn't land the ball on the green or it would run down the hill way past the hole. I couldn't land it short, or it would run down the hill right back to me.

I had to land it perfectly on a small spot on the fringe, so the ball would slowly leak down to the hole.

When I stood over the next-to-impossible shot, which would determine a tournament win or a second-place finish, chipping uphill to a green where I had no margin for error, I told myself, "Okay, Mister Choke, get out of the way and let the Hawk do his thing."

I struck it perfectly. It landed on the exact spot I had targeted and trickled down to the hole, stopping about two feet from the cup. I tapped in for birdie, while Rick made his par.

I collected the $30,000 and donated $5,000 back to Marino's charity.

It was a great golf moment for me, largely because Aris and Krista were there to see it. It's the only tournament they've ever seen me win.

The moral of this story is that Kenny Harrelson couldn't have hit that shot, but the Hawk could.

Dick's teachings rang true to me in that moment. I had embraced my choke side—Jack Nicklaus once told me everybody has a Mister Choke in them—which eliminated any self-induced pressure.

My alter ego had capped off a similar scene years earlier when I received a sponsor's exemption to play in the PGA Senior Tour event at Stonebridge Country Club in Aurora, Illinois. I announced before the tournament that I would give my earnings, along with the money six sponsors had promised to match, to the Century Club of Chicago to benefit fallen officers' families.

I shot 69 the first day and 70 the second, and as I arrived at the course Sunday for the final round, I thought I had a good chance of winning.

That was probably the worst mind-set I could have had. By thinking that way, I had just put more pressure on myself, instead of just relaxing and playing my game. Sure enough, I shot myself out of it by the time I double-bogied the 14th hole.

I hit a big shot off the tee on the 18th hole, a long par-5, leaving me 237 yards to the hole. I looked at my caddy, Roger Warren, and said, "Roger, give me my 7-iron."

I killed that shot, leaving me about 30 feet for an eagle. I walked up to mark my ball and I noticed there must have been 10,000 people in the grandstands surrounding the 18th green. I read the putt and saw that magic line many pro golfers always talk about. It was left to right.

As I stood over my golf ball, I still don't know why I did what I did next. Maybe it was the Hawk taking control.

I backed off the putt and yelled to the crowd, "Are you with me?"

The fans shot back in unison with a huge "Yes!"

I then rolled that 30-footer to the bottom of the cup for an eagle, as the crowd went absolutely nuts.

Larry Zeigler, playing in my group, walked over to me and said, "That's the craziest thing I ever saw."

"That wasn't me, Ziggy," I said. "That was the Hawk."

That putt bumped my prize money to $4,000, which added to the $24,000 the six sponsors matched, resulting in $28,000 for the fallen officers' charity.

My high and low experiences on the golf course and playing thousands of rounds over the years have helped shape who I am, not to mention the times I was enthralled with watching the legends of golf themselves.

I saw how Nicklaus thought his way around a golf course. I watched Arnold schmooze his way around a golf course, smiling and laughing with his fans from tee to green. I was in awe watching how my childhood idol Hobart Manley handled himself on the golf course.

And then there was this encounter with the one and only Ben Hogan.

A buddy of mine, Paul Richards, the former White Sox manager who lived in Waxahachie, Texas, invited me to play at Shady Oaks Golf Course in Fort Worth one time.

"You want to come down and play with Ben Hogan?" he asked.

I couldn't schedule a flight fast enough. I got to the course on a cold, drizzly, and miserable day. Ben and I shook hands and made some small talk. Eventually, the rain stopped and I went out to the range to hit a bucket of balls. I noticed he came out to watch me, but he never said a word. Then he disappeared back into the clubhouse.

When I walked inside, he told us, "Guys, I am not going to play in this weather. You go play and then come back in and we'll have lunch."

Over lunch that day, I wanted to talk golf and Hogan wanted to talk baseball. I learned his two pastimes were playing gin and betting on baseball.

I continued quizzing him about his mental approach to golf. He told me he believed golf instructors should teach the game from the ball forward, instead of what a golfer should do behind the ball on the approach. If a golfer thinks about things that happen behind the ball, like the mechanics of a swing, that golfer is doomed to failure, he said. A golfer should think more about the follow-through and envision where the ball will go once the club makes contact.

The more I thought about that, the more sense it made. It was similar to what Al Vincent, the hitting instructor Alvin Dark hired while with the Athletics, once told me about my approach at the plate. And I think that was one of the philosophies that helped me at the plate during my career season of 1968.

As I watched Tiger Woods during his prime, as he won tournament after tournament, he became the poster child for this philosophy. He usually stood behind the ball, envisioning where his shot would go. I don't think Tiger took practice swings as much as he rehearsed his finish, if that makes sense.

Near the end of our lunch, Hogan told me, "Give me your address. I will make you a set of clubs and send them to you."

The great Ben Hogan would design a custom set of clubs for me?

Within weeks, they arrived. They were, bar none, the greatest set of clubs I ever owned. Those irons were magical to me. Hogan had cut the irons square at the end, instead of his usual curved finishes. I went out and hit a few balls with the wedge, and after my very first swing, I knew I held something special in my hands. I never even mentioned to him what I liked and didn't like in a set of golf clubs. He watched me hit a few balls on the range that day and he figured what I needed.

I took my new clubs to Riviera Country Club near Los Angeles the following week. Peanuts Lowry, a former big-leaguer who was coaching at the time, was a very good golfer. He and I had agreed to meet there to play for some big Nassaus that day.

I just clobbered him.

We played the next day and the following day, too, and Peanuts never won a side as I put him in a big hole. My caddy, who worked at Riviera, told me I was hitting drives where he had never seen them hit before on that course.

I then flew to Washington, where I was scheduled to promote my buddy's travel agency. Not wanting to leave my new clubs in my hotel room, I placed them in a back room of the travel agency, thinking they would be secure. The next day, I rushed to catch a flight to Savannah to play in a tournament there, stopping by the travel agency to pick up the clubs on my way to the airport.

The clubs were gone.

I picked up another set after I arrived in Savannah, and as luck would have it, a writer for *Golf World* magazine was there working on a feature about my golf game. When the magazine hit the newsstands, it included a photo of me using the other clubs, not the Hogan-made clubs that had been stolen.

I knew that would mean trouble, so I called Hogan's Fort Worth office after it hit the newsstands. I explained what happened to his assistant but Hogan wouldn't even get on the phone with me. I can understand since he thought his gift had been so unappreciated.

A year later, I was in West Palm Beach at a nice restaurant. The maître d' approached and said Hogan wanted me to join him for a drink.

I walked to the back of the restaurant where Ben and his wife, Valerie, were sitting in a half-moon-shaped booth. We pulled up a couple of chairs and had a few drinks with them. He was as nice as he could be.

Finally, he said, "I heard what happened to the clubs."

He had forgiven me.

I played only three rounds with those clubs and that was it. They netted me some money from Peanuts, but I would have loved to get my hands on the SOB who stole those clubs.

Winning money on the golf course often supplemented my income.

I once had a good golfing buddy by the name of Carl Rosen, who owned Puritan Fashions. Carl also owned the famous racehorse Chrissie Evert. The tennis legend had endorsed Carl's clothing line, so he named a horse after her.

I called Carl "Satan" because of his appearance. With his shiny black hair and deep tan, he looked exactly the way I figured Satan would look. We frequently played a game called "whip out," because the loser whipped out his money after every hole.

One Saturday, we teed off very early at Doral Country Club in Miami. I played from the tees all the way back while Carl played from the member's tees. Carl was a well-heeled man and I considered him a good friend. He kept his Rolls Royce convertible at Doral and his Mercedes at the Jockey Club.

And he usually carried a Pan-Am bag full of $100 bills.

By the time we reached the 18th tee that day, my golf bag was full of Carl's Ben Franklins, but I was feeling bad for him.

The 18th at Doral is one of the greatest finishing holes in all of golf, a long dogleg to the left with water on the left.

"Satan, I will tell you what I will do," I told him. "I will give you a stroke and a half on this hole—all the money in my bag against that beautiful Rolls Royce convertible you have."

He looked at his caddy and nodded.

I knew he was a born gambler and he would take the bet. I hit first and burned one right down the middle. He got up to the member's tee and I could tell that he was nervous. He promptly poked his tee shot into the water.

"I'll give you a mulligan," I offered.

He then hit his second tee shot into the water. Now I felt even worse for him. Sure, I wanted that convertible, but I knew I wanted to keep his friendship even more.

"This is it now," I told him. "I will give you one more."

He hit his third tee shot in play. I had hit my second shot to about 30 feet from the hole and then I left my first putt three feet short. All I had to do was make the putt to win his beautiful Rolls. It was worth about $70,000 at the time.

I decided I wouldn't make the putt. I pulled it to the left, but I acted as if I was disappointed. He walked over to me and gave me a look, as if to say, "I know what you just did."

I dug out all of those $100 bills and gave them back to him. But that wasn't the end of our day. We left the course, hopped on his helicopter, and headed to Boca Rio Golf Course, about 40 miles to the north near Boca Raton.

I beat him from the first tee to the 18th green again. I had a bag full of cash again. We walked into the pro shop and I pulled the money from my golf bag when Herman Barron, the course's head pro, walked over to greet us.

"Herman, do you have any size-12 Foot Joys for sale?" I asked, noticing several club members gathering around, maybe attracted by the amount of cash I had displayed.

Herman brought me the new golf shoes. I paid for them and opened the box. I then tossed the shoes into the trash can and stuffed all of those $100 bills into the shoebox.

"Got a rubber band?" I asked him.

He handed me one, and I wrapped it around my shoebox full of cash.

"See you guys later," I said, walking out of the pro shop toward Carl's helicopter much wealthier than when we had arrived that day. At least Carl still had his Rolls Royce and we still were buddies, I thought.

As for the members at Boca Rio, I have heard through the grapevine that they have retold that story often through the years.

I didn't always win money on the golf course, however. The game of baseball was full of golf hustlers.

One time I played in Alvin Dark's tournament in Lake Charles, Louisiana, when legendary pitcher Dizzy Dean invited me to play a practice round with him.

"Don't bet with him," Alvin said. "He will hustle you."

I watched Dizzy hit some balls on the range and I figured beating him, even while giving him one shot per hole, would be a piece of cake.

I shot 74 that day—and I had no chance.

Dizzy had set me up: he killed me with that handicap. He obviously had done a great acting job, looking like a hacker on the range.

As many great days and stories as I have enjoyed from golf, nothing has compared to my time living near and playing with the legend of Bay Hill Country Club. We had relocated from Illinois to Orlando in 1988 and settled there, building a house near the 17th tee.

The course, and the entire property for that matter, was Arnold Palmer's baby.

He redeveloped it after buying it in the mid-1960s and then he redesigned every inch of the place, living there for the last 40 years of his life.

Arnold's lasting friendship became one of the highlights of my life.

I called him "Arnie" and he called me "Hawkie." We competed on the golf course, played cards, sipped cocktails, and laughed together for more than 27 years.

Everybody loved being around him, because he treated people the way you are supposed to treat people. He was gracious to fans, kind to any John Doe he met, and always a complete gentleman.

At times over the years, I have thanked my lucky stars for not making the cut at the 1972 British Open, because making it may have prevented Arnold and I from ever becoming close. As I have said, Arnie was a stickler for the rules and etiquette of the game, and if I had bolted for home after the second round because of my temper tantrum, it likely would have ruined our friendship forever.

A Red Sox fan once sent me a picture of me swinging a bat during my AL Player of the Year season of 1968. My left hand just happened to be covered with Arnie's signature umbrella-logoed golf glove.

I couldn't wait to take it to the clubhouse to show Arnie.

We played together that day and when the round was over, I handed him the picture. (He had won the Bob Hope Desert Classic and the Kemper Open the year the picture was taken.)

"Listen, I know you had a good year in 1968," I told him. "But I wanted to provide you with proof that you also helped lead the American League in RBIs."

"Where'd you get that?" he asked, chuckling. Then he had me sign it for him.

I first met Arnold in 1969 when he came to the Savannah Country Club to play an exhibition with Hobart Manley, Hollis Stacy—a future LPGA star who was only 15 years old at the time—and me. Hollis grew up in Savannah just as I had.

Arnold flew in on his private jet and arrived at the clubhouse early, so we ate breakfast together. Hobart had not arrived yet.

"Can I ask you something, Mister Palmer?" I asked. "Besides your-self, if you had to have someone play 18 holes and your life depended on him winning, who would it be?"

"I would take Hobart over any SOB on the planet," he told me.

He didn't say that because Hobart was on his way to play with us, either. Hobart had tour-winning talent and he was great under pressure.

That day, I noticed three drivers in Arnold's bag.

"Why do you have three drivers?" I asked him.

"This one is for a dogleg left, this one is for a dogleg right, and this one I hit dead straight," he explained.

Arnold's personality just captivated me that day.

The gallery that day in Savannah was huge. Arnie had his army, but Hobart always played in front of large crowds in our hometown. I real-ized that day I was playing golf with two of the legends of the game. One won majors and dozens of professional tournaments. The other was probably one of the finest amateurs who ever lived.

As the years passed after we moved to Bay Hill, rarely a day went by when I didn't either play golf with or wave to Arnie—if both of us were in town simultaneously.

We were both competitive and we never played golf with each other without something riding on it.

When Arnie was competing regularly on the PGA Senior Tour, I had a real streak going against him. I was just killing him on the golf course, taking his money every time. And I never, ever took one stroke from him in all the years we played, although to be fair, I happened to be 12 years younger. After every round during this streak, he promptly whipped out his cash and paid off, because that's the type of gentleman he was.

One day as I drove my cart down to the clubhouse for breakfast, I saw Winnie Palmer, who married him when he was still an amateur in 1954. She had a very serious look on her face and I thought something must have been wrong.

"Hawk, when are you going to let Arnold win?" she asked.

I laughed, but then I realized she wasn't joking. To that point, I had no idea his losses to me were bothering him, because he never showed any disappointment or frustration.

I didn't say much, but after I ate breakfast and returned to the house, I told Aris, "Arnie's going to beat me today."

I actually thought about throwing our golf game but it turned out I didn't need to. He shot a 64. I paid him $1,100, and never felt better about losing that type of money.

The next day, as I drove to breakfast, Winnie stopped me again.

"Are you happy now, Winnie?" I asked her.

She hugged me and thanked me profusely.

"I want you to know that I didn't give him anything," I told her. "He shot a 64!"

Arnold was the best at being welcoming and accommodating to whoever played with him. Whenever I had a friend come into town to play golf, I often asked Arnold if they could play together.

"Sure, put him in my group," he always would say.

That's just the way he was. He never, ever turned me down, and I know he did the same thing for many of his other friends. I played with him hundreds of times over the years, but I knew how much it would mean for anybody who loved golf to claim they once played a round of golf with the one and only Arnold Palmer.

Most of them—no matter how rich they happened to be, no matter how important their jobs were, even if they once had played in Major League Baseball—would tell me later, "I have never been so nervous in my life as when I teed off with Arnold Palmer standing next to me."

The only guy I ever asked if he wanted to play with Arnie who turned me down was White Sox general manager Kenny Williams. He was in town for baseball's winter meetings one year when I had already placed him in Arnie's foursome.

"I am sorry, Hawk, but I got a few meetings today," Kenny told me.

I called Arnold and told him, "For the first time in your life, you got turned down on the golf course."

He laughed that hearty laugh of his.

Arnie never refused an autograph, either. Not only did he answer all of his fan mail, but he secured it in a storage area at his home course at Latrobe, Pennsylvania. He never threw out one letter from a fan that I know of.

One day, we were sitting in the clubhouse after a round of golf, just shooting the bull as usual. I was turning Smirnoff into urine and Arnold was drinking his usual Ketel One vodka. Dick Ferris, the former CEO of United Airlines, was Arnold's closest friend and one of our frequent golfing buddies.

"Hawk, you have met so many people in your life," Dick said, winking. "Who's the most charismatic person you have ever met?"

He may have been setting me up, so I looked directly at Arnold and answered, "Well, you are No. 2!"

"Well who's No. 1?" Arnold asked.

"No. 9!" I answered.

I was referring to Ted Williams, the Red Sox great who could walk into any room and capture it within minutes.

But Arnold could do the same thing.

It was common for us to get a foursome and play match-play at Bay Hill. I always contended you learn a lot from a guy when it comes to winning, losing, and who pays off their bets and who doesn't.

One day, Bill Damron, a great guy and fellow member at Bay Hill, and I teamed to beat Arnie and Greg Norman. In the clubhouse after the round, Arnold was as gracious as could be, as usual, not showing he was bothered one bit by losing to two amateurs.

As soon as we sat down, Arnold pulled out his cash to pay off the match. Norman was nowhere to be found.

A few minutes later, Norman stuck his head in the door and said, "Okay, Arnold, I'll see you tomorrow."

He never said a word to us.

Arnie almost had a cow.

"Hey!" Arnie told Norman. "You get in here and pay up!"

Norman walked into the room, threw his money on the table, and walked out without saying a word. I had never liked him much anyway. He was known as the "Great White Shark," but I always referred to him as the "Great White Throatlatch" after he lost the 1996 Masters.

I always rooted for good people to win, no matter what sport, and it was tough for me to root for guys who were not.

While I told Arnold stories from my baseball career, he told me hundreds of golf stories. The successful golfers made huge amounts of money, on and off the course. He once told me that if Tiger Woods retired at that very minute, his monthly pension would be something like $330,000.

On Saturday, April 2, 2016, I walked into the clubhouse at Bay Hill and saw Arnold sitting in his usual spot.

"Hawkie, when are you headed back to work?" he asked me.

"Fly to Oakland tomorrow," I told him.

I sat down at his table and was taken aback by how old he suddenly looked to me. He just didn't appear vibrant, as I was used to seeing him. We sat there making small talk.

When I stood up to leave, he stuck out his hand and said, "I'll see you when you get back in the fall."

"Count on it," I told him.

I then bent over and kissed his forehead. When I walked out of the clubhouse that day, I truly wondered if he would be there that fall when I returned.

By the time I arrived home in Orlando following the baseball season, Arnold was in Pittsburgh. He was about to undergo heart surgery and I had heard he was not doing well.

On the night of September 25, I was relaxing at home when Aris called me.

"Honey, I am sorry to tell you this, but I just heard that Arnold passed away," she told me.

"Good," I replied. "I just knew in his heart that he was ready to go."

Then I hung up and sat in my living room chair, alone, crying like a baby.

Arnie was 87.

I had lost plenty of friends before, but this one hurt in spite of his age. Our relationship may have been much more special to me than it was to him, I was sure, because Arnold had hundreds of good friends. That's the type of guy he was.

That day, I felt just like I did when Mama passed in 1979. As much as I was saddened, I also felt relief, because I knew each of them was in a better place.

I couldn't attend his memorial service. I sat in my living room that day and watched it on television, crying as his grandson, Sam Saunders, delivered an unbelievable and touching tribute at Arnie's Latrobe Country Club course in Pennsylvania.

My neighbor at Bay Hill, Pete Luster, had been Arnold's long-time private pilot. After the service, Pete flew over the course in Arnie's airplane, spreading his ashes.

When he finished, a huge rainbow appeared on the horizon. Fortunately, somebody snapped a picture of it.

It is one of the most-amazing photos I have ever laid my eyes on.

I have it framed, sitting right next to that signed photo of me wearing Arnie's signature golf glove.

23 "I *AM* A HOMER, THANK YOU VERY MUCH"

I ALWAYS CONSIDERED BASEBALL A GAME MADE PERFECTLY for radio, more so than for television.

From the time I heard the voices of Jack Buck and Harry Caray bring Cardinals games into my tiny childhood bedroom, my socks stuffed into the screens to keep the mosquitoes from eating me alive, I loved listening to baseball on the radio.

Through their delivery, I could envision every home run, double play, and diving catch.

Both of those broadcasting legends are gone, of course, as are many of the legends of the broadcast booth. There have been many others like them, but in my opinion, I always considered Ernie Harwell and Vin Scully, who recently retired, as the greatest of them all.

And two of the highlights of my life were getting to know them well.

I also owe them a huge debt of gratitude, along with others such as Tom Hamilton in Cleveland, my former teammate Ray Fosse, who has called A's games for years, and my good buddy Bob Uecker, the legend in Milwaukee. I like to think listening to those West Coast games in the hours of darkness as I drove from the South Side of Chicago to my home in Granger, Indiana, following White Sox games, helped keep me alive.

Years ago, I sat down with Ernie, whose deep voice over WJR in Detroit reached across the Midwest for decades, at old Tiger Stadium before a day game. We talked about the many aspects of his life and I taped our conversation for a broadcast. I discovered that he was not just a broadcasting icon; he was an ex-Marine and an accomplished song-writer. He also had written a few books.

I really believe Ernie was one of the best, but even he got fired once (by incoming Tigers president Bo Schembechler, who later rehired him after an outcry by the fans).

As far as Vin, nobody on this earth dislikes him.

I always considered him a storyteller who happened to handle play-by-play. He was at his best when telling stories.

When the White Sox played an interleague series at Dodger Stadium in 2012, I wanted to pay Vin a visit, never knowing the next time I would bump into him since we worked in two different leagues.

I admired him so much that I wanted to give him a gift of thanks for what he has done for baseball all these years and for keeping me company on my nightly drive home. I knew Vin was a very religious man, attending Mass almost every day. I walked into his booth and asked him to hold out his hand. When he did, I placed this small wooden cross into it and I closed his fingers around it. He opened his hand and looked at it for about 10 seconds without saying a word. I could tell he was getting emotional.

Finally, he said, 'Hawk, thank you so much. I will treasure this gift until the day I die.'"

The game of baseball has been described over the radio airwaves for 100 years and it will be played for hundreds of years to come—and there never will be another Ernie Harwell or another Vin Scully.

Those guys, along with my childhood memories of Jack and Harry, helped shape my concept of how a broadcaster should act, what he should say, and how he should approach his job.

"Don't try to please everybody. You just can't do it."

When I started broadcasting in 1975 with the Red Sox, those were the words of advice from both Curt Gowdy and Howard Cosell, two broadcasting legends. I took them to heart, and I never looked back.

Well, there are plenty of guys in broadcasting today who obviously never were given that advice. There are some great broadcasters working today and there are also a few who are not.

One of the reasons I think I survived this long in the business is I hope I never came across to the viewers or the listeners as somebody who knew more than they did. I never wanted to act like I knew everything about the game, because nobody does. The best who ever managed the game don't know *everything* about it.

I also have given fans credit for knowing the game. A broadcast should not be a Baseball 101 lesson from me. I believed I should allow the parents out there to explain the game to their 10-year-old boy or girl watching the game with them. Some announcers may think they are the reason fans listen to the game. They're not.

I have received plenty of mail over the years, including some hate mail. Much of it has been complimentary. And there have been some expressing gratitude.

Despite what Curt and Howard once told me, I do reach out and call some critical fans once in a while, but only if their letter is well composed and void of vulgarities. I have done that throughout my career, especially since I first arrived in Chicago. I usually wanted to explain to them why I said something in a certain situation, sometimes offering an explanation of what I also couldn't say on the air.

I usually won them over, too.

One day at Fenway, when I called Red Sox games, Gowdy and I were talking with a few other announcers. He said I had it easy.

"It's the guys who work in the two-team towns—such as New York, Chicago, and Los Angeles—who have it tough," he said. "In New York, you have Mets fans calling the talk shows ripping the Yankees announcers, and vice-versa. In Chicago, Cubs fans will call in just to criticize a White Sox announcer. Same with the Angels and Dodgers fans."

Once I arrived on the South Side of Chicago, I discovered what he meant.

I always believed Cubs fans called those radio shows pretending to be White Sox fans just to rip me and my work.

And when I said in 2017 that Wrigley Field needed a vast renovation, the media made a big deal about it, and the criticism of me mounted. Truth is, I sort of loved stirring the pot between White Sox and Cubs fans, because I believed it has been a healthy rivalry that heightens the city's general interest in baseball. It's another example of how inter-league play has helped grow the game.

I told Jason Benetti, the young announcer the Sox hired to replace me on play-by-play, that he needed to be aware of that. Chicago is a two-team city, and someone will always be criticizing him, like they did me or Steve Stone or Harry and anybody else, but maybe for the wrong reasons.

At times, I have made comments that kept the fires burning between the two fan bases.

During the 2016 season, I said I thought Todd Frazier was having a better season at third base than the Cubs' Kris Bryant. The Chicago media went off on me, calling me the biggest homer in the world again. But I wasn't going to hold my opinion just because it offended some Cubs fans.

As it turned out, after Frazier was traded to the Yankees midway through the 2017 season, and Bryant continued to put up huge numbers in the early part of his career.

It was just one more reason for Cubs fans to hate me. In turn, I believe many of them are whiny complainers who behave as if their team has captured 27 World Series championships. Wait, that's the Yankees. The Cubs have one title since 1908, but because it was so recent, they are riding high for the moment. They've won the same number of titles in the past century as the White Sox.

It's not like I've never been wrong before. Show me a broadcaster who was right 100 percent of the time, and I'll show you a guy who was afraid to voice an opinion.

I have never been accused of that.

As fans know, "You can put that on the board!" is my signature home run call when a White Sox player hits one. Krista became a very good diver when she was young, and I attended all of her diving meets and would yell "Yes!" when she nailed a dive. Somehow, I combined those and it morphed into what it is today.

I have heard over the years that most fans love my signature calls, but believe me, I didn't plan them from the beginning. They just happened and then evolved. Such as "He gone!" That one always came easy for me, because I used to say it out loud when I was in the field.

I have used "Stretch!" when a White Sox batter hits a long fly ball that may or may not get out of the ballpark. That, too, came from the game of golf. Many times I stroked a putt that looked short and I yelled "Stretch!" to coax it to the hole. (Note it didn't always work.)

"Mercy!" was a well-known Southern saying I picked up as a kid. "Grab some bench" was a line that's been uttered thousands of times over the years by players after a guy struck out.

One of our producers once told me that some of the guys in the truck designed "Hawko" cards, similar to bingo cards. Each listed my catchphrases, and the first player to fill out his entire card won the game.

Of course, I never considered these catchphrases the meat and potatoes of my work. I loved to tell stories on the air, too, which are especially needed during those lopsided games. And I once in a while stumbled upon giving a player a nickname. Those, too, were never planned.

As I described earlier, there is no sport like baseball when it comes to nicknames. In fact, it's very unusual if a baseball player is called by the first name his parents gave him at birth.

In my day, we often called a guy by his number. I often refer to certain players I knew well that way. Ted Williams was "9" to me, Kaline was "6," and so on. I saw Al as recently as the 2017 season in Detroit when he walked into our booth, and I asked, "How are you doing, 6?"

Frank Thomas was a star from the moment I saw him get his first hit in Milwaukee. He hit the ball so hard so often that I started to say, "He's really put a hurting on that pitch."

One day, in the midst of one of his hot streaks, I just blurted out, "'The Big Hurt' just crushed that one."

It stuck. From then on, he was "The Big Hurt."

On one road trip, I noticed a reserve outfielder, Warren Newson, was all dressed up in a black suit.

"Warren, you look just like the deacon going to church on a Sunday," I told him.

That's how "The Deacon" was born.

Ellis Burks once approached me, requesting a nickname.

"Ellis, it just doesn't happen automatically," I told him. "You have to do something to get one."

Using one nickname over the air that I didn't come up with really got me in hot water years ago.

Jim Fregosi, who I later hired to manage the White Sox, had a nickname well known among other players.

It was "Dago," which obviously could be interpreted as a derogatory term used to describe an Italian American. As far as I knew, Jim had no problems with his nickname. Let's face it, not every nickname in baseball has been politically correct.

I was broadcasting Red Sox games when Jim played with the Rangers and he had a couple of hits one night. I happened to say, "Boy, Dago is really swinging the bat well these days. He's one tough out."

Again, like it had when I told the audience that Tim Foli had "big balls" during my first game over the air, the switchboard at the station lit up. But this time, the critics had the backing of the Italian American Society, which threatened to boycott our sponsors.

I had to apologize to those who were offended.

Another time, I used a term which I was unaware was politically incorrect. During a White Sox game at Boston, the Red Sox brought in a reliever by the name of Daisuke Matsuzaka, a right-hander from Japan. As I started my scouting report on him, I said, "Most of these Oriental pitchers have that same high leg kick."

At that very moment, the switchboard in the studio in Chicago lit up like a Christmas tree. Then the media spent a few days writing about my words. Truthfully, I had absolutely no idea it wasn't a proper term to use to describe someone from Japan. But from the reaction I received, you would have thought I used the worst racial term possible, or insulted the pitcher's heritage.

So I apologized—again.

Normally, if I ever said something objectionable, I usually could tell by glancing over at my broadcast partner's face.

Dick Stockton often had a sour look on his face. Drysdale usually smiled. Paciorek would raise his eyebrows. Steve Stone, who has been by my side since 2009, reverts to complete silence.

Everybody in Chicago realizes Steve and I have had our differences over the years. We got along great at first, then we hit a rough patch, but we had a meeting or two and aired things out, and now we get along great again.

The bottom line is, I always respected the guy. Outside of Drysdale, Steve knows how to articulate pitching better to fans than anybody I ever met. I think he is a terrific analyst. Many fans may not know that he won 25 games and the Cy Young Award with the Orioles in 1980, and he was one of the smartest pitchers the game has ever seen. If you show me a guy who can pitch up in the zone with good stuff like Steve did, I will show you a winner.

I watched the 1980 All-Star Game and Steve, who started it, put on one of the best performances by any pitcher in All-Star history. He faced nine batters over the first three innings and was perfect. I am sure that will never be done again, because managers do not use starting All-Star pitchers for more than an inning or two.

When he retired the ninth National League batter that night at Dodger Stadium, I stood in my living room and gave him a one-man standing ovation. Aris may have rolled her eyes at me, but I did that often in front of the TV if I saw a performance—in any sport—that deserved one.

I have experienced a lot of baseball over the years, but my time in the game is coming to an end. My critics won't have this "homer" to kick around in the future.

It was true that I wanted the teams I worked for to win. There were even times as a broadcaster I got involved with negotiations on a free agent.

Following the 1983 season, the White Sox wanted to re-sign second baseman Julio Cruz, a free agent who had an offer from the Angels.

I told Julio what I believed: he couldn't play for better owners or a better organization than Jerry Reinsdorf, Eddie Einhorn, and the White Sox.

"I really believe the Sox have a bright future," I told him, "and you are the one guy who holds this club together."

After our talk, he met with Jerry and Eddie and decided to stay in Chicago, signing a six-year contract.

They certainly didn't need my help to make their case, but it was imperative in my mind that the Sox keep Jose. I also was convinced it was the best thing for Jose, too.

Over the air, I frequently refer to the White Sox as "the good guys" and I won't apologize for that, either.

What my critics never realized was that a certain percentage of players on all of those teams probably couldn't stand me. You know why? I had been critical of them at times on the air. Did that make me a homer, too, or was that telling it like it is, when I saw a guy not hustle to first?

I could never stand laziness. There is no excuse for not running hard on ground balls or pop-ups. I never liked mental errors, either. Everybody makes physical errors, but mental errors shouldn't be made repeatedly at the big-league level. I have never, ever tried to fool the fans over the years and I think they understood that. After all these years, I think they learned they could trust me and I wouldn't purposely misguide them.

I also learned to let the cameras do the work at times. The viewers' eyes don't lie. They knew what they were seeing on their TV screens, and silence sometimes was my greatest tool. I called a lot of replays over the years, and if I saw somebody loafing down the line, I often hit my mute button and told our director Jim Angio, "Jimmy, let's see that again."

Jimmy would show the replay of a baserunner loafing down the line, and I wouldn't have to say a word. When that player got home that night, his family members may have told him, "Boy, Hawk really ripped you on the air again for not running hard," but it really wasn't me or my words.

The camera never lies to the audience.

Producing a game for TV has changed as much as anything else over the years. Now there are dozens of bells and whistles. There is a strike-zone box and more graphics and items that may not be entirely about the game itself. When I first started out, Bobby Whitehall was my director *and* producer. There is no way one person could do both of those jobs today.

But the sports television business has to continue progressing and evolving because there are just too many other things to watch these days besides baseball.

I have detailed my love for tradition and the old-school ways of base-ball repeatedly. But I violated one of those, at least according to my critics, when I called a game against Tampa Bay in 2009.

After the eighth inning, before we went to break, I said, "Call your friends, call your sons, call your daughters…Mark Buehrle has a perfect game heading into the ninth inning."

Of course, there has been a long-standing tradition to never mention a no-hitter or a perfect game while it was in process, as though the very mention of it would jinx the pitcher. That is taboo for teammates and coaches in the dugout—not for broadcasters in the booth high above the playing field.

I wanted to give everyone with a TV the chance to witness history in the making. My job was to give everyone the opportunity to see it. I also realized that with cell phones, almost everyone on earth above the age of 12 was reachable with one call.

In the months that followed Buehrle's perfecto, I received dozens of letters from fans thanking me. Thousands of people who were in the midst of doing something else that day tuned in to watch that ninth inning, because a friend or relative had called them, following my advice.

It was no secret I openly rooted for guys like Buehrle and A.J. Pierzynski.

Buehrle is one of the nicest guys I ever met, almost a clone of my favorite teammate, Catfish Hunter. I'll never forget the first time I saw Mark pitch. Don Cooper, a pitching coach in the White Sox organization since 1988, came up to me one day during spring training in the late 1990s.

"Hawk, there's a little left-hander warming up over there on a back field," he said. "Go over there and watch him. Then tell me what you think."

I walked over, watched him warm up, and figured the little guy didn't have a chance. He wasn't throwing very hard. He didn't have great stuff. I was wondering who signed him.

Then the game started.

I could tell within an inning or two he knew how to pitch. I wrote everything down back then. I watched his next start, too and when I looked at my notes, he had thrown 21 first-pitch strikes to the first 23 batters he faced in those two outings. I knew that he had great control and he was not afraid of anyone.

It was difficult for me to tout a young pitcher throwing 83 miles per hour, but I told everybody I knew that the White Sox had a guy who was going to win a ton of games.

The club called him up during the 2000 season and the rest is history. Fifteen years later, he retired with 214 career wins and he recently had his number retired by the White Sox. He was a five-time All-Star and pitched 200 innings or more in 14 consecutive seasons, a feat accomplished by Hall of Famers such as Greg Maddux and Christy Mathewson.

I sincerely hope Buehrle will be inducted into the Hall of Fame someday.

And by saying that, I realize I may enhance my reputation as the "biggest homer in baseball." That's fine with me.

24 SABERMETRICS AND STEALING SIGNS

THERE IS NO DOUBT BASEBALL'S REPUTATION AS AMERICA'S favorite pastime suffered once the players went on strike in the summer of 1994. For the next three years, attendance dipped and interest sagged—and I never blamed the fans one bit for their apathy.

I will forever claim that strike never needed to happen.

And then the Cardinals' Mark McGwire and the Cubs' Sammy Sosa came along, swinging for the fences.

McGwire hit 70 home runs and Sosa hit 66, both shattering Roger Maris' single-season record of 61, and that was all anybody talked about as the 1998 season progressed. The media attention on their head-to-head home run race was overwhelming, and suddenly, thousands of fans migrated back to loving the game again.

Then reports surfaced that their home run duel had been fueled by performance-enhancing drugs.

Seven years later, the two of them sat next to Rafael Palmeiro, testifying in front of Congress about steroid use in baseball. I always loved Mark but he looked bad that day, repeating, "I don't want to talk about the past. I am here to talk about the future."

It obviously was a rehearsed line, which I am sure originated from poor legal advice.

He wasn't the only one looking silly over this issue.

Commissioner Bud Selig, who I still believe was the best commissioner of the eight commissioners I've known, also looked foolish when he held a large press conference to address the steroid issue.

There were no microphones for the media and he could not hear the questions being asked of him. The lights were bright in Bud's face as he squinted and often asked the reporters to repeat their questions. At times, he also looked confused.

The entire thing didn't go off well, but it really wasn't Bud's fault.

I called him the next day. He agreed that the optics weren't good.

Neither Sosa nor McGwire ever admitted to taking steroids to my knowledge, but their numbers and careers came under suspicion by the media, and they have not been inducted into the Hall of Fame in Cooperstown, New York.

Neither have Barry Bonds, or Roger Clemens, or Palmeiro.

I have no doubt that long-term use of the juice isn't good for the human body, but when fans or the media ask me how I feel about steroids in baseball, I have one simple answer:

"The home run race *saved* baseball."

That response always throws them into a tizzy. But that home run race and the media coverage it generated brought thousands, if not millions, of fans back to the game, where they have remained.

It's ironic in a way, because if we ever lifted weights in my day, we faced a stiff fine. Clubs didn't want baseball players lifting because the common belief then was that we would lose the fluidity in our muscles.

With salaries skyrocketing in the 1990s, if a player realized taking steroids would take a few years off his life, but he also could secure his family financially for generations, would he still do it? That was the decision many players faced, and it really was tough for me to second-guess them.

When it comes to the Hall of Fame issue, I believe if players had Hall of Fame numbers before they ever touched the juice, then they should be inducted. If not, and steroids produced their numbers, they should not. But how would you know for sure when they started?

McGwire hit 49 home runs as a rookie for the A's in 1987. Look at pictures of him when he came up—he had a skinny frame, so there was no way he was taking steroids as a rookie. Mark often battled plantar fascia, which is very painful. I remember having a little bone bruise on my heel after the '67 World Series. I went home to Savannah and I couldn't play golf for two weeks because of it. So there was no doubt in my mind that if Mark used steroids, he used them to recover from those painful foot injuries.

I also believe Sosa, Palmeiro, Clemens, and Bonds should be in the Hall of Fame, since their production had been so impressive for many years before their bodies obviously changed.

On the other hand, I have no respect for Mark's former teammate, Jose Canseco.

He had great talent and a pretty good career, but then he ratted people out for using steroids in his book and lost everybody's respect. During his final season in the big leagues, with the White Sox in 2001, I happened to be in the clubhouse one day when he took off his shirt.

I stood there just staring at him, wondering if I had stumbled into the Bears' locker room by mistake. He had muscles on his muscles.

When he later admitted in his book how he got so big, it all made sense.

There was no drug-testing program through the years in baseball, and those players did what they could to gain an edge.

Performance-enhancing drugs aside, it has been a game conducive for what some would claim is "cheating," but that was the way the game always has been played.

Remember the time that the Yankees' Graig Nettles' bat busted open and a bunch of Super Balls bounced out onto the infield? Sosa, too, got caught one day in 2003 at Wrigley, with a layer of cork flying from his broken bat. Well, Nettles and Sosa weren't the first guys to cork their bats, either.

Many guys in my era did it.

Including me.

I have more shocking news for you: we also stole signs and tried to get "tells" on pitchers.

Is that cheating?

Not in my book.

It was part of the game, part of the culture.

It was, and is, *baseball*.

Certain pitchers would give away certain pitches without ever knowing it. For example, I knew when Luis Tiant was about to throw a curveball.

I think I had 40 at-bats against Luis in my career, getting only eight hits. Now, that average may be only .200, but seven of those eight hits were home runs. In his windup, Luis would drop his hands when he was about to throw a curveball. He didn't do it in the stretch, so I am sure most of my home runs were with the bases empty.

If a player wasn't in the lineup on any given day, Alvin Dark would tell him, "Watch this guy and see if you can pick up any tell on him."

I am guessing almost every manager in history has said similar things to his players.

It served two purposes—it kept a bench player in the game mentally, and if he discovered something, it could help win a game.

Joe Nossek was the best I ever saw at it. He could stare at a pitcher for a few pitches and discover something pretty quickly, and he stole signs from the other teams' third-base coach as well as anybody.

Of course, there were more artificial and elaborate methods, too.

If a club had a fast team, maybe it placed bases 91 feet apart at home. If they were slow, maybe they were moved up to 89 feet.

I know that a lot of clubs used lights somewhere in the outfield seats to help their hitters. They had somebody stationed in the bleachers with binoculars to steal the catcher's signs and then they would relay them with a walkie-talkie. If it was a breaking pitch, a light somewhere on the scoreboard would flash for the batter to see.

We had a guy in Cleveland who sat in center field, wearing a white sanitary legging on his right leg and looking through binoculars to see the catcher's signs. If the catcher called for a breaking ball, our guy would stick his right leg out into the aisle.

We were facing Minnesota one time in 1969 when Bob Miller was on the mound for the Twins. I could never touch his slider, but I stood in the batter's box in that game, staring into the center-field stands. After I saw that white sanny slide way out into the aisle, I sat on Bob's slider. I hit it into the upper deck in left field.

As I rounded third base I saw Billy Martin, the Twins' first-year manager, standing at home plate, holding my bat.

"You son of a [expletive]," Billy said. "You are strong, but you are not that strong. This bat is corked!"

"Hawk, is your bat corked?" the umpire asked.

"No," I told him.

"Okay, then," he said. "Just don't use it again."

I knew that slider was coming because of our sign-stealing system and Billy didn't have a clue.

Sign-stealing was an art, probably the biggest art in baseball, but knowing the location of a pitch would also be a big help.

I often asked the guy in the on-deck circle to use my name to let me know where the catcher set up behind the plate.

For example, if the catcher moved inside when the pitcher was in his windup, the guy behind me may have said, "Come on, Kenny!"

If he set up outside, he may have said, "Come on, Hawk!"

Using names or numbers also were and are very common methods to relay a message to the hitter. That's why you see catchers tapping their hands on the dirt in one direction and then moving to the other as the pitch arrives. The hitter likely is listening to where the catcher is setting up behind him. It has always been against baseball etiquette for the batter to turn and look at the catcher.

And when one pitch could mean the game, we tried anything to get an edge.

Certain guys in my era made the club because they were great bench-jockeys, especially talented at getting under the opposing pitcher's skin. We realized that if we could get certain pitchers, especially young ones, ticked off, we had a better chance to knock them out of the game.

Bobby Del Greco was the best bench-jockey I ever saw and that was one reason he was on our ballclub in Kansas City. Bob Uecker also was a big asset because of his fists. That may have been another reason he made the Braves' roster all of those years. The Ueck was as tough as they came and good with his dukes. Some people even called him "Hank Aaron's personal bodyguard."

This brings me to the numbers game that is being played today.

As Aris and I flew to Arizona for the beginning of spring training years ago, I made the mistake of allowing her to pick the movie we would watch.

Wouldn't you know, she wanted to watch *Moneyball*, the movie that glorified Oakland A's general manager Billy Beane's approach to procuring players based on a relatively new term: "sabermetrics."

Sabermetrics, as I understand it, basically tosses old-school scouting methods out the window to emphasize statistical analysis to determine a player's value. They call it "objective statistical evidence," versus judging players by the naked eye or with the experienced gut instinct and other factors scouts have used for more than 100 years.

I remember reading a newspaper story about the movie when it came out in 2011. Steve Stone was my broadcast partner at the time and he and I got into a discussion on the air that night in Toronto.

"This thing could get a lot of good baseball people fired if owners actually believe it is the way to go," I said.

"Will you watch the movie?" he asked me.

"Nope," I said. "I will never watch that thing."

Well, we had a long flight and I basically had no choice. I gave in to Aris, but nothing in the movie changed my mind. What jumped out at me is what was *not* in the movie.

If you know anything about baseball or watched the A's play from 2000 to 2004, pitchers Mark Mulder, Barry Zito, and Tim Hudson carried those teams. Mulder won 21 games in 2001 and 19 the following season; Zito, a three-time All-Star, won 23 games and the Cy Young Award in '02; and Hudson won 69 games over four seasons.

Those three arms had more to do with the A's success than any new approach Beane took to the game of baseball. When a team ran pitchers like those out to the mound every night, it could play any type of baseball and still have a good chance to win the game.

I know one thing will never change, however, and that is the average baseball fan's love of numbers. The fan wants to know if a player makes $20 million a year, or if he hits .300, or hits 40 home runs, or drives in more than 100 RBIs.

Numbers define the game for many fans, so it's only natural that they pay attention to sabermetrics.

I have talked to several managers in recent years fed up with this trend. Some won't allow it to be a factor when they make out their lineup cards, even if it gets them fired.

This would shock most people: there are plenty of general managers who send their proposed lineup cards down to the managers, based on their analytics. This practice has become more and more common.

There also is little doubt money has become a determining factor in making decisions that should instead be "baseball decisions."

As a broadcaster, I have stayed away from a player's salary and anything to do with money. That issue was none of my business. I believed big-name players who are making $20 million a year are earning it, because they put butts in the seats. On the other hand, I always had a problem with the guys making $7 million a year who couldn't play.

But I never, ever criticized a guy on the air for the size of his paycheck. That was a no-no in my book.

What I don't like about how much players are paid today is the fact that it has taken away a manager's leverage. Money has changed the culture of the game, simply because it took the power from managers and gave it to the players.

When I played, the highest-paid guy on the team *was* the manager. He could threaten a player with a trip back to the minors. Now, with guys having $50 million guaranteed contracts, if a manager ever said something like that, the player would tell him to get out of his face.

Other pro-sabermetrics people claimed the Red Sox won the 2004 World Series based on analytics, but they never mentioned the Red Sox had one of the highest payrolls in baseball.

In my time around Beane, he seemed like a good kid, but all I ever heard him talk about was the stock market.

Sabermetrics disdains bunting and the art of the hit-and-run. I believe the more that numbers and statistics are brought into the game, the more instincts and experience are taken out of it. People are inundated with too many numbers in baseball today.

This has been a kid's game and it will always be.

There is and has been a place in baseball for numbers, as I said, but they don't mean *everything,* as the sabermetrics' crowd would have you believe. Nowadays, there are acronyms such as WAR, BABIP, CERA, DIPS, ISO, VORP and so on. I don't know what most of them mean.

As I said, I am one of the few who always believed batting average was the most overrated statistic in baseball. I don't care what a player's average is. I want to know when he got those hits. Did he get a hit in the second inning with two outs and nobody on base, or did he get it in the seventh, eighth, or ninth inning with runners on base and the game on the line?

That is what made Yaz such a great player. He usually came through in the late innings during a tight game. How does sabermetrics measure Yaz? Or Don Mattingly? Or a hundred other clutch hitters?

What I really hate is that a lot of young kids have been learning the game through sabermetrics.

The most important abbreviations to me are W and L.

Can sabermetrics capture the value of leadership? When does the will to win—I call that TWTW—play a factor? What does experience do? Those intangibles add up to Ws.

Missing the cutoff man, missing a sign, not hustling, or failing to get a bunt down have nothing to do with numbers but they all lead to Ls.

Baseball is a game made up of 25 individuals on one team, and if they know how to play the game correctly, or at least better than the 25 on the other side, those efforts will result in a win on that particular day.

If a team does the right things on the field and thinks as a team, it probably will win a lot of games.

Take the Cubs' 2016 season, for example. Theo Epstein, the general manager of the Cubs when they finally broke through and won the World Series, held the same position with the Red Sox when they broke through. They say he uses sabermetrics.

I believe the best thing Theo did was hire Joe Maddon. Joe won in Tampa Bay consistently with lesser talent, because he is very smart, has superior instincts, and is a great motivator. Those Tampa Bay clubs always gave him 27 outs every night. They never took a play off.

I never believed the only mark of a great manager was the wins and losses—it is how hard his team plays day in and day out. On the other hand, the gauge of a general manager, like Beane or Theo, should be wins and losses.

The bottom line: I believe sabermetrics is the most overrated thing to come into baseball in a long, long time.

Today's game also has been driven by agents, who carry great influence with a club's general manager.

It is common today for an agent to call a team's general manager and say that their client's arm is sore. The agent also may tell his client, "Tell them your arm is not quite ready yet and you need to go on the disabled list." By doing so, the agent wants to extend the career of that pitcher in order to get him another large contract.

There were 9,900 player-days on the disabled list during the 2015 season. That number was exceeded by August the following season. The number increases with each season. Why? Are players today getting hurt more often than the players in my era?

Heck, no.

Players aren't playing hurt like they did in the old days. They don't want to take a chance, and the agents don't want them to take a chance, given the millions of dollars they earn. I know Drysdale would be rolling in his grave over the agents' influence. He pitched an entire season with a broken finger on his pitching hand.

I also know teammates are not as close today as they used to be. When I played, five or six taxis were all that were needed to get our team from the ballpark to whatever bar or restaurant we were headed to after a game. Today, they need 15 or 20 limos, and they probably are headed in 15 or 20 different directions. It has become more of a business and less of a game, but I don't blame the players one bit. They just don't realize how it once was. Today, they are much, much better players on average than we were, but I can guarantee you that they don't have as much fun playing the game as we did.

Off the field, players today are pampered and most may not even realize how great they have it, compared to the way it used to be.

All clubs have traveled on chartered flights for several years now, unlike my days playing for cheapskate Charlie. There is no waiting for flight crews or changing planes or layovers. All of the team hotels are the best in that city, mostly Ritz Carltons and Four Seasons. Nobody doubles up anymore (let alone the three-to-a-room Charlie required some places). Some players today even upgrade to huge suites.

Today, as part of the players' agreement, Major League Baseball clubs must employ an executive chef to prepare the food in the clubhouse. And let me tell you, it is every bit as good as any you will eat in the finest restaurant. Before a game, players usually eat a snack in the clubhouse, take batting practice, then come in and eat a little more before game time. After the game, a nice dinner buffet is laid out, featuring entrée such as filet mignon, grouper almondine, or chicken cordon bleu.

To say clubhouse fare has come a long way from my days would be like saying air travel has progressed since Orville Wright.

When I played with the Indians, our clubhouse guy would set out a bowl of potato chips, a roll of bologna, and liverwurst. He would lay out a few loaves of white bread, next to the mayo, ketchup, and mustard. And that served as our postgame meal. If we grabbed a beer or Coke out of the cooler, the clubbie put a check by our name.

We weren't even allowed to eat in the clubhouse before a game, because they figured we would play more aggressively if we were hungry. They thought we would be passive on a full stomach.

Clubhouses today are very plush, too. I think the Cubs' new clubhouse measures 30,000 square feet, including the players' lounge and training area.

I remember my first clubhouse in the minor leagues. The manager didn't say, "Go pick your locker." He said, "Go pick your nail."

We would find a nail, albeit a rusty one which had been hammered into a two-by-four, and hang our clothes on it.

Again, we didn't mind it because that's the way it was for everybody and we didn't know any better.

Players were supposed to tip clubhouse hosts. The most generous guy I ever saw was my roommate with the Senators, Frank Howard. I would like to think I was the second-most generous. You can tell a lot about a person by how he tips.

A few years back, I asked the White Sox visiting clubhouse guy, "I won't ask who the worst tippers are, but who are the good ones?"

"One has to be Alex Rodriguez," he said. "If the Yankees come in for a three- or four-game series, he may give me $3,000. And another guy was Cal Ripken Jr."

That was good to hear about A-Rod. Of course, he did have that $30 million salary to pull some pocket change from.

That was another reason I always loved jockeys. I have been around several over the years, guys such as Eddie Arcaro, and they never let anybody around them spend money. They always tipped generously. Football players were always decent, too. The worst tippers were golfers. Those guys on the PGA Tour believe everything should be given to them, but maybe it is because golf is an individual sport and they never had a chance to understand the team concept.

On the field, one of the biggest changes in strategy or the way the game is played today relates to the quality of the bullpens.

In the past, the starters were the best pitchers on every team and the bullpen was the place they stuck those who were not good enough to make the starting rotation.

It's certainly not like that today. The best pitchers come out of that bullpen every night in the seventh, eighth, and ninth innings, especially if that team has a lead. Thus, hitting in late innings is much, much more difficult than it used to be.

One change has been great for the game: interleague play. I would love to see it expanded with a realignment of both leagues.

As it is in recent years, the White Sox and Cubs face each other only four times per season. Wouldn't it be great if baseball realigned so the Angels-Dodgers, Yankees-Mets, Phillies-Orioles, A's-Giants, White Sox–Cubs, and all the other clubs in close proximity were in the same division in the same league?

That way, they would face each other 18 times per season.

To me, that is the final frontier. That change would help maintain the game's popularity for decades to come.

In many ways, the game has been based upon tradition. And tradition often overrules common sense.

How else to explain that there has been a designated hitter in the American League since 1973 and not a DH in the National? That has been the most ridiculous inconsistency for four decades. Because of that rule, the AL has played a different game than the NL.

I don't care if they get rid of the DH or keep it, but it should be the same for both leagues.

When it comes to rules and rule changes, I believe one of the latest changes—the institution of the "Buster Posey Rule," written to prevent home-plate collisions—as well as the new rule to prevent a runner on first from taking out the fielder at second base—were terrible changes.

First of all, the baserunner who tries to run over the catcher normally is the player who gets hurt more often. (Pete Rose and Ray Fosse being an exception.) With these changes, baseball has eliminated two of the most exciting plays in the game.

I have been privileged and honored to stay around baseball since the late 1950s. Fans tell me that the game has changed. Well, the players have changed. When they change, the game changes along with it.

I like some of the changes in the game, love a few other parts, and yet hate a few others.

I wish there were more African American players in the game. At the start of the 2017 season, of the 750 players on the 30 teams, only 62 were black. I don't know how to increase that number since there are few places to play baseball in our inner cities.

By contrast, 40 percent of the players today are from Latin America. That is one reason why if I was a general manager or owner today, I would prefer managers who are bilingual. Manager need to have the tools to communicate effectively with the entire ballclub.

Learning Spanish should be a requirement for any coach or manager in the minor league system. Guys like Lou Piniella had an advantage, in my opinion, because they were bilingual. Nothing got lost in translation when they were trying to communicate with players. The Latin kids grow up playing a different game than American kids do. They see the ball, hit the ball, and develop great instincts. They don't get off their islands to reach America's big leagues by taking pitches and coaxing walks. They get here by crushing a first-pitch fastball thrown over the plate.

When people say that I'm old school, I take that as a compliment. I don't like what I see in clubhouses today after a loss. Some guys just don't hurt like you are supposed to hurt after a loss. I have heard laughter, I have heard music, and I have seen smiles after tough losses. That always ticked me off. If you are playing every game to win, every loss should hurt.

Changes or no changes, baseball still is unique in so many ways: It's the only game with no clock, the only game in which a team cannot score on defense, and the only game where the team on defense controls the ball. These are the elements that make the game so beautiful.

The superstars of my era would be stars today, but the average player today is better. In my day, Luis Aparicio was the best shortstop in the game. Heck, there are five shortstops today better than him.

If I was a baseball fan and I was driving through Boston today, I would want to go to Fenway to see Xander Bogaerts play. If I was driving through Cleveland, I would want to buy a ticket to see Francisco Lindor play. If I was in Baltimore, I would want to see Manny Machado and Adam Jones. If I was in Anaheim, I would pay to see Mike Trout.

In my seven decades in the game, I can honestly say there have never been so many good, young players. The future of baseball is in good hands with these guys and dozens more I have not mentioned.

I don't see their huge salaries steadying or stalling, either. I think they will continue to increase. Team owners wouldn't pay what they pay if they couldn't afford it.

One thing I worry about is fans' safety.

I have seen dozens of fans over the years get hit by foul balls or by a bat that slipped out of the hitter's hands, or even a broken bat that splinters apart and becomes a lethal spear. I worry someday that a fan will get killed.

When a line drive flies into the stands these days, I'm afraid to even look. (Unfortunately, I saw a fan die at Yankee Stadium when I was calling Red Sox games. During a rain delay, some guy tried to climb down to a better seat. Fans were cheering him on, but then he slipped over the railing and fell head-first right onto the concrete.)

Those images sometimes keep me awake at night.

As a broadcaster for all these years, I have been honored and privileged to help deliver baseball to millions of fans.

For the average fan, watching baseball on the tube still may not surpass the experience of seeing the green grass of the outfield up close, smelling the aroma of ballpark hot dogs, or hearing the crack of the bat.

Sabermetrics, overzealous agents, and the DH be damned—even as the game changes through the years—the sights, smells, and sounds of baseball will always remain the same.

And they will never grow old to me.

25 "HE GONE!"

OVERMATCHED AND MOSTLY INEXPERIENCED, THE 2017 WHITE
Sox gave great effort in their first season under Rick Renteria, from
opening day to the final game, just as I expected they would. However,
they still finished 28 games below .500 with a 67–95 record.

They traded veterans such as third baseman Todd Frazier to the
Yankees, outfielder Melky Cabrera to the Royals, and pitcher Jose
Quintana to the Cubs to further their rebuilding process for the future,
which should be very bright very soon as their young prospects develop
into stars.

On the team's charter from Cleveland to Chicago after the final
game, a 3–1 loss ending the final road trip of my broadcasting career,
Renteria grabbed a boom box at the front of the airplane.

He then pushed a button to play Sinatra's "My Way."

While the song played, the players stood to give me a standing
ovation—and I had tears in my eyes.

That song always has been one of my favorites and it was appropriate
as far as I was concerned. The words describe my career in many ways.

"And now, the end is near, and so I face the final curtain..."

The final curtain is coming for this guy, who I am sure many of today's
players, broadcasters, or baseball executives regard as "old school," some
perhaps only because of my age and others because of my opinions.

I still take it as a compliment, even though I know when it comes
from a young executive, or maybe from a fan, it is meant in a demeaning manner. I have no doubt many of my critics claim I live in the past.

The truth is, life is about gaining experience.

And you know what they say about experience? It's something you gained through the years, which you didn't want to gain.

I never have been accused of holding back on my opinions, but my ability to speak my mind symbolizes what makes this country the best on the planet. We all have our opinions and are free to put them into words. As you know by now, I have put dozens of mine into this book. Thank God for the First Amendment.

To that end, I have always considered myself very patriotic and always cared deeply about our country. I believe all Americans should be thankful for those rights.

I always believed in what that American flag stood for, and stands for, as it waves before, during, and after a baseball game in ballparks across America. The nightly performance of our national anthem, and the presence of the flag, is worth standing for in my opinion.

This issue obviously had become a hot topic in the NFL, but not so much in baseball. I got to know former Bears coach Mike Ditka from my time in Chicago and I often wish Colin Kaepernick had played for him.

I think Iron Mike would have grabbed him and made him stand at attention, but who knows? I likely will be criticized for this opinion, too, since the PC element has taken control of how we are supposed to think and what to believe in over the last several years.

Like Ditka, I won't apologize for my beliefs.

During a road trip to Baltimore in 2014, White Sox radio play-by-play man Ed Farmer asked me if I wanted to take a tour of Air Force One. Ed, one of my favorite guys in the broadcasting business, had arranged the tour through his connections, so I jumped at the chance.

Just like when I drove down Magnolia Lane for the first time, when I walked into Yankee Stadium that first time, and when I walked the 18th fairway at the British Open in 1972, I walked up those stairs of Air Force One that day with tears in my eyes.

I knew then I was privileged to see the symbolic power and impressiveness of that airplane. I instantly was fascinated by the three sections of security clearance, with the carpets colored red where the president slept and worked, with a blue section for personnel and a white section for guests and media. (I read recently that system has changed since our tour.)

The man who conducted it was wonderful to us. He told us plenty of behind-the-scenes stories. I don't want to describe him in too much detail, or even say what his position was, because of what he told me when I quizzed him that day.

I pulled him aside and asked, "Who were the best people you ever worked for?"

He never hesitated.

"No question about it—the Reagans!" he said. "Nancy knew everybody's name and was so nice to us, as was President Reagan. They were wonderful people. The Bushes also were very nice."

Okay, he gave me that, I thought, but there was no way he would answer my next question.

"You might not be able to say, but who were the *worst*?" I asked.

The man shocked me, letting out an expletive before using a certain former first lady's name.

"Hillary!" he said. "She just treated everybody like crap! Every time she walked onto the plane, we had to back up against the side of the airplane and bow our heads until she passed by. That was the rule. Can you believe that? We all considered her an evil person."

I am not taking political sides at all—just reporting what he told me that day.

I do support our current president, no matter what his critics say, because I want him to be successful for the good of our country. I care about the future of my kids and grandkids. He has more critics than any president I can remember, but I call him "New York smart," and that's meant as a compliment.

It is sad, however, to see how divided our country is these days.

As I write this, I am nearing the end of my 55th season in professional baseball, whether as a player, general manager, or broadcaster.

I have seen it all and done it all, for the most part.

And I know, like the game of baseball, I too have changed.

For the better, I hope.

I am no longer the guy who goes out every night. I rarely, if ever, drink in public anymore. That part of the Hawk has been long gone. It has been a long time since I got into a good scrape. I suppose that's a natural part of the aging process, or maybe the maturing process.

I enjoyed my downtime on the road, although "getaway days" are tougher than they used to be. But when I traveled with the White Sox, I didn't even touch my bags unless I was packing or unpacking. Everything was done for me, as it was for the players, because the club has an excellent traveling secretary by the name of Eddie Cassin.

In the old days, I enjoyed a few drinks and played cards with my teammates during flights. In recent years, I have sat by myself and read or watched Netflix or played gin or hearts on my iPad.

I can guarantee you that nobody in Major League Baseball—player, manager, writer, or broadcaster—spent more time in his hotel room than I did. I always ate alone on the road, unless I was in the clubhouse, because that's the way I liked it. Steve Stone has been my broadcast partner for more than nine seasons and I have never had lunch or dinner with him. And anybody who knows me knows I don't even eat breakfast.

After a night game, I would kick back, mix a Smirnoff and diet tonic, and watch TV.

That describes the average night on the road for this guy, who years ago lived for the nightlife and was in more bar-room brawls than he can remember.

One thing hasn't changed for me—I still enjoy my interaction with fans.

And I don't want to be paid for it, either, although I have always been a big proponent of the aging baseball stars being able to sign autographs for money. If you think about it, they played the game because they loved it, not because of the money. They didn't make millions of dollars like today's stars, or even today's average players.

I have signed for money only once and that was because it was a signing with Yaz. I get about five or six requests for official signings each year and I pass on each one.

Most of today's players don't understand what the players of yester-year went through. There is much less player-fan interaction today; big money has changed everything. I would bet that I signed more autographs during recent seasons than most entire teams do, and that is sad. These players today pull out their cell phones and act like they are having a conversation when they walk through a hotel lobby, just so they don't have to sign. They disappoint me in how they treat the fans.

I don't mean all of them, certainly.

That is why I always appreciated players such as Cal Ripken Jr. and David Wright. I know there are many others who go out of their way to sign, too, just not as many as there should be.

The players of yesterday treated the fans much, much better, and I believe I am in position—having stayed in the game this long—to make that judgment.

As far as my future, Jerry Reinsdorf came to me at the end of the 2015 season and asked me what I wanted to do about my schedule.

I told him that the drive from Chicago to my summer home in Granger, Indiana, was a tough one after a night game. I had to endure 90 miles on an interstate with truckers riding my back bumper. I have learned they don't have much patience at that time of night, and neither do I.

What made the drive bearable over the years was listening to the radio voices of Vin Scully or my old teammate Ray Fosse, who calls the A's games, or the late Ernie Harwell doing Tigers games.

So I told Jerry I wanted to only call road games, beginning with the 2016 season, other than a Cubs series here or there.

It worked out wonderfully for me.

Whenever I do leave the booth for good, I may spend the next few years as some sort of White Sox ambassador, shaking hands and signing autographs for people.

If I make it to 2020 in some capacity, I will join an exclusive group.

There are only a few guys—Don Zimmer, Vin, Tommy Lasorda, Dave Garcia—who worked in baseball for parts of eight decades. All those men left quite a legacy.

I hope I will do the same, whenever I retire.

I turned 76 during the 2017 season, so one day I sat down and did the math that represented my broadcast life in sheer numbers. I had spent seven seasons doing TV for the Red Sox, two with the Yankees, and 32 with the White Sox. I don't know the exact number, but I probably have called more than 4,000 games, or at least 36,000 innings, over the past five decades.

That also adds up to thousands of nights on the road, room-service meals, flights, and getaway days spent packing and unpacking. I have endured the seemingly endless rain delays, extra-inning marathons, and pitcher-manager conferences on the mound. Those 3-hour-and-50-minute games that end at midnight can age you.

Vin, Uecker, and I frequently joke together about growing old.

Before he retired, Vin said, "When they say, 'Vin, you really look great,' that's when you know you are old."

It reminds me of how Jerry and I greet each other these days when we haven't seen each other for a while.

"Man," I'll say, "you look like crap."

"You do, too," he'll say. "Just keep on looking like crap and you'll be okay."

Truth is, Jerry is the youngest-looking eightysomething you will ever run across. He looks as if he gets younger every year and he is full of energy. I have already told you he is one of the smartest men I ever knew, but he was also one of the toughest. I was honored to be in a foxhole with him all these years.

I really never figured my broadcast career would last this long, but that booth became my second home. I felt alive in there, being able to communicate to baseball fans about this great American game. I am honored that I have been recognized for my contribution, but I certainly never got into this business to win any awards.

What did mean something to me was the White Sox naming the broadcast level at the stadium after me. They even placed a small plaque of my face on the wall. Whoever designed the thing has my prominent nose protruding slightly, which became a running joke for Bert Blyleven, the Twins' broadcaster, every time he came to Chicago.

"Hawk!" he'll say. "You owe me another shirt. I just walked by your plaque and your nose snagged my shirt again!"

Good ol' Dutchman. It's the same joke every time Minnesota comes to town. Friendships with guys like Bert, Paciorek, Drysdale, Uecker, Yaz, and a thousand other guys inside this great game have been very rewarding for me. I wouldn't trade a minute of all the good times and conversations we enjoyed over the last seven decades.

In the last five to seven years, several radio guys across both leagues have mentioned they were genuinely upset that I was not yet in the Hall of Fame as a broadcaster as a Ford Frick Award winner. I have been a finalist a few times, but never elected.

I believe my career—calling every season but four in the booth since 1975—speaks for itself.

Would being inducted into Cooperstown be nice? Sure it would. It would be a real honor to join men like Jack Buck, Ernie, and Vin. But I would love it mainly for my kids and grandkids. However, it was never a goal of mine nor is it something I stay awake thinking about. It may happen someday, maybe when I am gone, or it may not.

Let's face it, I have been pretty outspoken over the years. Perhaps I won't ever get into the Hall and I can live with that, too, because I did it my way. I did my homework, called the games as best I knew how, never pulled my punches, and told stories to entertain the fans.

The players are the focus of the game, more than any broadcaster. But I also know this: the game of baseball is nothing without the fans. Just as Rocky Colavito ingrained in me when he grabbed me by the collar that day in Kansas City soon after I came up to the big leagues, the fans make the game what it is.

Wherever he is, Rocky would be happy to know that I never forgot the lesson he taught me.

I have worked with the best producers and directors, like Bobby Whitelaw and Jim Angio. My partners on the air—Dick Stockton, Ned Martin, Don Drysdale, Bobby Murcer, Mickey Mantle, Wimpy, Darrin Jackson, who I love like a son, and Steve Stone—have been great to work with. They were all a huge part of my career.

I wish Don was still with us and I think about him often. The big guy was one in a million. Bobby and Mickey also left us way too early.

As for the others, I wish them the best.

"I've lived a life that's full. I've traveled each and every highway..."

I did do that. And I did do things my way, right or wrong, throughout my life. I realize that maybe I didn't make all the right decisions every time I needed to. I am human. But I did do things my way.

"Regrets, I've had a few, but too few to mention."

No, I can mention a few. Everybody has a few, if you live long enough.

From a baseball standpoint, I sometimes regret not accepting the offers to manage a team. But I did the right thing for my family. I regret fighting my buddy Douglas in the sixth grade, just before he died of brain cancer. I regret not getting the chance to ever meet Dean Martin.

I regret not keeping baseball memorabilia all these years to give to my grandkids, especially that ball signed by the Babe and Ty Cobb. I regret losing the glove Satchel Paige used when he pitched his final game. I regret not getting my $1,500 back from Denny McLain.

One thing I never regretted was marrying Aris.

We celebrated our 44th anniversary in 2017 and I can honestly say she was the best thing that ever happened to me. She changed me for the better. If I hadn't met her, I would have been killed by somebody somewhere a long time ago.

Not that we didn't have our arguments: I call her a strict contrarian. If I say left, she says right. If I say white, she says black. But we made it work all these years and we are still in love with each other. Every day, I realize how fortunate I am to have her and my kids, Krista and Casey, and my grandkids, in my life. They make everything complete.

Because of them, I have been trying to take better care of myself. I eat the right things and don't drink as much anymore. I can still hit the golf ball 300 yards, but I can't get in 18 holes because my wrists hurt so much. My equilibrium is not the same and I get wobbly if I get up too fast. Other than that, I feel great except for trouble with my eyes. Maybe I just wore them out, since I've seen a lot in my life. I've had four operations on each eye and detached retinas in each. I have had cataracts and doctors have stuck a small needle through my eyes plenty of times. Now I have very restricted peripheral vision.

If there is such a thing as reincarnation, I always joke that I want to come back as either Neil Diamond, a hockey player, or an eye-drop salesman.

I mean, who doesn't sing along to "Sweet Caroline"? And I love the way hockey players settle things when somebody ticks them off. Nobody breaks up their fights and it is perfectly legal to hit somebody on the ice simply because they deserve it. And did you know they get about $400 for a one-ounce bottle of those special eye drops?

"I've loved, I've laughed and cried. I've had my fill, my share of losing."

I've done a lot of loving, laughing, and crying in my life, and you know that by now. And I lost plenty, but as long as my butt is pointed south and my 10 toes are parallel to this earth, I will appreciate everything I have earned and everything that has been given to me.

I will always appreciate the unique experiences baseball provided me. I sometimes marvel at the people I met and was fortunate to know along the way.

Yep, it's been quite a ride.

I know I have been privileged to do the things I have done and seen the things I have seen, and especially made the lifelong friends I made.

Not bad for a so-called mama's boy with a crooked nose from tiny Woodruff, South Carolina.

When my journey ends someday and my obituary is written, I have often joked that this is the headline I want to top it: HE GONE!

On that day, I am confident Kenny Harrelson will walk up those steps to Heaven.

I just hope he brings the Hawk along with him.

"For what is a man, what has he got?

If not himself, then he has naught.

To say the things he truly feels and not the words of one who kneels

The record shows I took the blows and did it my way."

My old buddy Sinatra had it right, didn't he?

ACKNOWLEDGMENTS

PEOPLE I WILL ALWAYS REMEMBER AND APPRECIATE...

Bob Grim: One of the most loved people in the organization. I love him like a son.

Scott Reifert: Same as Bob Grim. Brilliant at what he does. I love him like a son.

Ed Cassin: Best at what he does in baseball. Invaluable to this organization. I love him like a son.

Mike Mazza: Runs a great and difficult department. Along with Pete Catizone and the rest of the Ticket office staff. Great people who I will always remember.

Christine O'Reilly-Riordan: The Queen of White Sox Charities.

Bob Beghtol: Another huge asset to this organization. He's terrific, and he has a great wit.

Roger Bossard: "The Sodfather"—nobody does it better!

Roy Rivas: What a wonderful job he's done for this organization for many, many years. I love him.

Nancy Nesnidal: She is absolutely fantastic. Love you, Nancy.

Ed Farmer: I love him like a little brother—and one of the toughest guys I ever played with! What great stuff he had, terrific knowledge about pitching and just a great person!

Darrin Jackson: I love him like a son. One of the most honorable people I've ever known and a great father. If you push him too far, you've got a big problem.

Steve Stone: A very competitive person. We've had our ups and downs but that all worked out. He's a former Cy Young Award winner (1980) and very knowledgeable about pitching and a lot of other things.

Wimpy: What's not to like about Tom Paciorek. Great athlete, terrific teammate, and a good player. I love Wimpy.

The Medical Department: Herm Schneider, Brian Ball, and Allen Thomas are the best not just in baseball, but in all sports, and they have the numbers to prove it!

Kenny Williams and Rick Hahn: What a great team!

Other White Sox Staff and Friends:

Ray Garcia, Tom Sheridan, Rob Boaz, Jim Muno, Gabe Morell, Greg Hopwood, Alex and Ursula Snelius, Gail Tucker, Martha Black, Rob Warren, Jo Simmons, Lindsey Jordan, Joe McNamara Jr., Sheena Quinn, Tony Colosimo, Jeff Szynal, Moira Foy, Bill Waters, John Corvino, Joe Roti, Ron Vesely, and Billy Russo.

All the guys at Savannah Golf Club.

Bob Witt: A dear friend.

Dick O'Connell, Jerry Fineberg, Derek Sanderson, and Randy LaMattina: What good guys!

A.J. Pierzynski: A Dennis the Menace.

Bobby Orr: Maybe the greatest hockey player ever! And what a sweet guy (off the ice).

Red Auerbach: Fantastic!

John Havlicek: Terrific person and terrific athlete!

Gino Cappelletti and Babe Parilli: Good guys to hang with.

Gino Cappelletti and Babe Parilli: Good guys to hang with.

Joe Hajduch: My great friend for many years. Like another member of my family.

J.J. Shearer: Great guy and a man's man!

Dick Ferris: The only man to ever turn the "Hawk" into a pigeon. A great mind.

Bill Damron: Love him like a brother. Love his whole family—Billy, Robert, Patrick, and Tracy.

Bruce and Jack Walters, Greg McDonald, Regis Hillow, and Charlie Bailes: One of my and my son Casey's favorites.

Chris Quarles: Best 12-year-old baseball player I ever saw. Hurt his arm, unfortunately.

All the guys at Bay Hill and Orange Tree.

Terry Hanley: One of the nicest people you will ever meet!

Mike Leary: Best producer I ever worked with. Also Dave Ross, Joe Grube, and Mark Harper—love them.

Jim Angio: Best director in the business and I love him like a brother.

All the guys at Trio Video: A great team!

John and Sally Draper in Chicago.

Shelley Solow: A great buddy and great lawyer.

Dr. Jules Victor and his wife, Barbara, from Savannah: Love 'em both.

Mo Norman: For the couple of rounds we played together. He was something to see.

Tommy Bolt: What a ball striker.

Ted Williams: The single most charismatic person I have ever met. (Arnie was second.)

My doctors: Chris Quinn: Wonderful doctor in Granger, Indiana. Tracy Williams: Couldn't do it without him. Kirk Packo, Jim Noth,

John Rubenstein, David Orth, and Dave Buchestki: They are all just awesome!

Hobart Manley: One of my idols.

Jerry Templeton and Ronnie Braddock: Two guys I'll never forget!

Vince Lombardi: Unforgettable!

Lou Holtz: What a guy and the best speaker I've ever heard. Played a lot of golf with him.

Bob Uecker: Love him like a brother and a very tough guy.

The 1967 Red Sox: A great team and even better teammates. Love you guys!

Dan Plesac: A super guy who should be considered for the Hall of Fame!

Bud Selig: A great commissioner of baseball.

All the people at MLB: What a fantastic job they do.

All my great friends around baseball who I will never forget. You know who you are.

A guy all of us loved, Jim Corno. God rest his soul.

Alvin Dark: What a baseball mind!

Ben Hogan: For the three hours we spent together at Shady Oaks.

Adam Motin and Noah Amstadter, for a job well done.

The Bertucci Boys: Bobby, Bruno, and handsome Anthony. It wouldn't be White Sox baseball without the Bertucci family!